Sam

Sam

Memories of a Remarkable Woman

Richard J. Toner

iUniverse, Inc.
New York   Bloomington

iUniverse books may be ordered through booksellers or by contacting:

iUniverse
1663 Liberty Drive
Bloomington, IN 47403
www.iuniverse.com
1-800-Authors (1-800-288-4677)

Because of the dynamic nature of the Internet, any Web addresses or links
contained in this book may have changed since publication and may no longer be
valid. The views expressed in this work are solely those of the author and do not
necessarily reflect the views of the publisher, and the publisher hereby disclaims
any responsibility for them.

ISBN: 978-1-4401-7600-5 (sc)
ISBN: 978-1-4401-7598-5 (dj)
ISBN: 978-1-4401-7599-2 (ebook)

Printed in the United States of America

iUniverse rev. date: 11/11/09

Considering the title, there is no one to whom this book could be dedicated other than my loving wife of fifty-one years:

Sam

But I would be remiss if I didn't also include the physicians, nurses, and other medical professionals, especially Dr. Paul Sherry and his nurse assistant, Patti Friesen, who contributed immeasurably to the added longevity that permitted Sam and me to be together for all those years. My heart and my gratitude go out to all of them.

Contents

Preface

This is the story of the bravest human being that I have ever known. When we met in Annapolis in the spring of 1956, she was Joanie Nobis, a senior at Boston College, and I was a second-class midshipman (a junior) at the U.S. Naval Academy. Joanie was a member of the Boston College dinghy sailing team that had been eliminated from the Eastern Intercollegiate Sailing Regatta that Saturday morning while I was a varsity baseball player, and our game had been rained out that afternoon.

Despite the Naval Academy regulations that prohibited alcohol consumption by midshipmen within seven miles of the academy, many of my classmates and I—all of whom were of legal drinking age anywhere in the country—would occasionally go to a small bar on the Severn River called Town Hall. While rules were rules, Academy officials tended to turn a blind eye to those who had a few beers with their buddies as long as they didn't overly indulge.

A classmate of mine, also a member of the baseball team, knew some of the BC sailing team members and invited them out to Town Hall, where Joanie Nobis and I first met. She enjoyed telling people years later that we met in a bar. And though that was factually correct, it was hardly a place where my friends and I would go to meet girls.

At the time we met, we were both "pinned" to other people—a quaint term of the era that meant you were a little bit more serious than going steady, but not yet close to being engaged. But we found a measure of attraction in one another, and when we discovered that our families lived within five miles of one another in suburban Boston (Medford and Arlington), we made a vague commitment to get together sometime when I was home on leave.

Two weeks later, my girlfriend called to tell me that the nuns would not let her take a final exam early so she would be unable to come to the Ring Dance, the most important social event in the four years at the Naval Academy. My disappointment was not enough to make me decide that I would skip the big dance, and my thoughts drifted to the attractive young lady from BC whom I had recently met. I called her on the phone to ask her to be my date, and was completely honest in explaining my reason for the late invitation. She told me that she would "get back to me" with her answer in a day or so. But I only had to wait until the following morning for her acceptance.

She told me sometime later that after her long weekend at Annapolis for the Ring Dance, she told all her friends that she had met the man she would marry. I was not quite so rash in my judgment, but the following Thanksgiving we became officially engaged and would marry fourteen months after we met.

This was the beginning of the most remarkable display of indefatigable courage, determination, and will to survive that I have ever witnessed. This story is dedicated to my lifetime hero: Sam.

Prologue

"After we get married, I'd like to have four or five children. Does that sound alright to you?" she asked me with that enigmatic smile that I had come to love many months before. "I'd like the first one to be a boy and we'll name him after you, if you agree," she went on. We were seated closely on the bench front seat of our "new" used 1954 Ford in the parking area of Big Sandy beach, looking at the moonlight on the waters of the Mystic Lakes.

"Sure, I guess that would be okay," I replied, all the while thinking that I wasn't even used to the idea that I was a newly minted second lieutenant in the U.S. Air Force and was about to take on the most serious commitment one can make in life—marriage—within the next few weeks. Worse yet, we had both been brought up strictly in the Catholic Church, were partially (on my part) or wholly (on hers) educated at Jesuit universities, and in the custom of our generation, had practiced abstinence throughout our year-long courtship. And she already wants to fill the house with little ones, I thought. But I didn't tell her that, of course.

"Since you've agreed that Richard John Junior will be the first son, you can name all the rest of the children if you want. I know you'll make the perfect choices, but you need to know one thing before we reach that day. For no reason that I know, I can't stand the name Sam for a boy, so I just hope you won't want to call our other son that," she stated with a degree of finality as if she were already pregnant with a second baby boy.

I couldn't help but laugh then, both because she was so utterly sincere as she spoke about the names and because naming a boy Sam would probably never have entered my mind. "I'll tell you what! Since you are so opposed to a son being called Sam, I'll make it my special name for you from now on. Certainly we can't have two Sams in the same house, can we?"

She leaned her head back on the car seat with an expression that couldn't have been more pained if I had struck her physically. Gradually, slowly, the expression evolved, first into reluctant acceptance and then came that unforgettable, enigmatic smile of a few minutes previous.

"Okay, it's a deal. But promise me you'll never let anyone else call me that and you'll never use that name when you're angry at me." Before I could reply, she put her arms around me, hugged me with all her strength, and we kissed deeply and passionately.

When we came up for air a few moments later, I looked directly into her lovely blue eyes and said, "I love you, Sam!"

And she's been Sam ever since that night. And no one else has ever been, or will ever be, allowed to call her that.

Chapter 1

Our Early Days

After I graduated from Annapolis and was commissioned in the United States Air Force, we had a span of about forty days before our actual wedding date on July 20, 1957. I kidded my classmates that Joan and I didn't want to rush into things like many of them did, getting married in the academy chapel immediately following the commissioning ceremony. But we spent my time on graduation leave most enjoyably, for the most part, even though a considerable amount of that time was dedicated to preparing for a large, formal military wedding at St. Raphael's Church in West Medford, Massachusetts.

Our wedding was, in my judgment, an overly extravagant affair and that didn't especially please me, but Aunt Dorothy[1] convinced "her Joan" that you only get married once and it needs to be a day you'll remember for the rest of your life. I had no choice in the matter, but I didn't suffer in silence—complaining only to Sam, however. She was always good at making people look at the brighter side of life, and I was no exception to her wiles. So I just continued to look forward to the day when all of this would be over and we'd

---

[1] Joan's mother had died when she was only ten years old and her father tried very hard to bring her up alone. But he finally gave in to Aunt Dorothy, Joan's late mother's sister, and allowed her to raise Joan and her younger brother to adulthood. She did so exceptionally well but became somewhat of an autocrat in the process and no one in the family ever had the temerity to challenge her decisions, including her husband.

head off on our honeymoon and then on to my first Air Force assignment. Then we would finally have the chance to start our own lives together.

But first, there was to be a major confrontation. At the wedding rehearsal, the entire party of matron-of-honor, best man, and six bridesmaids and six ushers (I guess they call them groomsmen now) were all gathered in the church for a quick run-through of the following day's proceedings. We kept waiting for Sam and her father to begin their march down the aisle. And waited, and waited. Finally, after many of the organist's false starts of the wedding march, I walked back to the rear of the church only to find that Dorothy was insistent that *she* would walk down the aisle, not Joan, who, by that time, was in tears when I reached them.

"You're Irish! You know full well that it's very bad luck for the bride to walk down the aisle at her wedding rehearsal, and I won't permit it," she blurted out. "I am going to stand in for her, as is only right and proper," she concluded, figuratively stomping her foot as she spoke.

I had reached the end of too many days of patient silence, and I responded bluntly, "You will do no such thing. We decided long ago that we weren't concerned with old superstitions and Joan will do her own rehearsing, thank you very much. Now you have one of two choices: You can either stay to watch or you can go home. But right now, get your ass out of the way so that we can proceed." I then kissed her tear-stained eyes and said, "C'mon, Sam, let's get this over with so we can get a good night's rest for your big day tomorrow."

The rehearsal went off perfectly and the St. Raphael's pastor asked if we would like to go to confession since we would be married at a High Mass the following morning. Joan's look clearly said to me, you go first. We hadn't totally given up the idea of abstinence, but had indulged in a full week of serious foreplay leading up to the wedding. Probably Bill Clinton would have had a clear conscience pointing an index finger and saying, "I never had sexual relations with that woman!"

Apparently the priest had seen Joan's apprehension before he entered the confessional, and when I told him that we had "nearly done it" many times, he quietly chuckled and said not to worry. "You're both to be commended for trying so hard to avoid temptation. Now go tell your beautiful bride not to be concerned about anything when she comes in here. And God bless you both. May you have a long and happy life together."

When I drove Sam home for the last time, Dorothy was standing at the front entrance, arms akimbo, and all ready to lash out in her most domineering form. But I beat her to the punch. All the pent up frustrations of the prior six weeks of having no opinions, and no say, bubbled to overflowing. With my forefinger pointing menacingly at her nose, I backed her across the entrance foyer, across the living room, and finally to the sofa where she had no choice but to sit because she could retreat no further. I'm not sure exactly what my continuing harangue was, but in mostly civil language, I made sure that the dowager empress knew she had lost her scepter as far as Joan was concerned, and she was never, ever again to give my wife orders to do anything. I would be her husband in the next twelve hours and any future conduct like Dorothy had displayed tonight—and for the entire time that I had courted her niece—would completely and unequivocally not be tolerated.

The wedding went off very nicely the next day, and as we arrived in our limo at the public country club where the reception was to take place, we discovered that we were the first ones there. As we entered the ballroom, I was shocked to see two waiters each pouring two bottles of champagne at a time into a bubbling fountain. "What in the world are you doing? Why have champagne if you're going to ruin it by pumping it through this cascade?" I asked them.

"Sorry, sir, that's what was ordered," one of them replied. And I knew there was nothing else to be said.

So I took one of the newly opened bottles from where he had placed it, picked up two champagne glasses in my other hand, and began to pour some unadulterated wine for the two of us. As I was looking into her eyes, trying mentally to compose a brief toast to us, I heard a familiar voice over my shoulder from behind. "You be very careful of how much of that you drink, Joan. There's a long day ahead of you and you certainly don't want to embarrass yourself."

I wheeled around, and through clenched teeth, I warned her, "I thought I made myself perfectly clear last night, but if you want me to continue, I'll be more than happy to do so in front of all the people who are arriving. Joan is making her own decisions and does not need you to tell her what to do. *Am I making myself perfectly clear?*" I concluded, my voice a little louder than intended in the final sentence. Then I turned and escorted my lovely young bride to a group of her Boston College classmates who had begun to gather nearby—while she looked at me adoringly with an expression that said both "thank you" and "finally!"

Before moving on to the next phase—the first phase of our lives together—I must clarify the relationship that I had with Dorothy over the next four decades. She was a very well-meaning woman and if it had not been for her insistence that Joan was to be the first in their family to go to college, I probably never would have met my bride in the first place. But my association with her was marred by contention that always simmered under the surface. She gave up trying to control Joan's life but resorted instead to showering Joan with guilt for not doing what her aunt wanted her to do or not "coming home" frequently enough. She also never forgave me for electing a career that would take us around the world, far from the Boston area. There was no doubt in my mind that she loved Joan deeply, but unfortunately, her love was both obsessive and possessive and she was unwilling to share Joan's love with anyone.

*   *   *

All of the love and passion that we had reserved for ourselves flowed over after the ceremony and reception were over. That first night, we never even got to the resort hotel on Cape Cod that we had reserved for the following week, but instead, we ended up in a hotel in Boston. Our fervor was blissful and couldn't have been more heartfelt, but I sensed that each time we made love, she said a little silent prayer that she had conceived her first child. But just in case, we gave ourselves to one another unstintingly as we traveled down the East Coast until we settled into my first assignment— pilot training at Bartow Air Base near Winter Haven, Florida.

Sam had spent a year teaching elementary education while I finished my senior year at the academy. She never hesitated to tell anyone who would listen that it took me five years to get my degree, versus her four, since after a year at Holy Cross College I, like everyone else, needed to start again as a freshman (plebe) when I entered the academy. Understandably, she didn't want her newly acquired skills to go dormant and just sit home alone all day. She was reluctantly hired to teach at Polk City Elementary School, where the majority of the parents of her children were orange-grove workers. The area was a hotbed of cult religions, most prominent of which were those who believed that they could handle poisonous snakes at their services and "The Lord would protect them"—thus the reluctance of the administration to hire "a northern lady who, worse yet, was a Catholic." However, as she had a talent for doing throughout her life, she won over the entire faculty, administration, and parents with her charm and grace, as well as her special ability to teach young, disadvantaged children.

Those were very good days for us and we delighted in our time together, as well as being full-spirited attendees at all the parties with my classmates. Our pilot training class was made up entirely of recent West Point and Annapolis graduates, and the age-old rivalry between the two institutions bloomed into lasting friendships that have endured over the years.

Perhaps our most memorable occasion during this period was the 1957 New Year's Eve party at the officers' club. Like everyone else, we went early and stayed late, with no restrictions on the alcohol that was imbibed. Sam had discovered her new favorite drink, a Moscow Mule,[2] and she drank it like water all evening, except for the midnight champagne toast, in which we heartily partook. We arrived home in the very wee hours of the morning and she was as drunk as I ever saw her, before or since. Suddenly she went into hysterics, screaming one minute and sobbing uncontrollably the next. After my trying at length to comfort her, she finally managed to blurt out the reason for her bitter despair: She still wasn't pregnant. According to her, she was a "failure" as a wife, she was "unable to fulfill her duties," and she wouldn't blame me if I "dumped" her and found someone else who could bear me a son.

The next day was grim, of course, but despite her inebriated state of the previous evening, she remembered her outburst and

---

[2]   The Moscow Mule was a specialty of the club bartender, consisting of vodka, ginger beer, and a wedge of lime served over ice. It was a very smooth drink that went down quite easily.

was still not very willing to be consoled. She finally accepted my assurances that she would become pregnant in God's good time. And she finally smiled when I said, "In the meantime, let's just be happy that we can continue to try."

But as I had suspected for many months, her ability to conceive was never far out of her mind and the most important thing in the world to her at the time, except for me, was her near obsession with becoming pregnant.

That also happened to be the time period when the Air Force made one of its worst personnel policy decisions in its young ten-year history, a decision that was to have serious ramifications for the next twenty-five years. Just days before we service academy graduates were to report to our pilot training bases, the chief of personnel, Lieutenant General Emmett "Rosie" O'Donnell, offered all of us the opportunity for "excellent, challenging assignments" if we would opt out of pilot training. There was a WW II and Korean War glut of pilots in the U.S. Air Force and they didn't need any more.

It seems patently obvious, in hindsight as well as to all of us lieutenants at the time, that it was a terribly ill-conceived policy, if only for the fact that we had not spent four tough years at the academies to deny ourselves the next important career progression. Of the nearly 250 of us in that training class, only a handful accepted the offer. So instead, over half of our class was "washed out,"[3] when the wash-out norm for academy graduates in prior years was less than 15 percent.

Unfortunately, despite being among the first in my class to solo at Bartow, I happened to be one of those eliminated, based on a trumped up catch-all charge of "dangerous tendencies." It happened just fifteen flying hours before my graduation from the two-hundred-flying-hour primary training program. Sam admitted to me later that she was devastated for me, but way down deep, was relieved because she had harbored an intuitive feeling that I would be killed in an aircraft accident or during wartime. I suspect most Air Force pilot's wives are not immune to that hidden fear.

---

[3]   The term "washed out" is military jargon for involuntarily failing to complete training.

With still three years of commitment left to serve, I was convinced that I would become a civilian as soon as I could. For my new assignment, I was offered the choice of either becoming a navigator or a civil engineer (termed installation engineer at the time). No way would I fly the back seat for anyone else, so I really had no choice at all. And in a matter of a few weeks I was on my way to South Ruislip, England (near London)—*alone*.

When we left Florida, there was a large going-away party for Joan at the Polk City Elementary School at which many people, including some of her students and parents, made short speeches about how much she had done for the community and that they would miss her a great deal. The school principal gave her the highest compliment—for those folks, at least—when he stated that she was "the nicest northern lady any of them had ever met."

Sam was very excited about going overseas, but deeply disappointed that with less than six months of married life behind us, we were faced with our first separation. Two weeks later, she bade me good-bye at McGuire AFB as I boarded a USAF C-118 for the trans-Atlantic crossing. As we parted, she hugged me tightly, and with tears flowing down her cheeks, but a bright smile on her face, she whispered, "I haven't told anyone until I could tell you, but I think I might be pregnant." And, as it turned out, she probably had been on that unforgettable New Year's Eve.

My first letter from her in England confirmed that she was "with child" and she was brimming over with joy. While I would have been happy to continue our married life simply just the two of us alone, I was equally pleased that she would finally rid her mind of the self-imposed guilt for going "so long" without producing an heir. Meanwhile, in London, I busied myself with trying to learn what the support side of the USAF was all about. Like most pilot trainees, I figured that knowing how to fly an airplane was my job, and I had done little or nothing to educate myself on the inner workings of the macro-organization.

After reporting in to Third Air Force, I quickly learned that I was to be a base engineering member of the Inspector General staff. Having asked, "What's that?" I was told that I would spend much of my time on the road at USAF bases throughout England and Scotland examining the base engineer's record keeping of the real estate actions that were underway on each base. Needless to say, I was totally ignorant of any aspect of what we were talking about and almost as excited as one can be watching corn grow. However, I worked with two very good technical sergeants who were both patient and kind in breaking in the untrained new guy.

After a couple of weeks of trying hard to be positive with my lot, I arrived in the office one Monday morning to learn that the big boss, the IG himself, wanted me to report to his office at 0900. My immediate boss, Captain Dave Ferree, assured me that there was nothing to be concerned about; the colonel was a very nice man, and he just wanted to welcome me to the headquarters and the IG team. I still had a little trepidation when I entered his office, but he very kindly put me at ease after the initial formalities.

"Well, I've been looking forward to meeting you and I see by your records that you're a recent graduate of the Naval Academy. We already have a rivalry going between us because my son was a contemporary of yours at West Point and he was commissioned into the U.S. Air Force as well. I also see that you're newly married. Congratulations. Have you and your bride been able to get settled in yet?"

"No, sir," I replied. "She's still back in the States."

"Good Lord, son, you've been assigned to one of the greatest places to be in the Air Force and you decided to leave your new bride back there? Why in the world would you do something like that?" he queried.

"I was told by the personnel clerk at my pilot training base that because there is no government housing here, my wife would have to wait until I found a place to live on the local economy before they could process her paperwork to get her a port call."[4]

"That's the most ridiculous thing I've ever heard, and I'm sorry for the mix-up. You must be the first officer to come here under those circumstances, and I'm going to get on that right after you

---

[4]   Since there was a backlog of people waiting to move from the States to their new European station of assignment, and the paperwork was ridiculously complex (applying for passports, getting shots, etc.), one could not travel until all that was done and one was issued a "port call," a time and date to be at the port (air or sea) of departure.

leave my office. We'll get her here as soon as possible—you can count on it," he assured me.

"Did you find the installation engineer course at Wright-Patt[5] interesting and worthwhile?" was the colonel's next question.

"The what, sir?" was the only thing I could answer.

"Goddam, this is a disaster. First you were deprived of the opportunity to bring your new bride with you, and now you tell me you're right out of pilot training and haven't even been given the foggiest notion of an introduction to your new career field. Some heads are going to roll over this, and you can bet on it," he asserted, growing redder in the face as he spoke.

"You must be totally confused trying to inspect people on a subject that you've never even been introduced to before. Absolutely asinine! Well, I'm going to get together with our personnel director before the day's over and get this mess straightened out. I'm not sure what the final decisions will be, but I know two things: First, we're going to get you and your wife back together again, and then we're going to get you the training that you deserve and need to do a good job for the Air Force. You've been badly screwed by our system, so I want you to keep your chin up while we work these problems."

And with that, he came around his desk, shook my hand warmly, and gave me a sound slap on my back to send me on my way.

Trans-Atlantic telephone calls were exorbitantly expensive in those days, but I couldn't wait until that evening to call Sam on the phone—collect—and tell her to start packing her bags. I walked on air for the next few days expecting to hear almost daily that the port call had been issued and my love was on her way. But the days turned into weeks and the weeks turned into months before I finally learned of her arrival date. It never occurred to me to follow up with the IG to find out what the hold-up was. We learned in our four years at Annapolis that one never questions a senior officer—a tradition that I made sure that my future subordinates would *not* honor—so I never asked for nor received a status report on the

---

[5]   Wright-Patterson AFB, Ohio, is the home of the Air Force Institute of Technology and holds both short-course training programs as well as multi-year master's and doctorate degree programs for selected officers.

progress. Who knows whether it would have helped. Now she was on her way, so it no longer mattered.

During the interim period, I busied myself trying to find a place to live that was both fitting for my lovely lady and something we could afford. I was referred by a co-worker to a "lovely little apartment" in Edgware, a northern suburb of London. Having looked at a number of places I didn't like, I was anxious to see if this was the "right place."

It turned out to be a lovely Tudor-style home on a cul-de-sac with a putting green on the side yard and a clay tennis court in the back, both carefully tended by a gardener who came weekly. It was an upstairs apartment over the landlord's much larger flat, with a bedroom, sitting room, and a small but functional kitchen. It was also nicely furnished. I immediately made a deposit but then began wondering if I had done the right thing. It was a typical English flat of the period—no central heating, gas-stack in the bathroom, which (barely) heated the water for a bath, a cistern on the roof for our drinking water, and a number of other limitations, at least as I perceived them.

So in my daily letters to Sam, I was constantly apologizing for where she had to live, and expressed the hope that she would find it acceptable. And when she assured me that a rat hole would be acceptable as long as we were together, I began to relax over the issue—though not completely.

As the big day approached, I prepared to go north to her arrival base, RAF Station Burtonwood, which was near Manchester in the English Midlands. This was a major U.S. logistics base for the United Kingdom (UK) and was the arrival location for all passengers and cargo flights coming into the country. My immediate boss called me into his office a few days before and told me that his secretary had already made bachelor officer quarters (BOQ) reservations for me, so I needn't bother with that.

"I also want you to go up there a day early and make a courtesy call on the installation engineer and take a cursory look at their real property records. And you need to borrow my wife's car for the trip. It's right-hand drive and I'm sure that Joan will have a bit of luggage with her. Come home with me for dinner the night before you leave and you can pick the car up then. I can't tell you how much we're looking forward to meeting her. Maybe you'll start smiling a little bit more after she arrives."

Bless his heart; I realized what he was doing. He was sending me there on official government business so the poorly paid second lieutenant could afford to make the trip. It was completely legal but there was no doubt in my mind that he must have been stretching the rules a bit. But he could count on the fact that I'd be smiling a heck of a lot more when we returned.

It was late April in the UK, but there was still quite a chill in the air when the big day came. And it was heavily overcast—not the best conditions in which to see one's new homeland. She had had a long flight, stopping in Gander, Newfoundland, and then Shannon, Ireland, enroute, so I was a little concerned that she'd be overly tired when she arrived on the commercial charter flight. I was as close as I could get when the passengers started down the mobile stairway that was backed up to the aircraft's exit door.

Then finally I saw her beautiful face in the doorway. And as she started down the stairs, I was stunned. *My God, that lady is wearing maternity clothes!*

When she reached ground level, we rushed toward one another, embraced as we never had before and both of us shed one or two tears of pure joy. In the process, she had dropped her camel's hair winter coat on the tarmac, but even though the pavement was perpetually damp at this time of year, no damage was done and we simply laughed at our excitement.

As we drove toward the BOQ, a heavy late afternoon fog was drifting in and I couldn't help mentioning that it reminded me of Heathcliff racing drunkenly across the moors at dusk searching for his beloved Catherine in Emily Bronte's enduring novel, *Wuthering Heights*. "That's an awfully morbid thought," Sam stated. "We're together again and hopefully we will be for a long, long time. So let's be happy and rejoice that all of that is behind us now."

The BOQ buildings were tar-paper-covered barrack-like buildings obviously left over from WW II. As the misty fog rolled in, the street lights cast an eerie glow. This setting hardly seemed the place for us to begin a second honeymoon. But the room's interior was not as gloomy, and I had purchased a fairly decent bottle of champagne to aid our celebration. I saw that she noticed the lone single bed in the room, so I told her that I would sleep in the chair when the time came.

"The hell you will!" she stated quite adamantly. "I'm not that big yet." And with that she began to take off the navy blue maternity outfit that still looked amazingly fresh despite her many hours of travel over the last twenty-four hours.

Apparently I had a very strange look on my face when she did that, because she chuckled lightly and came to enfold me in her arms. As she did, she whispered hoarsely, "I'm still the same person that I always was, dearest. I won't bruise or break and I already checked with the doctor and he told me that it's perfectly all right for another few months. Now take your clothes off and let's see how well we can manage in that single bed."

All the way back to London the next day, we talked about what we had done and seen while we were apart and what we were still going to do until she was too far along to be significantly active. But in between, I kept trying to prepare her for disappointment when she saw the flat I had picked out for her. But I shouldn't have been the least bit concerned.

When we drove up to the front and I told her that this was it, she covered her face with both hands and cried, "Oh my, oh my, it's absolutely beautiful. I love it! I can't tell you how thrilled I am to see it. I couldn't imagine a nicer place in my dreams. Thank you, my love, for finding it for me." And there was no pretense in what she told me because until the day I lost her, she always would tell me that the little flat in Edgware was one of her favorite spots of all the homes that we lived in over the next fifty years.

*   *   *

We spent only three months in her dream house, but one part of the "bargain" that the IG had made with me finally came to pass. As much as she loved London and reveled in all the things that we were able to do there, I was being transferred to a small base in eastern France near the village of Phalsbourg. The idea was that if I went to a base-level assignment, I could learn on the job what the career field was all about, rather than going back to the States to go to the school that I missed. As we did so often in those carefree days, we were not upset in the least by the change and actually looked forward to being on the Continent and experiencing all it had to offer.

Each weekend, we did all the touristy things that visitors do in London. We saw the Changing of the Guard at Buckingham Palace more than once. We strolled through Hyde Park and Green Park. We attended the theatre—an opportunity that was quite affordable in those days. We were most fortunate to get tickets to the Queen's annual birthday celebration, the Trooping of the Colours. And in 1958, as the young monarch did many years subsequently, HRH Elizabeth II reviewed the Horse Guards, seated sidesaddle on her favorite steed of the moment. It was a spectacular display of British pageantry at its best and it was not until many years later that we learned how fortunate we were to witness the actual event—rather than the queen-less rehearsal that was open to the public a few days before.

We also managed a week of leave so that we could fly across the English channel to Brussels where we would be enthralled by the 1958 World's Fair. From climbing to the top of the centerpiece structure, the Atomium, to visiting every national exhibit in the fairgrounds, we did it all. Sam's stamina at the start of her third trimester was remarkable, but on those rare occasions when she tired, I would hire one of the ubiquitous reverse-rickshaw-like vehicles and wheel her around the grounds. It was truly a glorious holiday—one of just dozens and dozens yet to come.

But before we actually moved our tiny household across the Channel, we wanted to do one more thing in London. Julie Andrews and Rex Harrison had just opened at the Drury Lane Theatre in the European debut of *My Fair Lady*. Having been familiar with all its wonderful music from its opening in New York a year previously,[6] we were determined to see it before we left. We obtained scalper's tickets in the top balcony for a Saturday matinee performance and it was

---

[6]   Playing of the music and selling the recordings from *My Fair Lady* anywhere in Europe prior to its opening in London, was forbidden by law. And unlike the present day of pirated music and other various scoff laws, laws were obeyed and the Continent was just being introduced to songs we already knew by heart.

well worth the price—which was probably about one guinea (about four dollars at the time) for each of us, though these seats normally sold for just a few shillings (less than a dollar). Not disappointed in the slightest after the show, we sang the tunes together all the way back to Edgware.

When we arrived at the house, Ronnie Bunsley, our landlord, met us at the door and invited us to accompany him and his wife, Ruth, to their local haunt—the Green Man Pub.—a few blocks away. When we agreed, he asked, "By the by, where have you been on such a smashing day?"

When we told him, he responded, "Pity, you've missed summer!" That turned out to be a lasting memory of Jolly Olde England and has been a standing joke that we've chuckled over in various forms ever since.

One of the ex-pat U.S. government civilians who worked in the same office complex with me, fairly drooled when he learned where we going. He was a Francophile through and through and began bringing me brochures, travel books, and the like each day before I transferred.

"Surely you're going to have a layover in Paris for a few days on your way, aren't you?" he inquired in his slightly British-influenced accent, which was impossible not to acquire for long-term American residents of the UK. "I have just the place for you to stay, if you'd like. It's a delightful little hotel, L'Hôtel de Nice, and it's right in the middle of where you want to be. It has all you need for a long weekend in Paris—wonderful bistros nearby, museums, and on and on. I stay there all the time and I'd be delighted to make reservations for you," he gushed.

When I told Sam, she was thrilled, "Oh, could we please?" she begged. "I've always dreamt of going to Paris since I was a little girl, and even though I'm as big as a cow, it will still be terribly romantic."

It took no convincing for me. I had been to Paris as a midshipman and loved the city. And I do even more so today. So the reservations were made at L'Hôtel de Nice. We reserved a flight from Dover to Calais on a newly organized airline that took two small cars and its occupants across the channel at wave-top height in just twenty minutes. We had purchased a left-hand drive car, a used Hillman

Californian for six hundred dollars to take to the Continent—a big mistake since it was a lemon and I could have bought a new Volkswagen sedan at the base exchange for five hundred dollars more. Live and learn!

As one of her very last acts before we left England, Joan had her final check-up with the obstetrician at the South Ruislip base hospital. He estimated that she was nearly eight months along—a very inexact process at the time based on the first known missed period—and safe to travel to our destination. Unfortunately, as we were to recall later, she had forgotten to bring a urine sample with her to that final appointment and blood tests were virtually unheard of for prenatal care at the time.

On the flight over, I shocked her by telling her that it was common practice in France to stand at the roadside behind one's car and urinate, as there were no public restrooms and, often, not even the petrol stations had them. And wouldn't you know, one of the first views she had of France as we left the outskirts of Calais was a man relieving himself by the side of the road. But this wasn't just an ordinary chap. It was an *abbé*, a local Catholic priest, with his cassock hiked up to his waist, letting it all hang out.

"I think France might take a little getting used to," she laughingly offered, "but I already know that we're going to love it here. It's all so new and fascinating to me."

The little hotel was all that we hoped it would be: a lovely little Parisian hideaway. It had one of the old open-cage elevators that two people could barely fit into—a particularly interesting challenge because she was in the full bloom of her final days of pregnancy. The concierge got us settled and—well prepared by my friend who had made the reservations for us—he was especially kind and helpful to us. He spoke no English, as was the case in most small Parisian hotels before the great influx of American tourists began, but we got along very well with my basic fluency in French from high school and college studies.

After a traditional dinner of *steak et frites* at a nearby bistro, Sam wanted to sit at the sidewalk tables in front and watch the Parisian world go by. To cap off the evening, I suggested cognac and espresso as we sat there—neither of which she had ever experience before. But she was game for most anything in those days. As she took her first sip of Courvoisier, she nearly gagged and her eyes watered as she tried to choke it down.

"I hope the coffee is not that bad," she joked as she tried her first sip. "I think they both need a little sweetening," was her conclusion after trying the espresso.

She went on to reveal that Nana Wood—Aunt Dorothy's mother with whom Joan had shared a bedroom throughout her college years—often asked Joan to get a wee dram of brandy for her when she had "chest pains," which apparently occurred most evenings before bedtime. Nana always had a bottle tucked in her closet, a shot glass on the nightstand, and paper-wrapped sugar cubes in the top drawer. She would always put a cube into her brandy and dissolve it before she drank, and then her chest pain would miraculously go away.

"If it worked for Nana, it should work for me too," she opined. The local people seated near us, and the waiter standing nearby, nearly went apoplectic as Sam blithely took a sugar cube from the bowl on the table and dropped it into her snifter. It still didn't solve her instant dislike for the spirits, and it took many more months of French living before she became a believer. Unfortunately for me, I was not about to finish hers with sugar in it so the glass went relatively untouched when we left to return to the hotel.

Sam brought her most lovely gossamer nightgown and peignoir set with her and when the street noise of next morning woke her, she got up, slipped on the peignoir, and threw open the floor-to-ceiling glass paneled doors wide to greet the beginnings of a new Parisian day. She motioned for me to come beside her as we looked out on the push carts, street vendors, and all the other bustle that was typical of this *arrondisement* (a precinct of the city).

"Despite the way I look, I have never felt so romantic and so much in love with you as I do now. Promise me that we'll come back soon after I have the baby."

That was not a difficult promise to keep and we held ourselves to it many times over the rest of our lives together.

I had noticed that for the last few days in England, and ever since we had arrived in France, she seemed insatiably thirsty. Neither of us thought very much of it and just assumed that it was simply a symptom of late-term pregnancy. So when we headed east out of

Paris two days later, we had a few liter bottles of water in the car to slake her thirst as we made the five-hour drive to our new home. She delighted in the French countryside and was enchanted as we went through the many villages that dotted the Route Nationale No. 4 between Paris and Strasbourg, the nearest large city to where we would live.

When we arrived at Phalsbourg Air Base, which was named for the modest town just a kilometer to the east of the main gate, we learned that there were no temporary base quarters available. But many of the newly arriving married couples were staying at a nearby resort hotel, we were told, and the base had arranged for special weekly rates for the newcomers. The hotel was located just five kilometers south of the town in a lovely picturesque valley.

Lutzelbourg, where the hotel was located, lay in a deep valley in the foothills of the Vosges Mountains. It was a very tiny village that was completely dominated by the hotel where we were to stay. The hotel was three stories high and must have had close to thirty rooms. And it was, in fact, a resort hotel but mostly for trout fishermen who flocked there for allegedly one of the finest trout streams in eastern France. The fast-moving river happened to flow just behind the hotel. We were soon to learn that the SNCF[7] main passenger line between Paris, Strasbourg, and other points east, ran through the village as well. The trains shook the valley floor as they passed, but the hotel put us in a rear room facing the small river and we slept very well, listening instead to the gentle ripple of the trout stream.

Our room charge included both breakfast and dinner, each of which was a superb example of the wonderful Alsatian cuisine— among the best in the world, in our well-formed personal judgment. And the *vin de la maison* (house wine) was not only excellent but actually cheaper than bottled water, which Sam was drinking constantly by then.

I needed the car to go to and from the base so that left Sam isolated in the little village each day. But she didn't care. She was delighted by the serenity of the hotel, and when I came home on the second evening, I found her seated outside with two older

---

[7]   SNCF is the Sociètè Nationale de Chemin de Fer, or the National Railway of France.

women (probably thirty-five or forty years of age) from the hotel staff, helping them to prepare *haricots verts* (tiny green beans) to accompany our evening meal. Sam had not yet learned any French but no matter; the ladies spoke only *Alsacienne*—a heavily Germanic language that reflected the history of Germany and France warring over the Alsace-Lorraine region for centuries. German possession or occupation, depending on your perspective, had been dominant for most of the past century, and the language had evolved accordingly.

But no one seemed to mind. They were obviously communicating very effectively and thoroughly enjoying one another's company.

At dinner that evening we met another newly arrived couple who had moved into the hotel that day. He was an USAF non-commissioned officer (NCO) and she was a nurse who hoped to gain civilian employment at the well-staffed base clinic. It was to prove a highly fortuitous meeting.

A few more days passed and I drove around with Sam early each evening so that we could both discover the lovely countryside together. In the middle of the night on our fifth day there, she suddenly awakened me to tell me that something was seriously wrong. The bed was soaked and, even as naive as we were, we soon came to the conclusion that her water had broken and she was about to go into labor. As a neophyte in all of these matters, I ran to the room of the couple we had just recently met, and asked for their assistance. When I told the nurse what had happened, she smiled and told me to relax; everything was going to be fine.

When we reached the base clinic, Captain (Dr.) Kaplan was on duty and I think he immediately sensed that he was soon to bring a little one into the world. This had not been the normal practice at the clinic heretofore. Usually, the expectant mothers were taken to the USAF general hospital in Wiesbaden, West Germany, a week or so before the delivery date to assure that both mother and baby had the best possible care, especially in the case of an unexpected emergency.

The doctor left to examine Sam for a few moments—husbands were not allowed to be present in those days—and returned with a deeply troubled expression on his face. "I'm so sorry to break the news to you so bluntly, but I don't hear a heartbeat," he told me, "and I'm quite certain that the baby is already dead. I'm not going to tell her that because the baby is definitely full-term, and it will be a terribly difficult delivery. I will heavily sedate her and send her by ambulance right away to the Army hospital at Landstuhl (Germany), which is much closer than Wiesbaden. I want you to go with her and encourage her however much you can, but please don't tell her yet what is happening. You may have lost your first child but you certainly don't want to lose your wife too."

Over the next few minutes, they arranged her as comfortably as possible and we set off in the wee hours of the morning for the two-hour drive. The hospital corpsmen—one drove while the other monitored her vital signs—were previously informed of the situation and mercifully kept quiet throughout the drive.

Sam was hurried into the labor annex to the delivery room as soon as we reached the hospital, the staff of which was already fully aware of the situation thanks to Dr. Kaplan's call. An OB doctor and nurse assistant examined her thoroughly. When they completed their exam, the doctor told me I needed to go back with the ambulance and gather a change of clothes. He also advised me to come back as soon as I could and plan to stay here for a while.

"She's not in labor yet, and we're going to induce her in a few minutes. But it will be a long process and you're one of the most important elements in getting her through this. If she gets into any trouble, we'll take the baby by Caesarian section,[8] so don't worry and please drive carefully on the way back."

I returned to the hospital as quickly as I could about five or six hours later, and while she was in heavy labor, she was nowhere near the point of delivery. Contrary to normal hospital policies and because of the circumstances, I was allowed in the labor room with her where I spent the better part of the next twenty-four hours by her side. She alternated between squeezing my hand so tightly, I thought she would crush it, to panting breathlessly and occasionally, dozing off briefly from exhaustion. A doctor or nurse came by frequently to check her and finally, the most important words I could imagine at the time were said, "I think she's ready now."

---

[8]   A Caesarian section was considered a highly risky procedure at the time and was rarely used except for emergencies.

There was no policy exception in the delivery room, however, and I spent the next two hours with the expectant fathers in the adjacent room. When the doctor finally came out, gowned and with a mask below his chin, he asked me to join him in the corridor. Clearly, I concluded, he wanted to avoid the prying eyes of others.

"It was a beautiful, fully developed baby boy," he told me, "and your wife will be just fine once she gets over the terribly difficult ordeal she's been through. She doesn't know that the baby didn't survive. And I think you should tell her that so that you can grieve together. But she does know that it was a boy and she smiled weakly just before we put her to sleep. One of the nurses is a Catholic and she conditionally baptized your son after the delivery. You need to know that. Now you go get a room at the BOQ and get some sleep yourself. She won't awaken for another five or six hours. She'll be in a private room, not on the maternity ward, when you come back and you should be here when she wakes up.

"I'm very sorry for you but there was nothing we could do. The baby was gone perhaps even as much as two days ago. But you're both very young and there'll be much more time for you to start your family all over again."

With that he shook my hand and disappeared back into the delivery room area.

I was by her bedside when she began to waken, but not unexpectedly, she was dazed and disoriented. She saw tears rolling down my cheeks and didn't need to ask. And we dissolved into each others arms sobbing for what seemed an eternity.

Her indomitable courage and bravery became evident to me over the next few days as we planned our immediate future steps and tried to look out even further than that.

*   *   *

She was up, moving around fairly comfortably, two days later when a doctor came into her private room. "Mrs. Toner," he began abruptly, "have you lost any appreciable amount of weight in the last month?" he asked. We didn't know.

"Have you been especially thirsty recently?" That answer was, of course, an emphatic yes.

"I know you want to go home as soon as you can [as if we even had a home at the time], but we're going to keep you here for a while. Your blood sugar was extremely high when you came in here, and it still is right now. That's a clear indication of diabetes, but before you worry needlessly, diabetes symptoms are not at all unusual during pregnancy—it's called gestational diabetes—and we just want you to return to your normal metabolic stability before we release you. It should only be a few days and your husband can be with you any time he wants."

He then went on to tell us that the diabetic condition—hyperglycemia (high blood sugar) manifested by her incredible thirst—had very probably led to the demise of the infant that was so close to being born alive. The blood sugar problem had likely deprived the baby of the oxygen he needed, as extreme hyperglycemia reduces the ability of blood to be oxygenated. We both reached the same stunned realization at the same time: Sam had forgotten to bring the urine sample to her last OB appointment, and her doctor told her it was not a problem. But in fact, a routine urine analysis would have revealed her nascent hyperglycemia.

We were crestfallen, but as is the case in so many situations like this, there was no turning back the clock and any anger, bitterness, or recrimination would be just a waste of emotion. But the term "diabetes" immediately raised both fear and horror in her mind.

As a young child, shortly after becoming Aunt Dorothy's ward, a man came to live with them known only to Joan as "Uncle Happy." She knew he was not related in any way, but had been told little else. He was essentially an invalid—a severe diabetic. He had already had one leg amputated, had lost most of the toes on the other foot, was nearly blind, and he had died not long after Joan became part of the family. Her instant thoughts all revolved around the fact that she dreaded the idea of becoming another Uncle Happy.

In an ironic interlude, Joan remembered that Aunt Dorothy had lectured her many times while we were engaged, telling her that she ought to "think twice" about marrying me because I had "a history of diabetes" in my family. And here she was—rather than me—fearfully faced with the possibility of becoming a diabetic herself.

To put her fears into the perspective of the times; diabetes mellitus was a relatively rare disease in the 1950s, not the raging epidemic that it is in this age of obesity caused by poor diet and lack of exercise. Diabetics were considered by a naive world population as freaks of some sort and few people, medical professionals included,[9] were aware of the cause, effects, or treatment of the disease, other than the fact that it was somehow related to sugar. In fact it was known for many years as "sugar diabetes," a clear misnomer.

Many even thought it was a communicable malady and, therefore, no one who was afflicted with it wanted the fact known lest they be ostracized. After all, Frederick Banting, a Canadian, and John J. R. Macleod, a Scot, had only invented insulin—for which they were awarded the Nobel Prize in 1923—just slightly more than a decade before Joan and I were born. Prior to that time, one who contracted diabetes—the failure of the pancreas to function for whatever the cause—was destined to go blind and die within a very short period of time. Understandably, just the word itself sent figurative shivers through Joan's mind, particularly in her weakened state.

Sam ended up staying in that hospital for two weeks while the internal medicine physicians tried desperately to get her pancreas to function once again and return her to a proper metabolic balance. Meanwhile, I moved our meager possessions into an on-base trailer— euphemistically termed a mobile home today—where we were to live for the next two and a half years. I visited her as frequently as I could, sometimes leaving in mid-afternoon to drive to Landstuhl and returning that night so I could be at work by 0700 the next morning.

When Sam's physicians saw a glimmer of hope in her condition, they released her to the care of one of the physicians at our base clinic, Captain Bill Holladay. She was given a very strict diet in the hopes that she would be able to control the disease by diet alone, and equipped her with the only home method at the time of checking her blood sugar: urine test strips.[10] She also went to the base clinic

---

9   We estimated, based entirely on our own empirical evidence over the early years, that fewer than one in ten medical doctors and one in fifty registered nurses were sufficiently well qualified to care for a seriously ill diabetic patient.

10   The test strips were blue and when dipped in urine, if they remained blue, her blood sugar level was acceptable. If they turned pink or red, it meant that her kidneys were spilling excess sugar into the urine— not a desirable sign.

weekly for blood tests that were a much clearer indicator of her condition. And weekly, she would sit down with Doc Holladay to plot her progress, adjust her diet, or take whatever action might stave off the ultimate need for insulin injections.

Sam was so desperate to avoid being insulin dependent that she resorted to "cheating." In order to avoid or prevent high blood sugar readings, she steadily decreased her food intake over the next three months to the point of eating virtually nothing. When she went from her weight of 112 pounds on our wedding day down to just under ninety pounds, it became clear that the time had come to act. She was admitted to the USAF hospital at Wiesbaden—which was much better staffed for the challenge ahead—where she was regulated on daily insulin injections and trained for her own self-care. For obvious reasons, I was also included in this latter phase of training.

After getting over the initial disappointment of becoming insulin dependent, we both studied everything we could get our hands on about the disease, and probably became equally if not more knowledgeable than most medical professionals we encountered over the next two decades. Sam didn't have any compunction about giving herself insulin injections but that didn't necessarily mean she liked it. So I soon began each day by giving her the morning shot in her buttocks.

Self-care for a diabetic was hardly an easy task in those days. There was only one type of long-acting insulin and determining her daily dosage was little more than an educated guessing game. It was not until the mid-1970s that the disposable insulin syringe was patented in the United States, and not until a few years after that until they could be obtained at military hospital pharmacies by prescription. Prior to that time, a diabetic was equipped with reusable glass syringes and reusable stainless steel needles. They had to be sterilized by steaming them over boiling water for at least ten minutes. She used them over and over until the needles became too dull, or the piston on the syringe froze up with contaminants from the steam.

But throughout this difficult period in her adjustment to her chronic condition, she revealed one of her most enduring, endearing, and admirable qualities—she never once uttered a word of complaint. In the decades that followed, I discovered that she had the most remarkable combination of qualities of any person I have ever known: indomitable courage, unflagging optimism, a determined will, and a gentle loving disposition.

These setbacks were merely temporary, however. It was not more than a month or so later and she was ready and willing to face another pregnancy and eager to conceive again, though hardly with the same zealous fervor that she had evinced initially. And perhaps the less fervid emotions over the effort helped to bring her to success more easily. But once again, it was not to be. She hadn't even reached the end of her first trimester when she miscarried. The loss occurred at home, just two days prior to Christmas of 1958.

A number of us had planned to go to midnight Mass on Christmas Eve at the base chapel, but she didn't feel up to the traditional ritual so soon after the miscarriage. Instead, she listened to midnight Mass at home on the radio while one of our bachelor friends, Lieutenant Bobby Tarleton, kept her company. Bobby was not a Catholic and probably had little idea of what was going on as the Mass was still in Latin at the time. But he sat with her most respectfully throughout the service, even joining Joan as she knelt during the consecration. She never forgot his kindness that night, and hardly a Christmas Eve ever took place for the rest of her life that she didn't recall that night.

Earlier that same fall, one of the newly hired elementary school teachers in the Department of Defense Dependent School (DODDS) on the base was critically injured in an automobile accident and had to be medically evacuated back to the States. Joan had already been selected as the primary substitute teacher for the elementary grades and was immediately hired to replace the injured woman for the remainder of the year. In this capacity, we became welcomed members of the male (primarily fighter pilots) and female (primarily school teachers) singles group, and led a very active and fulfilling social life with them. It was a period of high spirits, wild (for the era) times, and wonderful camaraderie.

At one point, the new Catholic chaplain on base, Lieutenant (Ch) John Cmiel, observed that we seemed to be inseparable and wondered aloud when he was going to get the opportunity to officiate at our wedding. After he learned that we already were married, he became a not-infrequent dinner guest at our trailer, taking proper advantage of our standing invitation.

We also became exceptionally close friends with the (intentionally, temporarily) childless couple across the street from us in the trailer village—Shirley and John Leaphart. We were constant companions, dining out together, sharing cocktails each night, and going on vacations with one another. That winter and the next, we became avid skiers and often could be found leaving the base late Friday afternoon and heading to Feldberg in the *Schwarzwald* (Black Forest) of Germany, the closest ski area to where we lived. The Leapharts and we have remained especially close friends ever since. And Shirley and Joan have had eerily similar medical histories over the years.

Sam became pregnant for the third time in the spring of 1959 and once again she experienced another first trimester miscarriage. By this time, we had become apprehensive about what these frequent miscarriages were doing to her physically, how much the onset of diabetes was affecting her ability to sustain a pregnancy, and whether it would be prudent to continue this pattern of unsuccessful pregnancies. We remained devout and obedient Catholics and the idea of using any form of artificial birth control was beyond the realm of our consideration. So we began what some of its practitioners call Vatican roulette—the rhythm method of birth control.

It worked, at least for nearly a year but despite being exceptionally cautious, mid-winter of 1959–60 found her pregnant—the fourth time in less than three years. As soon as the doctors at our on-base clinic—who were almost as anxious as we were—confirmed her status once again, they ordered bed rest for the entire duration of her gestation period. To add emphasis to the regimen, she was sent to the Wiesbaden hospital where she was to be under the constant care of a senior, well-renowned OB/GYN specialist. Once again, I was on the road to Germany every weekend and Sam's doctor was kind enough to give her a weekend pass each time I arrived so that we could luxuriate at the Von Steuben Hotel, a U.S.-forces-leased four-star hotel in one of the loveliest resort capitals of Western Europe. We loved Wiesbaden and we spent every weekend joyfully together, but we were much more careful in our romantic endeavors.

Sam always enjoyed retelling the story of my first weekend trip from Phalsbourg to Wiesbaden. I was filling up with gas at the Esso station at the foot of the hill on which the base was located, when an attractive young woman came over to the car and asked if I happened to be going anywhere near Frankfurt in Germany. When I told her where I was headed, she asked if she could ride with me and I agreed. We were hardly underway when she began to cry and tell me that she had just been kicked out by her English boyfriend with whom she had lived for the past year. He happened to be working in the area at the time and probably considered her little more than excess baggage since he was headed back to the UK.

"I loved him so much and we were so good together," she told me. "He even bought me a Coca-Cola every Friday evening." That certainly must have been true love.

By the time we reached the German border, she had stopped sobbing, and focused on me instead of her woes. Of course she wanted to know what was drawing me to Wiesbaden on a Friday evening, and when I told her, she had all sorts of questions about what it was like to be married and about our marriage in particular. She was also interested in how long Joan would be hospitalized, and what for, and then she finally conceived a brilliant plan. I could rent a small apartment for her in Wiesbaden and when I came up there to visit my wife, I'd have company and a nice place to stay. I'm afraid I simply smiled at her offer, but Sam laughed uproariously when I told her that evening in Willi's piano bar at the Von Steuben. And she told the tale many times in the years that followed.

February, March, and April went by swiftly for me, but I'm sure they dragged for Joan. She was allowed to get up for a few hours each day and occupied most of her time helping out on the maternity ward, though not with the babies. We enjoyed our weekends together as if we were on a mini-honeymoon each weekend. And more importantly, she was holding on to this baby well into the second trimester, and with each week that passed, our hopes became elevated.

But then one evening in her fifth month, I received a message from the hospital: I had better come quickly as Joan was having contractions. It might be false labor, the doctor said, but with her history, they were concerned that she was going to be cheated by fate again. I arrived just in time to be there to try to comfort her yet once again. She had an unsuccessful pregnancy for the fourth time.

The following morning, after we'd had a little time to grieve, the deputy hospital commander, a physician and an U. S. Air Force colonel, paid a visit to us in her room.

"I'll apologize in advance for being as blunt and outspoken as I'm going to be. But someone needs to speak candidly to you kids. You both, especially you Mrs. Toner, have some serious soul-searching to do. As directly as I can say this to you, you're seriously endangering your life by these frequent unsuccessful pregnancies. I don't think there's a physician anywhere in this world who would guarantee that you can make it through another pregnancy, Mrs. Toner, and I'm not just talking about success in having a baby. I'm talking about your personal survival."

He turned to me and continued, "And I don't have to tell you that you play a major role in this either, Lieutenant. Your wife's physical well-being is fragile to say the least and if you get her pregnant again, you may well be making yourself a widower at the same time. I know that you're both very upset over this most recent loss, and I don't want to upset you any further. But the gravity of the situation your wife is in right now might just impress you more by my doing this now rather than later.

"I realize that both of you are Catholics, and I will tell you right up front that I'm not. I don't have the same religious convictions that you do and my lot in life is to save peoples' lives, not their souls. But if you continue to refuse to use some form of birth control, or take some more positive approach to this situation like having a tubal ligation, you're simply gambling on the duration of your life together. I apologize for talking to you so toughly, but I can't in good conscience let the day go by without informing you of the general consensus of all the doctors who have been working with you for the past few months. I hope you'll consider very carefully what I've told you."

And with that he left her room.

We were a bit shocked and dumbstruck by his message, but he certainly seemed to answer our previous dilemma over whether these pregnancies were causing her physical harm. When the Catholic chaplain came in later that morning, we told him what had happened earlier and he became very upset. He mumbled a few platitudes about God never giving us a burden we couldn't bear and God having a purpose in life for all of us, and then he too left. As we were to learn later, he went directly to challenge the colonel for his lecture on a subject that was "uncalled for" and "completely out of line." We later learned that the confrontation was not private and had caused a whispering campaign throughout the hospital. However, we did not have any comments directed to us.

Meanwhile, we didn't dismiss out of hand what the deputy hospital commander had to say, by any means. In fact, it may have been the first chink in our religious beliefs that would manifest itself more directly as the years went on.

With regard to the chaplain's brief message, I had questions arise in my own mind that I never did convey directly to Sam. How did we know that God's "burden" for us was not her death? Wasn't it possible that God's "plan" for her was more unsuccessful pregnancies until Sam was unable to survive the final one? I quite surprised myself that such doubts even entered my mind, but they were there and not easily dismissed. I loved her dearly and the thought of losing her at such a young age outweighed all other rational thinking on my part.

The following day, Sam told me that she felt fine and was ready to get out of the hospital as soon as she could. But since they were reluctant to release her for a few more days, she suggested that we go shopping. She knew that "shopping" was hardly my cup of tea. But when I asked her what she was interested in looking for, she responded with an impish glint in her eye and a two-word answer—sports cars. Our good friends and backyard neighbors in the trailer park, Josie and Paul Cianci, had just purchased a new Mercedes 190SL, one of the sexiest high-performance cars in the world at the time. We loved it with its glistening black finish and hand-tooled red leather seats. And it drove like a dream.

During that same time period, a group of the bachelor officers had formed a one-time only corporation and purchased twelve Porsche sports cars directly from the factory in Stuttgart. We were suitably impressed by the look and performance of the Porsches, but five of the new vehicles had been wrecked—accidents alleged to be caused by the unusual handling characteristics of the vehicle—in the first year that they were purchased, one of which was responsible for the severe injury of the teacher Joan had replaced. She wasn't interested in a Porsche—probably for that reason alone—but wanted to look at some others that she had heard or read about.

When we entered the Wiesbaden Alfa-Romeo dealer's showroom, there was an Alfa 2000 Spider on the floor and Sam's reaction to it was almost the equivalent of love at first sight. It was bright red with a tan "rag top" as they were known at the time. It had natural tan leather upholstery with a five-forward speed gearbox on the floor. She sat in it. We went for a test drive in another demonstration car, and I thought she was all ready to suggest that we put a down payment on the thirty-five-hundred-dollar impractical toy.

"Let's think about it for a while," was my advice, even though I was nearly as taken by it as she was. She gathered up all the literature available and we headed off to dream about it.

The following day, the Catholic chaplain again came to visit Sam, but instead of any lectures or clichés, he suggested that we give some consideration to adopting a child. There was a military family adoption coordinator right here in nearby Lindsey Air Station,[11] and she might help us get more facts to aid us in our deliberations, he suggested. Adoption was a course of action that never even occurred to us before, and I felt certain that Sam would still see herself as a "failure" if we took that route. But it was a worthy idea and having a child, whether or not she was the birth mother, just might placate Sam's intense longing to be a mother.

That very afternoon found us in the office of Miss Elisabeth Dommermuth, a middle-aged German national who had the immense responsibility for uniting orphaned or unwanted German children with American military families. Miss Dommermuth was a small, slight woman with prematurely graying hair and a smile and charm that immediately told us that she was enraptured by her duties and took huge satisfaction in her prior accomplishments.

She had already been advised of the reason for our visit by the chaplain, but she wanted to hear directly from us why we had

---

[11]   Lindsey AS was the location of the headquarters of the United States Air Forces in Europe at the time and it was just down the street, within walking distance from the hospital.

come to her. When we told our story, but admitted that we were not necessarily sure of our decision to adopt, she smiled sagely and told us that she didn't think anyone in our position was ever sure on their first visit. But she went on to tell us that she had never had a dissatisfied customer in the many years she had been in this position. She then took out an album of an endless number of infants and toddlers who she had placed and told us the names of each one and their adoptive parents as she turned the pages. The expression in her eyes was of sheer ecstasy as she turned the pages, and we recognized instantly that this saintly woman could not have been better suited to her job.

"When are you scheduled to return to the United Sates?" was her first question. And when we told her that it was the following January, just a little less than nine months away, she frowned.

"Is there any possibility that you might extend your tour of duty in France?" she asked, "because it usually takes a year to eighteen months to complete all the details. You have only a few more months left here, and according to German government regulations, you must be stationed in Europe in order to adopt.

Extending my tour of duty at Phalsbourg was out of the question. General DeGaulle had already told the United States that all foreign forces—including NATO headquarters—were to leave France, and plans were already in the works for our gradual withdrawal. Phalsbourg was to be one of the first installations to close and the projected date was roughly at the time that I was slated to return to the States.

In addition, I was more committed than ever to leave the air force as soon as my commitment was over, and any delay in reassignment was just another delay in my ability to start a civilian career.

Miss Dommermuth was clearly lost in thought for some moments and she eventually brightened and suggested, "If you decide you want to try to adopt, and if you get very excellent references within the month, I'll do everything I can to help you. You can't be particular about a girl or a boy, and you'll need to have some extraordinary support from people who have known you for much of your lives, but there is an outside chance we might be successful."

As we left, she shook our hands warmly and advised that we needed to let her know as soon as possible of our decision.

We spent the entire rest of the day talking about nothing else. Our first decision was to determine if we even wanted to adopt. The second was to decide who those extraordinary references might come from and how best to obtain them. As I told Sam, we still could buy that impressive Alfa if there simply was not enough time to complete the adoption process. So, late that night, we decided to give adoption a try.

We called both families and explained our predicament. And we started naming those folks who we thought would carry the most weight: high school principals and teachers; Boston College and Holy Cross Jesuit priests for both of us; city government officials who had known us for some time, and on and on.

I don't know if the debate over who was responsible for getting the clincher was ever resolved, but Miss Dommermuth called us in France two weeks later and told us that our references were overwhelming and she was all but certain she could arrange for us to adopt a child. But the one letter of reference that impressed her the most was an unequivocal note of support from Richard Cardinal Cushing, the Archbishop of Boston, courtesy of my old parish priest who once was his secretary.

It was late May—Memorial Day, the thirtieth, to be precise— when we received the message from Miss Dommermuth that we had attained German and U.S. government approval. She told us that it would be a month or so before we would know that a specific child had been selected for us, but it would be a good idea to start preparing for a new baby.

Then on the last day of June, she instructed us to go to Bad Waldsee, a small mountain spa village on the eastern edge of the Black Forest, in the state of Badem-Württemberg. There we were to contact the jugendamt[12] who would handle all the details from then on. He would be expecting us. She then reminded us that we were in no obligation to accept the five-and-one-half-month-old baby girl after we had seen her. It was to be completely our decision and ours only.

---

[12]   The jugendamt was the child welfare officer for the district.

By dawn the next morning, we were in our car headed east and eager for the four-hour drive to come to an end so we could see our baby for the first time. We hadn't even spoken to any extent about girls' names, so we spent much of our time on the drive making that decision. We already knew the baby's given name, Ute Maria Etz, and we dismissed keeping any of her birth name as such a Germanic sounding name would be too hard on the child as she grew up and went to school in the United States. Then Sam reminded me of her promise three years before that I should name all but our first son. And since we already had our Richard John Junior, and lost him, it was up to me to select a name for our daughter.

I told her that I never took that commitment seriously and that the baby's name was to be a joint decision on both our parts. But I also told her that I had always loved the name Christine because I used to babysit for neighbors who had the sweetest little girl by that name. I'm sure that influenced my suggestion greatly. Then I asked for her ideas.

"Well, ever since we met the Reaves during the time we lived in London, I've always thought that their little baby, Bonny Sue, was one of the nicest names I could think of. But since that's a name that strongly suggests the south, and we're not Texans as they were, I guess that wouldn't be a good idea for our daughter. So Christine will do just fine," she concluded.

On Friday, the first of July, the jugendamt brought us to a Catholic orphanage that was immediately adjacent to a monastery with a magnificent onion-domed church in the middle of it. We were met by the Mother Superior and after a brief exchange of pleasantries with her, she rang a little bell she had hidden in her habit. Moments later, a very young, pretty nun came into the room, carrying the most adorable little baby either of us had ever seen. The nun handed the baby to Sam and then stepped back with tears running down her cheeks.

"I just love her and she's so beautiful," Sam crooned. And there was no question that I agreed with her completely.

"Of course we'll take her," we both said together.

The jugendamt cleared his throat nervously, and told us that we would have to wait until Monday to take little Christine home with us. Today was our decision day, to tell him whether or not we wanted her. It was late Friday afternoon and there was a great deal of paperwork that still needed to be done; that would have to wait until Monday morning. Half apologetically, he told us that we were in one of the loveliest areas of Europe and we should enjoy our weekend by touring around the nearby Bodensee (also known as Lake Constance) and seeing the sights, implying that we'd have our baby soon enough and our opportunities for adventure were about to be curtailed somewhat.

When we left the orphanage, we went directly next door to the lovely monastery church that was covered with Bavarian-style murals inside and out. As we knelt to say a brief prayer of thanksgiving, the sounds of a Gregorian chant filled the church. Soon a large group of monks wearing light beige robes with brown cowls that all but hid their faces entered in single file. The line of entering monks split at the rear of the sacristy and they proceeded down the two outside aisles of the church toward the altar, filling the interior of the church with their hauntingly beautiful harmony. They had come to sing their late afternoon prayers which, we were to learn, preceded the tolling of the Angelus. As we knelt there listening, Sam glanced at me with an angelic expression on her face and said, "What more confirmation do we need to tell us that we've done the right thing?"

Christine Leslie Toner became the newest member of our family on the morning of July Fourth, which to this day, she considers her real birthday, rather than January 16, her actual date of birth. Joan hugged the young nun who had been Ute's loving and dedicated nurse since the day of her birth while I held Christine. I knew that Sam deeply empathized with the young nun, having gone through similar wrenching losses herself so recently, and she was trying desperately to soothe the nun's evident anguish over saying farewell to "her baby." But Mother Superior nodded gently as if to tell the young nun that she would soon have another child on whom to lavish her love and affection, and she ushered us to the door of the convent with her blessing and well-wishes. Both Sam and I noticed the small tear that was welled up in the corner of Mother Superior's eyes as she bade us good-bye. She clearly wasn't immune to the sense of loss either.

By noontime, we had reached the main west-bound autobahn that would take us back to the Rhein and into France. We stopped at an American forces gas station where we would fill up for the remainder of the trip, have a little bite to eat ourselves, and most important, feed our new baby for the first time. The nuns had prepared food for us to feed Christine for a day or so. When her food and bottle were warmed, Sam looked at me with a very embarrassed expression and said, "I don't know how to do this because Aunt Dorothy never allowed me to babysit. Would you please show me how? I promise I'll learn fast, but I don't want to make any mistakes in my first attempt here in public."

Arriving at Phalsbourg late in the day, we were greeted by our trailer court neighbors with a wonderful, touching welcome. There were all the oohs and aahs that normally accompany the arrival home of a new mother and baby, and Joan was thrilled. And she learned very quickly indeed, not hesitating with the first messy diaper and all the other baby-care chores that go along with it.

Chris, as we had already come to call her, was a beautiful child who smiled and laughed all the time. She was also exceptionally active and was soon scooting around the trailer in a walker or bouncing in a swing that we set up in the lean-to attached to our small trailer to add a little more living and storage space. In anticipation, Joan had bought a lovely, traditional English pram with a fringed canopy and a rain hood that she had purchased before we left London. Now she finally had a chance to use it. She was out proudly pushing her baby all over the neighborhood every day she could.

It soon became clear that Sam simply wanted to be a mother and it didn't matter a whit how it happened. At last we had a child, and I had never seen her so happy.

*   *   *

The next few months flew by and Sam assumed the mantel of mother just as I knew she would. She loved to hold Chris when she wasn't absorbed in other household chores, but Chris was far too active to settle with being cuddled. She wanted to laugh and play and crawl, even attempting her first steps.

In late September, we received a surprise call from Miss Dommermuth who got to the point quickly. "The officials with whom I work are so impressed with your references and how nicely your daughter has fit into your family life that we're prepared to offer you another child. This time it's a boy and in fact it's Christine's half-brother. They both have the same mother."

Miss Dommermuth then went on to report that the half-brother was actually six years old, spoke only German, and was already enrolled in a German grammar school. He was living with a foster family[13] in the Black Forest region and would be available immediately.

Sam paused a long time and finally told Miss Dommermuth that we'd have to think about it, but that we would call back as soon as we were able to make a decision.

The idea of Chris having her own blood brother as part of our family was exciting, but ripping a young boy away from the only culture and education he had known seemed a daunting challenge. Not to mention the fact that we had only been married for three years, and some unscrupulous people would conclude that he was illegitimate—a rather silly concern in the enlightened era of today, but a genuine stigma that bore consideration at the time. And while our logic, in retrospect, was both convoluted and not terribly rational, we called her back the next day to decline her offer.

But our patroness was not to be deterred. She called two weeks later to offer another boy for adoption. This one was less than six months younger than Christine, she told us, and he too was available immediately. Joan (and Chris) were off playing bridge at the officers' club when I took the call so I went off to find her and tell her what had happened.

We excitedly left for home immediately—well, not exactly immediately. She had to tell her fellow bridge players that we were

---

[13]   The West German social system, by this time, had evolved to where the parents of every child received a not-insignificant stipend until the child reached the age of eighteen. The policy was clearly intended to rebuild the German population after the devastating losses of manpower in WW II. Those families who took in foster children received a double stipend for each foster child. This policy had both very good and very bad results over time.

going to be parents again. On the way home, Sam said, "It's just three months before we're due to leave to go back to the States, and we'll never have this opportunity again. I think we should do it, or at least go to see him right away and make our decision then."

Two days later, we had stocked up on more diapers—the cloth type that you had to wash every day—plus a number of changes of clothes for a three-month-old boy, and we were on our way back to southern Germany. This time, however, it was to Kempten im Allgäu, a town that most archeologists believe is the oldest settlement in Germany. Though it was only about fifty kilometers east of Bad Waldsee, it was in the state of Bavaria. Interestingly, we were to discover that the jugendamt, a federal position was the same man who had officiated when we gained Christine.

When we entered his office we could hear a child crying in a distant part of the building, and that continued for all the time we spoke to the official. "I'm afraid that Dieter [his given name was Dieter Bruno Stohr] is not in the immaculate condition in which you found Ute," he confided. But that was to prove a severe understatement, yet not the only shock we were to receive over the next few minutes. Instead of being six months younger than Chris, he was in fact six months older than her.

When Dieter was brought into the room, we discovered who the pathetically wailing child had been. Not only was he crying hysterically, his clothes were filthy and his shoulder-length blond hair was matted to his head with food and other filth. He was unquestionably the most pathetic little creature we had ever seen. The official could sense our complete dismay and quickly assured us that the right to refuse the child was our decision to make alone, with an expression on his face that asked, how could you possibly do anything else?

When Sam attempted to pick him up and hold him, he screamed even louder and raised both of his hands to his face as if to defend himself. When I picked him up, he didn't assume that defensive position, but he still sobbed uncontrollably.

With a demeanor that spoke of a bear sow defending her cubs, Sam said that we were going to take him back to the hotel with us, and would be back with him in the morning—if that was alright with the jugendamt. He nodded somberly. We set the time for 0900 the next day and returned to the hotel.

The first thing we did was strip off his filthy clothes to wash them in the bathroom sink, since none of the clothes we had brought with us would fit him. When his diaper was removed, we were incredulous. Every inch of skin in his diaper area was covered with festering sores. Heaven only knows how long since he had been bathed, but that was not the end of our unbelievable discoveries. At eighteen months of age, he could not sit up by himself, he was skeletal with his ribs showing, and his legs were not much more than skin and bone. It was clearly apparent that this pathetic little creature had been systematically starved, neglected, and physically abused, more than likely so that the greedy foster parents could get their grubby hands on the double stipend they were awarded for his care.

"We can't take him, Sam!" was my conclusion after these morbid discoveries. "We're far too close to going back to the States and caring for him is going to take away from Chris and just be far too much for you to handle."

With bitter tears of anger in her eyes, she stared at me and in a voice that almost sounded threatening, she let me have it. "What are you thinking of? Do you want to condemn this poor innocent child to death? I never dreamt that a baby could be so horribly abused and I refuse to allow it to continue. Yes, we're going to take him. You're damned right we're going to take him. And if you don't want to, I'll do it by myself. But I hope that the people who have done this to this poor little soul will rot in hell for eternity."

She still hadn't lost her fervor the next morning when we returned to the jugendamt's office to sign the necessary papers.

"Here is a list of the abuses that this child has suffered and I'm sure we will find more when we get him home and examine him more thoroughly. You saw the way he recoiled when I tried to pick him up yesterday," she went on, "and there's no doubt in my mind that the fiend who is supposed to have been his foster mother beat him on the head with great regularity. We're not simply adopting this baby; we're preventing him from being murdered. I'm not sure how much authority you have in this position, but I hope to God you will initiate charges against those people and, if nothing else, prevent them from ever having a foster child again."

She was to say essentially the same things to Miss Dommermuth not long afterward.

On the way home to France, Dieter finally ran out of tears and strength and, after being fed, he slept most of the way. He didn't resist when we brought him into the house and seemed relatively at peace for the first week or so—though he still reacted defensively whenever Joan attempted to pick him up.

We had already decided that this little one would be named Scott Michael Toner, but for the first weeks we had him, he was known simply as the poor little baby. And Sam's intuition that more damage would be found proved to be precisely correct. When I shaved the mass of filth from his head, his entire scalp was littered with scars where he had clearly been struck repeatedly. Not only could he not sit up on his own, he had never eaten solid food before and resisted being fed out of fear.

And we soon found that his acquiescence to his new surroundings was short-lived. Each time we would take him out of the trailer house, whether for a pram ride or to a doctor's appointment, he cried hysterically until he returned home and crossed the threshold. So I began coming home at lunch hour each day, putting him in his car seat, and driving around the eight-kilometer perimeter road of the base. Finally, after six weeks of doing that daily, he discovered that he was at home when we were with him, either in the house or elsewhere. And the crying finally stopped.

Within a month of our bringing him home, he gained enough strength to sit by himself, and just a short while later, he was standing and taking hesitant steps while one of us held his hands. Scott also became able to pull himself to his feet in the playpen. And despite continuing rejection on his part, Sam lavished him with kindness, love, and affection. She truly became his mama bear—the person who two pediatricians of the time credited with literally saving his life.

Chris thought that this new family member was a very interesting novelty and quickly learned that she had no trouble pushing him around in the playpen, even though he was quite a bit older than her. But she was also quite affectionate with him as a rule and quickly became his most ardent protector—then, as well as all the way through their teenage years to adulthood.

When the time came for us to take our flight back to the United States, we were very concerned about the abrupt change of everything in his life—waiting at the airport, being enclosed on the plane, and the like—but fortunately the fact that one of us was with him or near at hand all the time seemed to provide him with the security he needed so desperately.

We had prepared for the flight very prudently with three changes of clothing for each child. We properly decided that two children under the age of eighteen months could be challenging, and were prepared for the worst. And as it turned out, Christine became air sick a number of times on the flight and was destined to meet her new grandparents in Scott's clothes.

But as well as we had planned, we were not prepared for the weather. We sat in the Rhein-Main (Frankfurt, Germany) terminal for six hours while a raging snowstorm delayed our takeoff over and over again. Finally, a window in the storm cleared just long enough for us to get off the ground and on our way.

We flew in an USAF C-118,[14] with no amenities to speak of and minimally comfortable web seats. The babies were accommodated by cardboard boxes about thirty inches long and sixteen inches wide secured by seat belts. The boxes contained a thin disposable mattress and were the closest thing to a crib available at the time. The range of the aircraft was not long enough to complete a trans-Atlantic flight, so we had to stop in Keflavik, Iceland, to refuel—at 0230 in the morning, local time. Military regulations at the time required that each passenger had to deplane while refueling took place, so the little ones, who had barely settled down for the night, had to be rousted out to go into the terminal.

This terminal served both the military as well as the commercial flights through Iceland. And one of the first things we saw when we entered the building was a bar. If ever there was a time that we

---

[14]   The C-118 was a militarized version of the Douglas DC-6, a four-engine propeller driven aircraft that was then well along in the process of being phased out of commercial airline use. It was the same type of aircraft that had flown me to England three years previously.

needed a stiff drink that was it. So we took turns. While one of us walked the children—one on each hand—the other relaxed briefly with a cocktail. Both Chris and Scott had begun to walk, so they seemed to enjoy parading through the small terminal. And the exercise would certainly help to tire them out for the remainder of the flight.

When we were passing over Newfoundland and beginning our travel down the east coast, the pilot told us there was a major snowstorm in the northeastern part of the country, and we could possibly be diverted to someplace other than McGuire AFB in New Jersey, where the runways were closed. The date was January 20, 1961—Inauguration Day for John Fitzgerald Kennedy—so there were thousands of people concerned about the raging snowstorm, not just many of our family members and friends who happened to be waiting for us to arrive at McGuire.

But the weather gods eventually smiled on all of us, and as we passed over Boston, the pilot informed us that the weather had lifted. It was a clear, crisp, cold day all along the eastern seaboard, and most important of all, the runways at our destination had just reopened.

As we taxied in toward the terminal, we had no doubt that the reports of the storm had been accurate. Snow was piled so high along the taxiways that you couldn't see anything other than snow banks out the windows. This was before terminal jetways had been developed, so each of us, with diaper bags hanging off our shoulders, carried a child as we descended the roll-up stairway from the plane. Other than Chris's unfortunate air sickness episodes, both of the children had been angels the whole time. But that was soon to end, at least for Scott.

When we entered the terminal, an announcement was made that children under the age of six did not have to go through customs and immigration, and if there were family members on the other side of the barriers, we were encouraged to hand the youngsters out to them. We saw both my mother and Aunt Dorothy, so eager hands awaited both of our little ones. But poor little Scott wanted no part of these strangers, and he began to cry with the same plaintive wail that we had heard when first we met him four months before. Happy-go-lucky Chris, by contrast, was delighted to go to these strangers and be smothered with their attention and affection.

Before long, we had to have one of the flight attendants bring Scott back to us, where he eagerly thrust himself into his mother's arms—a far cry from the defensive posture that he used to take with Sam. Unconditional mother's love, in his case at least, had overcome that terrible insecurity he had felt when we first brought him home.

With both Sam's and my family living in the Boston area, there was always something to do or someone to see. There were lots of questions raised and concerns expressed over our decision to adopt— especially foreign children—but we left no doubt in anyone's mind that these two little ones were "selected, not expected." They were every bit ours and we wanted them to be regarded that way. This statement of our beliefs seemed to quell the comments, but we were to head to my next assignment ten days later not fully convinced that our two families looked at Scott and Christine through the same eyes we did. And this bothered Joan quite deeply.

* * *

Our next station couldn't have been much farther away and still have been in the United States. I had been assigned to Vandenberg AFB in California, the recently opened home of the new intercontinental ballistic missile (ICBM) research and development program. We had to drive across country and because it was still wintertime, we chose the southern route to avoid any blizzards and the risk of getting marooned en route. We had plenty of travel time allotted to us, but travel in a small car with babies was no time to do any sightseeing. Fortunately, except for a sandstorm crossing the Mojave Desert, the trip was relatively uneventful.

Vandenberg was so new and there were so many better-paid civilian contractors being brought to the immediate region that finding affordable housing for a young first lieutenant and his family was next to impossible. So we ended up in a two-bedroom apartment in the lovely Danish-replica village of Solvang, in the foothills of the Santa Inez Mountains, not far from the ranch that President Reagan made famous some two decades later.

Sam truly loved the village, mostly because it reminded us of Europe, which we had come to love. She didn't mind the fact that I had to have the car to travel the daily fifty-mile round-trip to the base. Sam wasn't bothered at all, she told me. She had the pram and it would be great exercise for her to take the children to the small village center, pick up the mail at the post office, and enjoy the wonders of California. But it wasn't long before we discovered some serious downsides to the arrangement. As soon as we learned of an affordable vacancy in Lompoc, the nearest town to the base, we took it. There, at least, Sam could drive me to work in the morning, pick me up in the evening, and have the car for errands and other activities each day.

We continued our flirtation with Vatican roulette and were successful for well over a year, but our romantic involvement suffered seriously with both of us checking the calendar each time the moment seemed right. In retrospect, this preoccupation with her not becoming pregnant affected more than our sex life. It affected our ability to be honest and candid with one another and that spilled over into other aspects of our relationship—even though our individual motives were primarily out of consideration for the other.

But that was not much of a consideration any more after we learned that the rhythm method had failed once again. But the OB/GYN physicians at the Vandenberg base hospital were able to help Joan sustain a pregnancy through term, through the use of a new drug on the market. The drug they prescribed was a recent development by a German pharmaceutical manufacturer. It was primarily a sedative-hypnotic that had been found to be highly effective in reducing morning sickness for pregnant women. Early research also found that the drug, available under a variety of trade names around the world, also appeared to assist women in sustaining their pregnancies.

Though the drug Joan was given had a different trade name, it was in fact a derivative of thalidomide.[15]

---

[15]   Thalidomide was widely prescribed during the late 1950s and early 1960s for pregnant women to combat morning sickness. Before its release, inadequate tests were performed to assess the drug's safety, with catastrophic results for the children of women who had taken thalidomide during their pregnancies (*Encyclopedia Britannica*)

As the months went by, Joan thrived on her new status, but we remained understandably skeptical of her chance to fulfill her deeply held desire—to deliver her own normal healthy baby, regardless of what sex it happened to be. But as she approached the end of her eighth month, an event occurred for which I have never been fully able to forgive Aunt Dorothy.

Dorothy had begun working for American Airlines as a reservations agent, and with that position came a very important perquisite—she and George would be able to take AA flights on employee passes. At the time, the passes were free except for the need to pay the federal tax on the value of an equivalent ticket. And one of the first trips she and George took was to visit an old friend and her husband who had moved some time before to the Los Angeles area. It also seemed an opportune time to drive up the coastal highway to Vandenberg to see Joan—and the rest of us. But instead of renting a car or taking a bus, she convinced the friends with whom they were staying that they should come too. And not only that, their adult daughter came with them as well.

They spent the better part of three nights and four days in Lompoc, housed in a nearby motel, but virtually every waking hour was spent in our small home. And to my disbelief, they expected to be entertained. They played with the children and took them out for a walk when the un-California-like Lompoc weather permitted, but did essentially nothing to assist in preparation of three meals a day and other household chores.

Dorothy would occasionally tell Joan, "Just tell me what you want me to do," but continued to ignore the obvious and visit with her friends. She did tell George to help with the dishes each evening but never turned her hand at all herself, even to assist with the care of the children. After all, she was on vacation, was the clear message that she sent.

When they left, Sam was exhausted and deeply hurt that Dorothy had been so inconsiderate. After they left on the following Monday, she awakened in the morning with very minor contractions and had begun spotting. The first thing I did was to call one of the secretaries in the office, Georgeanna Carter, a lovely young eighteen-year-old who had occasionally babysat for us. She voluntarily chose to take her own vacation hours and come to the house while I took Joan to the hospital.

As soon as Joan's obstetrician heard what she had to say, he admitted her to the maternity ward and told her she needed to make the necessary provisions to remain hospitalized until she delivered. I then went home and called my mother in suburban Boston and told her what had happened. Without prompting, she said she would come to stay with the children for as long as I needed her, and she arrived at our home three days later. Meanwhile, Georgeanna (or Gidget as she had been nicknamed by her former high school classmates since she looked a lot like Sandra Dee, the star of the recently popular movie) continued to take her vacation time to care for Scott and Chris. My mother and Dorothy had never been close, primarily as just one more outgrowth of Dorothy's jealousy and obsessive love for Joan. But when my mother learned of Dorothy's recent inconsiderate visit, the aloofness of their relationship turned to an enduring animosity on my mother's part.

My mother remained for the next five weeks, thoroughly enjoying the chance to care for her two new grandchildren and, I suspect, reveling in her ability to care for me as well. I spent all my time either at work or visiting Sam at noon or after work.

When I arrived home each evening, the kids were fed and ready for bed, but still had a little time left to spend with Dad before I put them down for the night. Then Mom and I would share the meal together that she had prepared and review our day, with the primary focus on how Joan happened to be doing that day. In many ways the time period reminded me of the days not long before when I was back and forth to Wiesbaden each weekend. But so much had changed in that brief interlude.

As Sam approached her natural due date, her doctor told us he was no longer going to trust nature, but instead had to decide what would be best for both her and the baby. He said that the following Monday morning he was going to take the baby by Caesarian section. Despite the inherent danger that existed, I was relieved to hear that. I think the memory of the thirty hours of futile agony that Joan had undergone in 1958 was still paramount in both our minds, even though her extant situation remained positive. I think we also both thought of the doctor's warning in Germany not long before of the danger that existed for Joan, not just the baby.

I was present before she went to the delivery room, of course, and she smiled broadly as they wheeled her in. Clearly she was not only looking forward to ending the time she had spent away from her babies, she was also eager to become a successful birth mother for the first time as well. It was not long before her doctor emerged to announce that we had a healthy baby boy, and both mother and baby were doing just fine. And this time, Joan was able to hold her newborn, even for just a short time, before she was given a sedative to let her sleep for a while.

But there was something strange in the doctor's somber demeanor when he told me the news. He just didn't seem as pleased and enthusiastic as I expected him to be.

"But there is a problem," he went on to say. "Your baby has a rather badly deformed right arm and leg, I'm afraid, though he is completely healthy and normal in every other respect. I'm sorry to tell you this, and after all you've been through together. I'm going to let you tell her when she wakes up in three or four hours."

Then he escorted me to the nursery to see the little guy for the first time. He was a little angel all wrapped in a blanket. He had a remarkable shock of black hair that extended from his hairline to his eyebrows. He even had dark fuzz on his ears, but he was beautiful to me. His skin showed the usual reddish tint of most newborns, but he also seemed to have a darker complexion than I might have imagined. Sam jokingly referred to him as "the Mexican gardener's son" after she saw him the first time.

But when I saw his hand and his leg moments later, I was devastated. How could God do this to her? was my first thought. Then it occurred to me that this would cause the poor little innocent even more problems throughout his life. Months later, we were to learn of the horrors that thalidomide—or other derivatives of it by different names—had been causing around the world. We were just one more family that had to face the reality of this drug, many with far more complex and debilitating problems than our baby.

When I told Sam, she looked at me incredulously and just turned away as I gently held her. But after a long while of silence on both our parts, she looked at me with those loving blue eyes of hers and stated, rather than asked, "You've seen him haven't you!"

I assured her that I had and described his looks to her.

"And you promise me that there are no other surprises. That he really is healthy, otherwise?"

She considered my confirmation just briefly and told me, "Well, that's all that really counts, isn't it. He's healthy. He will have his difficulties as he grows up, but we've managed greater disappointments than this since we've been married, and he's our son. With our help and support, he'll grow up to be a fine young man who will make us proud." Then she cradled my head against her cheek, and we stayed that way without speaking for a long, long time. She was always much stronger than I in times like this.

I had been graced with an above average tenor voice as a youngster and had been a soloist in a college glee club at one time. My specialty, if that's the right term, was singing "The Londonderry Air" or "Danny Boy" as it was more commonly known, and I was frequently asked to sing the song at family gatherings or parties. So when our latest family member was baptized, Sam again took the prerogative of determining the name and she would hear of none other than Daniel John Toner—and of course he immediately became known by all and sundry as "Danny."

In just his second month, we were referred to the Letterman Army Medical Center at the Presidio of San Francisco, where the reputed top pediatric orthopedist in the military medical service was practicing. The doctor seemed very well suited to his role and he thoroughly and compassionately examined Danny's arm and leg. In his judgment, with just a minor operation, Danny's hand could be made almost as functional as that of anyone else.

"He'll never be a concert pianist," he observed with a gentle bit of levity, "but otherwise he'll do just fine as he goes through life. I'm afraid that a therapeutic amputation of his lower leg will eventually be necessary, however. His knee looks fine, so I'm sure he will adapt very easily to a prosthesis. It's just a matter of determining the right time to do that, from both the standpoint of his continued growth as well as his psychological ability to adjust. But in my judgment, it should be done sooner rather than later. And when you decide that the time is right, you should look into the possibility of the Shriners Children's Hospitals. They're the best in the business!" he concluded.

We returned from the San Francisco trip considerably buoyed by the diagnosis and a darn sight more relieved and optimistic. And

Sam even had time to go by the City of Paris department store where she was able to purchase some fresh croissants and *reblochon* cheese, two of her favorites from the time we lived in France.

She accepted the role of being the mother of three little ones less than thirty months apart in age with amazing love, affection, and enthusiasm. Scott remained shy and relatively insecure but he improved steadily under her care. Chris and Danny were very happy little ones and seldom were a problem or proved difficult. In my biased but humble opinion, no mother could have been any more capable under the circumstances than my Sam. And all the while, she was coping with the difficulties associated with her diabetes.

* * *

Another revolution took place at this same time in our lives. My boss at Vandenberg was a salty, "old" colonel, John Everhart by name. He apparently saw something unusual in me personally, and took it upon himself to be my mentor. He had another desk brought in and moved me into his private office, with an admonition that I was to learn everything he knew, and more, about our responsibility for developing and constructing the launch facilities for the Atlas, Titan, and Minuteman missile systems. Whenever he traveled out of town, he put me in charge of the whole staff of five other officers, all of whom were considerably more senior in rank than I was.

"He's the only one other than me who knows what's going on in *all* the programs," he told them, "so he's the only one fully qualified to make the necessary decisions in my absence." No one questioned Colonel Everhart regarding his edict, and surprisingly to me at least, none of them seemed to resent the snotty-nosed kid having the authority to make decisions.

My boss also made me the chief spokesman for the office, whether that was in briefings to the wing commander,[16] escorting

---

[16] Our office was part of the 6565th Test Wing that had the on-scene mission to develop all of the ballistic missiles that were poised to become the first line of U.S. strategic defense. The wing commander was one colonel among dozens of others and was soon to be promoted to brigadier general, commensurate with the responsibilities that he held.

generals and senior civilians from Washington, or even, on one occasion, escorting President Kennedy on a tour of the launch facilities that had been developed, providing him with running commentary en route. As a son of Massachusetts, the president thought it was pretty special that a young officer from suburban Boston was his guide. And I agreed with him, even though I was scared to death by the gravity of the situation.

Under John Everhart's tutelage, I gradually learned that there was a possible place in the Air Force for me after all, and he inspired me to accept that challenge and stay around for a few more years. Shortly after making that commitment, I was temporarily assigned to a fourteen-week leadership development course at Squadron Officer School, which was a part of Air University at Maxwell AFB near Montgomery, Alabama. Normally, this was an unaccompanied period of professional education, and though the government would not pay for families to travel there temporarily, the school encouraged their new students to bring their families for this first echelon of career development.

Joan unhesitatingly declared that she and the children needed and wanted to come with me, even though we could hardly afford to live where we were, let alone the additional financial burden of a temporary home away from home. But Sam was nothing if she wasn't resourceful and soon came up with a couple who wanted to sublet our furnished house for the four months we would be gone, and she even obtained the landlord's permission to do so. And that was hardly the last time she proved the adage that "where there's a will, there's a way" whenever she wanted to do something badly enough. So we were off to Alabama—for the summer no less.

It's fortunate that we took a few extra days to travel cross-country by car, because we needed the time as it turned out. We had traded in our little French sports car some time before and had purchased a well-used 1958 Chevy station wagon, which in accordance with the times, was not air conditioned. In an effort to cause the least wear and tear on all the children, we spent the second day of our travels in a motel, and crossed the California and Arizona deserts by night.

But traveling with the windows rolled down apparently left the two older ones with a mild case of pneumonia, which forced us to stay over in Fort Worth for two nights while they were treated with antibiotics. And then when we arrived in Alabama, five-month-old Danny contracted the same problems—but much more seriously—and was in critical condition in the hospital with respiratory complications for nearly a week. And through it all, we were very anxious of course, but Sam took everything in stride and soon she had made our temporary little house—with a single window air conditioner—as comfortable and homey as possible. And she never regretted having made the decision and effort to accompany me.

During the final week of school, the commandant called me into his office and told me that my instructor, and everyone up the chain of command, thought that I had established an excellent record there. He then asked me if I was interested in returning to the school one day to become an instructor myself. He went on to say that since I was still a first lieutenant, and all of the instructors were either captains or majors, it would be some time before I would be transferred back to Maxwell. He simply wanted to know if I'd like to do it—someday.

I talked the offer over with Joan that night and her reaction was instantaneous. "I'd love to. I can't think of a nicer area to raise our children over the next three or four years, and I know you'd be an excellent teacher."

So the next morning, I returned to the commandant's office and officially declared myself to be a volunteer to teach at Air University's junior school, Squadron Officer School, or SOS as it was universally known throughout the Air Force.

I had spoken to Colonel Everhart before we left Alabama and told him our plans for the return. "Well, we're looking forward to having you back," he told me, "but unless you scream and holler like crazy, you're going to have a new job when you get here. Much as I hate to lose you, Joe Cody [the Test Wing commander] has just pinned on his new star, and he wants you to be his aide-de-camp. It'll give you another different perspective on the Air Force and you're the perfect fit for the job."

There aren't many jobs that are more career enhancing for a young officer than to become a general's aide, but it wasn't going to be a piece of cake by any means. After the exposure that John Everhart had given me, I was a bit apprehensive but pretty confident that I was up to the task. And General Cody was a jewel of a guy to boot. Sam was so proud when I told her, and to me, the combination of her pride and my apparent success certainly corroborated the decision that we had made months before to become a career Air Force family. We were anxious to get home again.

The trip back was fortunately uneventful and our house had been very well cared for, with everything neatly in its place when we returned. My first days on the job were challenging but fun and I knew it was the place for me.

Before the week was out, however, General Cody called me into his office and he greeted me by saying, "Damn, Dick, we've hardly had time to get to know one another and here I get orders from the personnel center reassigning you to Maxwell to become an SOS instructor. You must have done awfully well there," he went on. "I've already protested the move and I can still take it higher if you want me to. But I'll have to be perfectly honest with you. I fully expect to be transferred myself before long, so if you want to take this assignment, you'll do so with my blessing. You still have about six weeks before you're due to depart, so I want you to stay where you are. And if I don't have orders myself by that time, you can help me find your replacement and break him in."

So that's the way it would be. I told the general that I had volunteered and he thought it would be an excellent career move for me. Interestingly, as it turned out, Joan was the more valuable aide during that six-week period. Joe Cody had been a lifelong bachelor and had been married within the past year or so to one of his former secretaries. Hardly a day went by that Betty Cody wasn't on the phone with Joan, asking her what the protocol was for an upcoming event, what was an appropriate thing to wear, her favorite recipe to prepare for a visiting senator or congressman, and so on. Being the wife of her husband's aide, it was hardly unusual for the general's lady to consult Joan on such matters. But, more important, Sam and I knew that Betty was less experienced than Sam was, and she had complete trust in Joan's judgment and advice. In all likelihood, she also may have been too embarrassed to ask these questions of a more senior officer's wife.

In any case, Joan was pleased with the confidence that Mrs. Cody placed in her and they quickly became close friends. But it was not long before that relationship came to an end as it was time for us to depart Vandenberg AFB. The older children had already flown across the Atlantic, had crossed the United States three times by car, and we were about to do so for the fourth time. And Christine and Scott were still a long way from reaching their fourth birthdays. But this time, we would make a side trip on the way. Allegedly the most renowned pediatric orthopedist in the world was at Children's Hospital in Boston, and we were going to bring Danny to see him.

Danny's examination and later diagnosis turned out to be less than reassuring. After spending a few minutes looking at x-rays and physically manipulating the child's leg, the doctor's first comment corroborated the earlier recommendations that we had received. He needed a therapeutic amputation if he was going to lead a reasonably normal life. But the rest of his recommendation came as quite a shock. In his judgment, we needed to place the highest priority on permitting maximum growth of his limb before it was amputated. In his terms, that meant that he needed to wear a brace on his leg that would permit some amount of mobility until he was fifteen or sixteen years of age. Then, and only then, should his leg be taken and he could be fitted with a prosthesis.

We thanked the doctor for his time and consideration, but when we were leaving Children's Hospital, Sam nearly exploded. "Dammit, he may be the very best orthopedic doctor in the world, but he doesn't know a thing about children. Little kids can be the cruelest people in the world, whether or not it's done intentionally, and the bullies would have a field day with Tiny Tim hobbling around on a brace until his mid-teens. I'll be damned if I'm going to subject our baby to that, no matter what this idiot's reputation might be."

I chuckled at her outburst but at the same time hugged both her and the baby for her saying exactly how she felt. I had exactly the same feelings she did when we were in his office and couldn't have agreed more with her evaluation of what we had been through. Joan repeated her conclusions to Aunt Dorothy—who had originally recommended this orthopedist to us—when we got back to her house. Like many in her generation, she was amazed that we could even think to question the judgment of such an eminent physician. Clearly she disagreed with us, but our minds were made up. It would be much, much sooner than later that Danny would have his surgery.

*   *   *

SOS was designed to teach young officers some of the basics of communicative skills, [17] teamwork, and leadership, and to provide them with a broad framework of the entire U.S. Air Force and how it functioned on a day-to-day basis. This latter goal was important because most junior officers had had narrow exposure to their career field and command in their careers, thus far. So getting the bigger picture would be a new experience for most and knowledge they would need as their careers progressed.

A variety of methods were used to instill these goals. Each class was broken down into eight wings with eight sections of twelve or thirteen officers in each section. Each section had a section commander (instructor, critic, evaluator, and advisor all rolled into one) and that was to be my job. Competition was a cornerstone of the educational system with wing competing against wing and section vying for top honors in the wing as well as school wide. The competition was based on academic tests every two weeks, field leadership evaluations, and daily fitness exercises and sports contests. Formal and informal social activities were held frequently so it was a fully active, participatory, high-pressure environment for fourteen weeks.

In my personal opinion, SOS was the most valuable of all the professional development schools at Air University.[18] It broadened the perspective of the junior officers considerably, it provided them with basic skills that would endure throughout their careers, and for the first time, it introduced them to their peers and gave them an

---

[17]   All officers are college graduates and are reasonably well educated in English language skills. But it was important that they learn the U.S. Air Force way of writing (e.g., use of topic sentences, proper paragraphing, and absolutely no passive voice) as well as speaking (e.g., briefing meant exactly that, how to be persuasive, and again, with emphasis on organization).

[18]   The other schools were the Air Command and Staff College (for selected majors, usually at about the twelfth year of service) and the Air War College (attended by selected lieutenant colonels and colonels at the sixteen-to eighteen-year service point). Both colleges were of ten months duration. By contrast, SOS was for selected lieutenants and captains with three to seven years of service and lasted fourteen weeks.

insight into the high level of ability and skills of the people against whom they would be competing for assignments and promotions over the next twenty to thirty years.

About three-quarters of the students brought their wives and families with them for the school term, and this was where Joan (and all the other section commanders' wives) had a distinct role to play. Our wives were jokingly referred to as "den mothers" by both the faculty members and the students. They helped orient the temporary families to the Montgomery area, they were deeply involved in the planning and execution of social activities, and when necessary, they helped resolve any family difficulties that arose and assist in the event of an emergency. Joan was truly in her element and was well liked and respected by all who met her.

Sam's and my own social life was, like most other faculty members, made up of three different components. In addition to our interaction with the students, we had a separate relationship with the other wing and school faculty members. Most of us also had our own neighborhood or church social structure; so needless to say, it was a very busy period in our lives.

Everything considered, our three years at Maxwell were some of the best in our lives. We bought our first home, a newly built three-bedroom, brick ranch, in a new residential development of south Montgomery. Sam was like a little girl with a new doll house. She loved decorating the interior and found new skills that even she wasn't aware she possessed. Our neighbors were all roughly our age and lasting friendships blossomed overnight.

But all was not necessarily sweetness and light. At age four, Scott had made an amazing physical recovery from the horrible early start he had had. In fact, he was exceptionally dexterous for his age and showed early signs of being a skilled athlete. But at the same time, he still didn't talk, not even to call either of us by name. Instead he would just point and grunt. He made a variety of very distinct oral sounds, much of them guttural in nature. Somehow, Chris always knew what he meant or wanted and she served virtually as his translator—even though we were never able to decipher what he was saying.

As a teacher and a mother, Sam became more and more concerned about his lack of linguistic acuity and brought him to a child psychiatrist. Following a battery of tests over a period of time, the doctor provided us with his diagnosis: Scott had an IQ in the range of sixty to sixty-five and was barely educable. The doctor advised us to consider institutionalizing him.

Once again, Sam's protective instincts soared and she became incensed. She may not be a psychiatrist or psychologist but she did know children and she refused to accept this judgment, particularly as it applied to Scott's being placed in an institution.

"No damn way will we ever do any such a thing to this sweet child," she insisted. "He may be slow right now but he's far from stupid and I'm going to prove that doctor wrong if it takes the rest of my life."

She immediately began looking for private schools in the area that specialized in, what we would call today, children with "special learning needs." I think she must have visited at least three, along with Scott, and one evening when I got home she was glowing with excitement.

"I've found just the place," she gushed. "The teachers were wonderful. The headmistress was not only very nice, but she convinced me in no time that she was not just knowledgeable but had trained the staff exceptionally well to care for youngsters just like Scott. Best of all, they're convinced they can help him. We're going to have to cut some corners to afford the tuition, but I can't think of a better or more important way to spend what little savings we have."

The little academy was a day school and even had mini-bus service that would pick Scott up in the morning and bring him home in the evening. We were welcome to come any time we wished so that we could observe, and Joan often took advantage of that. In fact we were encouraged to do so in order that we might be able to reinforce what he was learning in the school when he was at home.

In just a year, they were able to work wonders with Scott. He developed language skills fairly rapidly, and with those skills, he was able to demonstrate clearly that he not only was well beyond being educable, he could very likely keep up with his peer group in a public school environment. Sam was probably a significant part of his development as she worked with him constantly to improve on the training he received in school—all with tenderness and patience that he was able to relate to. If I hadn't already, I certainly learned to trust Sam's judgment implicitly in matters pertaining to our children. Looking back, I can't imagine a greater mistake than if we had followed the psychiatrist's advice—and she knew it would have been, intuitively.

While all this was going on, we also reached the point in time when Danny's leg had developed sufficiently to support his therapeutic amputation. He was now nearly two years old. He would normally be walking—though he was highly mobile with just one useable leg—and our local orthopaedic doctors considered it a propitious time.

Between Thanksgiving and Christmas of 1963, we headed off to Greenville, South Carolina—the closest Shriners hospital in the southeast region—for a pre-arranged appointment for Scott to be reviewed by the hospital physicians.

On our drive through Georgia, we were stopped by the Georgia state patrol for going 70 mph in a 65 mph zone. The officer required us to follow him back to the nearest town, where I was arraigned before a kangaroo court of the worst kind. The "judge" had his feet up on the desk, wore a tobacco-stained, collarless white shirt that was open at the neck, and appeared not to have shaved for four or five days. He quickly found me guilty, fined me fifty dollars and told me, "Just make the check out to me personally, boy!"—pointing to his name plate on the desk.

On the way back to our car, the state patrol officer, trying to be decent, asked Sam if we were headed north for the Christmas holidays.

"No, we're not," she replied stiffly. "We're taking our baby to the hospital in Greenville to have his leg amputated. And that crook back there just took Christmas away from Tiny Tim."

"Lord, ma'am, why didn't you tell me that before? I would have let you go with a warning," he told her.

She just glared at him and got in the car and slammed the door in his face. And she couldn't wait to get to the motel that night to send a letter with a similar message to the governor of Georgia—whose staff, of course, simply ignored it.

The Shriners' doctors agreed that the time was right. Danny would have the surgery, would be given a short time for the stump to heal, and then he would be fitted with a prosthesis and taught to walk—all in the space of a few weeks. And in January, we brought him back. We spent the following days worrying our way through his surgery, but there was no need. He was seemingly just as happy after the operation as he had been before.

Danny had received a toy harmonica as a stocking gift at Christmas time and he just loved it. He kissed us good-bye and waved as we left him there, and he smiled and began playing his harmonica as we went out the door. No worries about that kid. He obviously had inherited his mother's indomitable courage and optimism.

While we have never been in the habit of airing our problems in public, word quickly got around the school of the difficulties that we had been facing. One day, a major in the faculty came to me and suggested that when it was time for us to pick Danny up from the hospital, he might save us a little money by flying me to the Greenville-Spartanburg airport during his monthly training flight. He was sorry that he couldn't wait and bring us both back, but as I was well aware, dependent family members were not authorized to fly on training missions. That way, at least I would only have to pay for the little guy and me on the way home. His thoughtfulness did help out, and I gladly took him up on the offer a week or so later when the hospital called to say that Danny was ready.

A nurse had me wait at the end of the corridor, and with a broad smile on her face, she briefly left me there. Soon, around the corner came a little cherub, pushing a small child's chair for balance, but walking right along on the tiniest prosthetic leg I could ever imagine. This was clearly one of the proudest moments of Danny's short life, as he grinned broadly when he saw me. Within a few steps of reaching me, he let go of the chair and walked the rest of the way unaided, holding up his arms to be picked up, while he fairly chuckled with pride. He couldn't understand why I had tears streaming unashamedly down my face as I clasped him to my chest.

That afternoon, when we arrived at the airport in Montgomery, I carried him most of the way from the gate, but when I saw Sam, I put him down and held his tiny hand as we walked the rest of the way. If anything, her joy at seeing this little guy finally walking on two legs was even more profound and emotional than mine had been. And it was only a matter of moments before a small crowd of travelers had gathered around us to share the joy and emotion of what was obviously a special homecoming. It was one of those remarkable, singular moments that neither of us could ever forget.

Our personal relationship during the three years at SOS was close and loving but the dark specter of another pregnancy was constantly our Sword of Damocles. It was a complete reversal from the days just five or six years previously when Sam was an ardent and passionate lover. The spontaneity of our romantic life was essentially gone and even on those times when we were "safe," there was an unintentional reluctance on her part. She had far too many psychological scars to be able to set them aside at will. And while I understood intellectually, I didn't like the change and we were destined to confront those demons for decades to come.

Chapter 2

For Better or for Worse

The summer of 1965 found me changing status from teacher to student when I was selected for a one-year master of science degree program at Rensselaer Polytechnic Institute (RPI) in Troy, New York. With her usual enthusiasm for new experiences, Sam packed up our growing household and we made our way north. She was happy that we would be close enough to Boston so that the children would have a chance to get to know their grandparents a little better, but happier yet that it would be for one year only.

As one of the foremost engineering schools in the country, RPI was in direct competition for prestige with its big sister school in Cambridge, the Massachusetts Institute of Technology (MIT), and I knew that the year was going to be difficult. Days were spent in class on the campus that was a few miles away from where we lived, and my nights were spent for the most part studying, usually late into the night. But we set aside a brief period of time for me to play with the children each evening and I would usually put them to bed. Meanwhile, Joan had a figurative "off limits" sign on Dad's office/study room where I was not to be disturbed.

Scott and Chris were now old enough to begin kindergarten and their school was just a block away, so they walked to and from school each day. Scott did as well as we hoped he would, and our expectation that he could hold his own in the public school system was greatly reinforced.

After the first overwhelming (for me, at least) summer school term, I adjusted somewhat and we began to set aside one evening a week for us to be together and relax. We often went out to dinner, to the theater in Albany or some similar diversion, a habit that was clearly good for both of us. All things considered, it was a busy and focused time of life for us, though the bugaboo of our stifled intimate relations continued to haunt us both. But not sufficiently.

Sometime around Christmas it became apparent that our worst fears were realized. Despite a terribly guarded existence as near to abstinence as possible, Joan was pregnant for the sixth time. While I knew that she was even more devastated than I was, she regarded the turn of events with her characteristic optimism.

"Maybe I might have broken the spell when Danny was born," she rationalized, trying to convince herself at least that a successful outcome was not beyond the realm of possibility. And she progressed with little or no difficulty well into her second trimester.

In early April, in preparation for our upcoming graduation, the USAF personnel system started generating assignments for the small handful of us officers who were in school together. Despite majoring in research and development management, and having been either an instructor or a student for the past four years, we learned that I was being reassigned back to a civil engineering billet—and this one was going to be as a combat construction engineer in Vietnam. The Johnson Administration had begun its big build-up of American forces there.

Joan's condition was of great concern to me as we were always conscious of the warnings that we had been given about her becoming pregnant again. So contrary to my normal principles, I called the personnel officer responsible for my assignment and explained the predicament we were in. He was both understanding and considerate and a few days later, he called me back to report that my remote assignment to Vietnam had been cancelled. He then told me that they still hadn't determined a substitute posting for me but I should know within the next month.

But well along into her fifth month, history repeated itself. Only this time it took on a somewhat different twist. Labor pains began in earnest shortly after I took her to the hospital in Albany and she was taken to the delivery room not long after our arrival.

When her doctor emerged an hour or so later, I knew from the expression on his face that once again, we were faced with the same outcome: a spontaneously aborted pregnancy. The difference this time, however, was that the baby was a perfectly formed little boy who was born alive. With today's advances in medical technology and procedures, the child would most certainly have survived and would have grown to have a normal healthy life. But that wasn't the case then. They had tried as best they could but simply were unable to save him, I was told.

The disappointment and sadness were scarcely any different than they had been in all the previous losses. How Sam had the courage and determination to persevere and avoid the deep depression that might be expected in such a situation was a glowing testament to the remarkable qualities of her character. She quickly shifted her focus back to the three little ones she had at home and within a few days, she was back to being the caring, loving mother she had always been.

Little was said about our loss after the initial emotional letdown, but a week or so later, as we had a late supper after the children were in bed, she looked at me directly and said, "I guess you need to call the personnel center back and tell them that you're available once again to go to Vietnam."

I was stunned. "I can't do that," I replied, after the shock had worn off. "You're just starting to get over a heart-wrenching period of grief, and there's no way that I can go off and leave you for a year under these circumstances."

"Look, you know full well that there are still six weeks before we'll leave here and that I'm going to be just fine by then. I also know you too well," she went on. "You are 'duty, honor, and country' personified and I'll not be responsible for your failure to fulfill what your sense of obligation tells you that you must do. Do I like the idea of our being separated for a year? Of course I don't. Am I frightened that you'll be going into a war zone and might be killed? You're damned right I am. But when I married you, I knew what our life would be like and I knew that we'd possibly face a time like this. Well, now we have, and it's time that both of us did the responsible thing."

In the eight years we had been married, I already knew that she was an ideal military wife and that she shared the same sense of values and duty that I felt. But this expression of love and willingness to sacrifice went well beyond my expectations. And the following day, I did what she had encouraged me to do.

The new construction engineer squadron[19] to which I was being assigned was to form at Forbes AFB in Kansas where we would undergo four months of individual and unit specialized training. We learned that the former Schilling AFB near Salina, Kansas, had been reopened and was being staffed as a "waiting wives" housing and support installation for military families whose husbands and fathers were being deployed to the war zone. With the promise of weekends together—Forbes and Schilling were only two hours apart—we made the decision that she would stay in Salina.

Aunt Dorothy was totally chagrined when she learned of our plans and badgered Joan daily to change her mind and come "home" to live with her. When this tactic failed, she turned her intense anger and frustration on me, accusing me of deliberately preventing Joan from staying with her. But Joan would not have done that even if it were not a matter of four months of weekends that we could be together. She had become far too independent to subject herself to Dorothy's smothering dominance for what would become a sixteen-month separation.

We made our expected trip to visit with family members back in the Boston area and then proceeded on to Bolton, Connecticut, where my parents had moved a year previously. On our last evening there, my mother asked Joan how she was going to fare while I was in Vietnam for a year, and whether she was deeply concerned for my welfare. She, of course, replied that she was a bit fearful and had given a great deal of thought to the possibility that I might never return.

This perked up my father's attention and, possibly in an effort to calm her concerns, he told her rather cavalierly that she shouldn't worry about it needlessly. "Ah, for goodness sakes," he assured her, "you can get killed just crossing the street here in the States."

---

19   The newly created construction units were similar to the navy construction battalions (better known as CBs or more commonly, Sea Bees) and the name given to them was RED HORSE, derived from the somewhat contrived acronym for Rapid Engineer Deployment—Heavy Operational Repair Squadron, Expeditionary.

Sam had always been my father's pet. She was a teacher, as he was; she was a Boston College graduate, which he had always wanted to be; and she was always sweet and kind to him. But this time she flew into a complete rage.

"Who the hell do you think you're talking to, some stupid ninny?" she screamed at him, getting out of her chair and pointing her index finger menacingly in his face. "Goddam it, no one's shooting at you when you cross the street; no one's firing rockets at the area where you live night after night. You're damned right I'm worried, and I'll be worried about him every minute he's gone. And if you used your head and gave it a few minutes thought, you'd be worried too. Crossing the street! That's bullshit and you know damned well it is."

A normal reaction to an outburst like that would be for my father to apologize profusely and try to say something that would ease the stress that he had caused. But my father was not a normal person. He was always "right" and could not tolerate anyone disagreeing with him. Before Sam had exhausted all she had to say, he got up from where he sat, went down the corridor to the bedroom and loudly slammed the door after himself.

The following day, as we had breakfast, the ambience was frigid. Again he refused to utter a word of apology, but instead acted as if Joan had somehow insulted or affronted him. I had always had serious issues with my father since I was a teenager, but Joan never did from the time they had met. Needless to say, the relationship between the two of them was never the same from that time forward.

As we drove away that morning, I told Sam how proud I was of her for taking the stand she did. But I knew that once again my mother would take the wrath of his unjustified anger before we got many miles away.

Not long after getting the family settled in Salina, Joan made one of the best and most important decisions she could ever have made under the circumstances. She decided to teach for the year that I'd be gone, and with the small population explosion that Salina was experiencing with the opening of Schilling Manor, as it was termed, she was instantly hired to teach sixth grade. We were also extremely fortunate to find a nanny for the children, the Panamanian wife of an U.S. Army sergeant who had no children of her own. Mrs. Payne could not have loved and cared for Scott, Chris, and Danny any more than she did. And the kids loved her as well—and still do to this day. On some weekends, Mrs. Payne would stay with the children while Joan came to Topeka to stay overnight with me.

I was the training officer for the squadron and took a group of about forty airmen and NCOs to Fort Riley—mid-way between Forbes and Schilling—for two weeks of basic combat infantry training to prepare them for our unit self-defense in Vietnam. Following that, I brought the same group to Smoky Hill Gunnery Range (known as Smoky Hole to the troops) for two more weeks of field training under simulated aerial attacks. Coincidentally, Smoky Hill was only a thirty-minute drive from Schilling Manor and Sam and I had a few unexpected weekend nights together at home.

*   *   *

After an emotional tug-of-war between our allegiance to the precepts of the Roman Catholic Church and the incredibly sad and perilous personal history that Joan had endured throughout our nine years of marriage, we finally elected to end our flirtation with Vatican roulette. We still attended Mass each Sunday and we were definitely committed to raising the children in the religion of our forefathers, but we neither could nor would receive the sacraments any longer. We tried a few of the available methods of birth control and found most of them to be unsatisfactory to our needs and mentality. But finally, with the advice and assistance of Joan's current OB/GYN, she began to use the relatively new development in medical technology: The Pill.

Joan seemed to tolerate it well during the short time we had left together, and its use seemed to lift a gigantic burden from our shoulders. But after so many years of being conscience-driven in our intimate life, it was hard to dismiss that little voice in the backs of our minds, telling us that we were doing something wrong. So I guess in the search for a silver lining, we were able to put that voice aside for the moment, enjoy the time we had left together, and plan to the long-term aspects of the practice after my Vietnam tour was over.

When the time came for me to deploy to Bien Hoa Air Base, we were both very pleased with our decision for the family to remain in Kansas. Joan had become quite friendly with some of her fellow teachers—all natives of Salina—with whom she worked. The kids were delighted that Mrs. Payne was their surrogate mom, and I would leave for Southeast Asia with the solid confidence that they would be safe and well cared for while I was gone.

When the training period was nearly completed, our commander selected his deputy, a lieutenant colonel, and me to take an advance party of nearly fifty NCOs to Vietnam to set up our squadron cantonment area in preparation to receive the other 350 members of the squadron when he or she arrived three weeks hence.[20]

Our small cadre left directly from Forbes AFB in a turboprop C-130 that had web seats along the sides and litters erected down the center of the fuselage where we could "hot bunk" for the eight-four-hour trip across the Pacific. We stopped at Travis AFB, California, Hickham AFB, Hawaii Wake Island, Guam, and Clark AB in the Philippines. Crew changes and refueling took place at every stop while we passengers had just enough time to stretch our legs and then get back on board again.

We all put on clean, starched uniforms, red berets, and neckerchiefs and shined our boots before our arrival at our new home, Bien Hoa Air Base. No way were we going to look like a bunch of slobs getting off the aircraft when we were a highly trained, solidly cohesive band of professionals. Little did we know that we would arrive at 0300 in a drenching monsoon rain and a simultaneous mortar and rocket attack on the base. And to top it off, no one seemed to know we were coming. Not an auspicious start—but it was just a matter of a few days before everyone at the base had heard of us and coveted the extensive capabilities represented by our arrival.

As I'm sure most of the men aboard that aircraft did on the long flight over, I thought a great deal about our family, the prospects for what life would be like on my return, and on how much I missed

---

20   The primary task for the advance party was to level an area and prepare plywood floors and frames on which we would erect a sufficient number of twelve-man tents to house all of our personnel.

Sam already. And while everyone going into combat is convinced that it's always the "other guy" who doesn't make it back, a few thoughts also occurred to me about how my little family would fare if I just happened to be someone else's other guy.

More as a process of hedging my bets than anything else, I guess, I decided I needed to go to confession at the first opportunity and begin receiving the sacraments again. And I knew that Joan had reached the same conclusion, though perhaps not for the same reasons, while she waited back in Kansas.

I had met the Catholic chaplain, Fr. Featherstone, in the dining hall a short time after we arrived and he seemed like a very nice guy. I asked him when he heard confessions and he told me that he was prepared at a moment's notice, but his regular time was for a half hour before Mass each Sunday. So the following Sunday, I arrived early at the little makeshift chapel and waited my turn. After I revealed the fact that my wife and I had practiced birth control, I suspected he would give me a brief penance and absolution. But that was not the way it evolved.

"How long have you been here?" he queried, "and what are your intentions regarding birth control when you return home next year?"

I told him that I hadn't really given that much thought and I imagined we would cross that bridge when the time came—probably knowing deep down in my heart that we would likely revert right back to the same practice when the time came. Sam was far too dear to me to do anything else.

"Then I can't give you absolution," he told me. "As you well know, your sins cannot be forgiven unless you have a sincere, firm purpose of amendment—that you are committed to not sinning again."

Initially I was shocked. Here we are in a combat zone and he wants me to make a promise about a time that may be more than a lifetime away. Then I got angry. "Well, it looks like I've wasted both your time and mine!" I fairly growled at him, stood, and left the confessional.

"Wait a minute," said his voice behind me and I turned to see that he too had left the confessional and was hurrying after me. "Somehow it seems to me that there's a lot more to this situation

that you're not telling me. We need to talk about this a lot more and
if you're able, I'd like you to come over to my hooch[21] at about 1900
this evening so we can give this the time it deserves."

After an afternoon's work—we gave the troops Sunday morning
off if they wished to attend religious services—I showered and made
my way to the chaplain's hooch. He had cold beer ready for both of
us and I soon got into all the details—how we had been observant for
the whole period, how many failed pregnancies Joan had experienced,
the stark warnings about her health, and particularly what havoc
they had raised with her mental outlook and the pressures on our
marriage. When I finished, he just shook his head sadly.

"I knew there was far more to it than the simple fact that you
had practiced birth control. And I'll tell you very candidly, if I were
in your position, I would do the same thing you have done—and
probably a lot sooner than you did. You have already adopted two
orphaned children and I simply cannot believe that God wants you
and your wife to suffer fruitlessly when you are otherwise as faithful
to your religion as you are. I also know that there are many priests
and bishops who would strongly disagree with what I am about to
tell you, but you can and should do whatever you can to ensure the
well-being of your wife and the mother of your children. And if that
includes the practice of birth control, you should do so with a clear
conscience."

And with those words, he gave me absolution and encouraged
me to pass on the same message to Joan.

Before the days of satellite telephone communications and
emails, our best hope to hear one another's voice was to use a small
reel-to-reel tape recorder. It took two to three weeks for the U.S.
Postal Service to shuttle the tapes between Kansas and Vietnam,
and we often experienced misunderstandings with the time delays
of overlapping tapes going back and forth across the Pacific—one
of us thinking that the other was answering a question that had

---

[21]   Hooch is a term that was used for the housing on the base, usually
consisting of a small building with open louvered sides, screening and
a shingled roof. They were of varying sizes and the chaplain's was the
smallest of the sizes so that he would have the privacy needed for his
continuing ministry.

previously been asked, only to find out that it was a different question entirely. But it was sheer heaven to hear each other's voice and to have the kids send periodic messages to me as well. We both must have listened to each tape ten or twelve times before making a new one to send back.

I couldn't wait to devote one of the first tapes that I sent to tell Sam about the evening conversation with Fr. Featherstone and the ultimate relief of his having told me what he did. But in the intervening five or six weeks before I had a reply from Sam, her consultation with the Schilling Manor chaplain turned out to be an exact opposite opinion of the situation. He accused my chaplain of being a "rogue" or a "renegade" and told Joan that under no circumstance could his advice be taken as a valid position of the Church.

It bothered the two of us intensely that two military priests could possibly be giving totally contradictory advice. But as we later resolved after a series of trans-Pacific exchanges of tapes, it really didn't matter anyway. We had crossed that bridge already and we were not going to turn back. And even though Sam agreed with me intellectually, I knew that deep in her soul it still bothered her a great deal and an aura of guilt was destined to surround the issue for some time to come.

During the Vietnam War, the Congress decided that a special privilege should be granted to the men and women serving there and authorized a week-long rest and recuperation (R&R) leave to a number of locations in Asia and Hawaii. The government would pay for the traveler's transportation aboard government-chartered commercial aircraft and the eligible personnel would not be charged for leave. It took us no time at all to decide that my R&R would be in Hawaii and Sam would meet me there. We also concluded that it would make the second half of my deployment a lot shorter and easier to tolerate if we met at the eight-month period of my tour.

Joan had always been a master at planning trips—usually from one assignment to another—and she applied herself to our Hawaii meeting with special enthusiasm. We were going to stay at the Ilikai Hotel on Waikiki Beach in Honolulu. And her planning was so precise that we were to arrive in Honolulu within just a few hours of one another. Obviously I was not traveling by a USAF C-130 this time.

Our initial meeting was one of the most blissful moments of our lives together. I had never seen her look more beautiful and we smiled and laughed constantly from the relief of being safely together again. All the attendant fears of pregnancy instantly became a thing of the past, and we returned to the very earliest days of our marriage in our ardor for each other.

Following a brief afternoon nap to combat our jet lag, we checked the hotel schedule and discovered that there was a torch lighting ceremony each evening at 1800 on the hotel's lanai that faced the beach. She put on her newly purchased long sheath dress in a beautiful bronze and orange Hawaiian pattern, while I dressed in the white duck trousers and green and black Hawaiian shirt she had bought for me, and off we went to join the celebration. We rode down the outside glass elevator that brought us to the lanai and we arrived just in time for the beginning of the ceremony.

Unfortunately, the ceremony began with multiple strings of fire crackers being set off all over the spacious lanai, which, from force of habit, sounded for all the world like small arms fire to me. I quickly dove behind a large concrete planter, which held a small palm tree, and dragged Sam to the ground behind me. She instantly recognized that she was witnessing a conditioned reflex, and reached over from her "safe" spot beside me and kissed me, assuring me that I had nothing to fear.

To my embarrassment, a number of people who were nearby quickly realized what had happened as well. It wasn't difficult for them to see, from my appearance and deep tan (except for the place on the top of my head normally occupied by a steel hat), that I had obviously just arrived from Vietnam. Eager hands quickly helped us to our feet and there was even a smattering of applause. In early summer of 1967, the anti-war, anti-military sentiment had not yet become endemic and we quickly discovered that we couldn't buy a drink for the entire evening.

We parted after a glorious week together, having done any number of wonderful things but, happiest of all, walking barefoot on the beach after dark each night holding hands. Our renewed separation was with optimism that the separation would not be as long and we would soon be back together again. And after we returned to our own daily routines, the time passed eventually—but ponderously.

Shortly after returning to Vietnam, I wrote the following letter[22] to Sam, in which I tried to apologize for the many years of failing to understand her personal struggle with our recent reversion to using birth control.

Sat., 10 June 1967

My dearest—

I've had a most difficult and emotional day today which I guess can best be described as the final symptoms of getting over Hawaii. It seems that I must accept the fact that it's over and I'm here for another four months.

Probably the catalyst for my mood was an article in *Look* (the current issue). It was entitled "A Priest Criticizes His Church" and is a most courageous effort to plead for resolution of the problems of the modern Church. I have never read a more incisive description of love that only a happily married man and woman can feel for one another. It said many of the things that I wish I were articulate enough to think of.

The most significant section of the article, to me, dealt with birth control. The reason that it was so significant was that it made me realize where I've failed you—even though you will never admit to this failing. You told me that you could still not go to communion after taking the pill without first receiving absolution. I passed this off by some innocuous comment relative to my belief, yet still leaving you with no resolution to an emotional battle inside yourself caused by years of mental conditioning as to what is "right" and what is "wrong."

This particular subject—birth control, or at least the potential results from the lack of it—has been the only

---

22   The letter was found among Joan's small cache of treasures after she passed away in 2008.

single thing that has caused a rift in our marriage. I've accused you in the past of being frigid. I've stated that we were "sexually incompatible" and said and done God knows how many other selfish things.

I never fully realized until we were together in Hawaii just how hard you've been fighting this in your own mind. More importantly, I realized that this was for me that you were fighting—a completely selfless effort on your part to make me happy. Then when you needed me to help you on the last leg of your battle, again I did nothing.

Since we must keep this question within the parameters of "the teachings of the Church," about the only way that I can find a rationale for being guiltless is through the conditions for a mortal sin. If I remember my religious courses, there are three conditions: to know that it is a serious sin; to give due consideration to committing it; and then to commit the sin anyway. I can't concede that preventing mental anguish and possible physical harm to you is a serious sin. I won't concede that the prevention of conception of a child that may be deformed or mentally retarded is a sin. The Pope or a bishop doesn't have the opportunity to see you spend sleepless nights wondering if you're going to survive. Nor have they had the opportunity to see you tearfully apologize in a recovery room because you (erroneously) have convinced yourself that you've somehow failed because the child didn't survive. If these are sins, then I'm the one who's guilty since I'm that one who has put you in those positions. However, I doubt that the most fundamental legalist would say that that is sinful conduct. There never has, is not, and can never be an absolute standard of what is moral in the sight of God. The act itself may be a sin, but the motivation behind the act must be the criterion by which it is judged to be sinful. Because of this factor, I will never again confess the "sin" of practicing birth control, and I intend to continue receiving the sacraments regularly. I hope that this will help you to feel the same way. For my own peace of mind, I humbly apologize for years of failing to try to understand the anguish that you have consciously and unconsciously endured. I know as I say this that you will disagree that such an apology is necessary, but that is just one more example of your completely unselfish love for me.

Please don't feel that I am going through a traumatic period of self-recrimination, because I'm not. There are just occasions when some people wake up to the realization of what's going on around them, and this happens to be my time. It's also a good opportunity to say "I love you" without using those familiar words. I thought I knew what love was before this past year, but our wonderful week together woke me up to the fact that the ideal of love, for us at least, has become a reality. I thank God for giving me the most wonderful woman who ever lived.

Yours forever,

Finally, October of 1967 arrived and my year in Vietnam was coming to an end. Those of us in the advance party a year before were among the first to depart, but in order to have some amount of overlap with our replacements, others had their tours of duty curtailed a few weeks early. It turned out that four of us were scheduled out on the initial departure, but almost as a parallel to my arrival a year earlier, we were to leave on an Air Force C-141 instead of a shiny, more comfortable commercial charter jet that carried most returnees to the States. But that really didn't matter. We were going home.

Each of my other three friends had wives scattered all over the United States: Gail Narum's wife was in North Dakota, Bill Jones's in Texas, Bernie Cavender's in New York, and of course Joan was in Kansas. So we decided that after what we had all been through together and the camaraderie that develops in a situation of shared danger, we would have one last hurrah together. All of our wives would meet us as we arrived on the same commercial flight in Kansas City.

On our way back across the Pacific, we took the northern route and landed first at Elmendorf AFB in Alaska—wearing our short-sleeved summer uniforms in the midst of the arrival of Alaskan winter. We proceeded after refueling to Travis AFB in California, where chartered buses took us to the nearest large commercial terminal, the San Francisco International Airport. It was there that we encountered our first inkling of the growing anti-war movement that began in that city. We were jeered by passers-by and a couple of us were actually spat upon. I recall Bill Jones saying, "Well, welcome home, and f___ you very much for your service to our country."

When we got off the plane, the four wives—most of whom had never met before—were together waiting for us. Each of us received an eager hero's welcome, but when I first saw Sam, I couldn't believe my eyes. In just four months, she had gained a huge amount of weight—nearly 25 pounds I was to learn later—and the stunning beauty that I had seen so recently in Hawaii was no more. I said nothing about it at the time, but Sam clearly noticed my surprise and disappointment.

"I'm sorry, I know you don't like to see me so badly overweight," she told me, as soon as we were alone. "I had tried so hard to look good for you in Hawaii, but after we parted, I had a terrible premonition that we'd never see each other again. And I just ate and ate whenever I got nervous, which was most of the time I was awake. Each time the news mentioned something that happened at Bien Hoa or the other places where you had worked—a rocket attack or something like that—I was convinced that I was going to get the dreaded visit from a casualty reporting officer. But now you're back and I promise you that I'll do better."

The final evening together with my Red Horse mates—in the best steakhouse in KC, which we had promised ourselves—was a fitting tribute to our combat-honed friendship. Tales were told continuously of our experiences, but as is usually the case with returnees from every war, they were only the funny stories. The waiters recognized who we were and what we were celebrating, and the management went out of its way to make our homecoming—and later departure from one another—a most memorable occasion. These were middle Americans, not the yahoos we had encountered in San Francisco.

It's amazing how much a young child can grow in a year, and even though Sam had regularly sent me pictures of our children, I couldn't believe they had gotten so big. Their mom had kept me very much alive in their eyes and it was such a thrill to hold them all in my arms again. And having their daddy home again seemed just as important to them as it was to me.

When I went into our bedroom to change my clothes, it seemed so nice to see my own bed again that I lay down for just a moment to reflect on the luxury of it all. And then promptly fell asleep. Moments or perhaps hours later, Sam came in to the bedroom and began to crawl stealthily, she thought, up the bed from the bottom to lie down beside me. But before she could get her second knee on the mattress, I sprung up in a fighting position with my leg cocked in position to kick the intruder in the face. When I recovered my wits and the realization dawned of what had almost happened, we both devolved into gales of laughter.

My orders for our next assignment finally reflected my recent education and we were going to Wright-Patterson AFB near Dayton, Ohio. I was to be a research and development director at the Aeronautical Systems Division—the home of the design, development and procurement of all the Air Force's new aircraft and related systems. I was thrilled to know we would have a stable home for a time in a great area to raise children. But first, I had thirty days of leave scheduled so that my family and I could have the time to reunite and for Sam to get used to having her man around the house again.

*   *   *

We settled in a northern suburb of Dayton called Huber Heights. By this time, all three children were in school. Danny had already outgrown three prosthetic legs and was as active as any other youngster his age. Scott was an eager participant in a midget football program and looked very intimidating wearing his full set of pads. Christine was, like many little girls her age, captivated by the idea of being a cheerleader as her mom had once been and proudly showed off her red and white uniform every chance she got. And Mom decided that with all of her little ones in school, it was time for her to teach full-time again.

Joan was back on the pill and showed no adverse signs from its use. When her more positve response that I had expected hadn't materialize, at least to my satisfaction, I became convinced that Sam was again showing indications of guilt over the use of birth control, not to mention her fatigue of being both a mother of three and a teacher of thirty. What I didn't realize, and was not to learn until many years later, was that long-term, insulin-dependent diabetics experienced a significant decrease in stamina and libidinal energy. What I did realize, however, was that I was not especially happy when we went to bed at night and she would kiss me good-night and then turn over with her back to me.

We would try to talk about it from time to time, but it was clear to me that she was uncomfortable with the conversation, and often would end it with a statement that began with, "It's not that I don't love you as much as I ever did, but …"

My job as the plans officer in a system program office caused me to travel a great deal after I had been there for only a short time. Not to anyplace exotic or exciting, though, since more often than not I was going to Air Force Systems Command at Andrews AFB, Maryland—our higher headquarters—and to the Pentagon. My trips were often three or four days during the week, which was by no means as bad as my being gone for a year, but it put an additional burden on Sam when I wasn't around to help out—which I normally did when I was at home.

The system program to which I had been assigned[23] soon became a higher priority with things escalating in Vietnam and the prospects for brush-fire wars elsewhere in the world a growing reality. As a result, all of the officers assigned to the program office were designated as "mission essential" and were assigned to four-year stabilized tours of duty. This designation was supposed to insure that we all remained in place until the system became operational.

We had lived in a three-bedroom, two-bath rental home for the first year and this new turn of events indicated that we'd be better off if we bought a new home and developed some equity. Among the

---

[23]   The program designation was the Bare Base System Program Office and it had the mission to develop and test an air-mobile air base, one that could be flown to anyplace in the world where there was a runway and a source of water. It could within seventy-two hours. The facilities under development ranged from aircraft maintenance shops to mess halls and from operations buildings to showers, latrines, and chemical toilets.

many pastimes that Joan enjoyed was looking at new home models and she was in her glory when we made the decision to buy. And within a couple of weekends of looking, she had found her dream home. It was not far from our current residence, it was in the same school district for the children, and I fully agreed with her judgment when she took me to see it. It was a beautiful new home. And as soon as the loan was approved, we gave our notice to the owner of our rental.

Moving to the new home was a fatiguing process, since we moved ourselves,[24] except for the very heavy, bulky pieces. The home was on the terminal end of a new cul-de-sac, our neighbors were all new arrivals to the street with children the same age as ours, and it was a lovely place to live. Joan was in her element, decorating another new home from scratch. The lot was a large, partially landscaped yard with plenty for me to do for the rest of the summer as well.

But as we changed homes once again, I had a personal change in my outlook on life. The human mind has a remarkable way of rationalizing decisions, and I became able to convince myself of the idea that if sexual satisfaction wasn't available at home, there was plenty of opportunity elsewhere. Perhaps it was my way of saying, "It's not that I don't love you as much as I ever did, but …"

Washington was, at the time, and probably still is, one of the easiest places in the world to "hook up" (to use the terminology of today). And the Andrews officers' club bar was just one of the many places where you could meet someone of the opposite sex for a one-nighter or a relationship of indeterminate duration. And though this was a whole new world to me—I hadn't been in the habit of picking up girls even when I was in college—I found the transition to be surprisingly easy, to my way of thinking at least. And I also found that I was hardly alone in these pursuits.

Was I being self-centered in my internal debate with myself? Unquestionably! Did I give adequate consideration to the potential ramifications of my actions? Of course not. But as the ancient adage goes: a stiff willy has no conscience, and I was living proof of that. But my rationalization also included the adage that what Joan didn't

---

[24] The government only pays for military household moves when it directs those moves to be made, as in a reassignment.

know wouldn't hurt her—to the extent that I even convinced myself that it would actually be to her advantage if I were unfaithful. If I were to stop becoming angry or demanding when she didn't choose to be intimate, she would feel no guilt for refusing me. Right? So why shouldn't I continue this behavior with a guilt-free conscience?

As I write this today, I am astounded by my logic process at the time, but even today I know that there are thousands if not millions of people—both male and female—who have reached these same conclusions through the same arcane process.

Eventually, the Bare Base Program had a full dress test in South Carolina in the fall of 1969 and it was a complete success. Literally days after my final report was delivered to the board of general officers that I had been briefing each week in Washington, I was told that the chairman of that board wanted me transferred to the Pentagon right away. Apparently I had made a favorable impression, because there was no opting out on my part. My stabilized four-year tour of duty at Wright-Patterson was cancelled, and the new house that we had barely begun to settle into would have to be sold at a loss so that we could afford to buy another new home in the more expensive Washington area.

My reporting date was for early January 1970. Since Joan was teaching and the children were only halfway through their school year, we agreed that I would go to Washington by myself, and they would join me when school term ended in June. There was a shuttle flight each weekday between Wright-Patterson and Andrews AFBs—it was far less expensive to run this shuttle for the large numbers of daily travelers back and forth than for the travelers to go by commercial flights—so I could come home on weekends. I lived in BOQ at Andrews. And, yes, I continued to frequent the officers' club bar with its willing companions.

One weekend when I was back in Dayton, Joan confronted me with her suspicions that I had been "playing around." I knew that this day would probably come eventually and I dreaded the thought—though not enough to change my behavior. While I had been *living* a lie for nearly a year, I was not a good *liar*. So I admitted she was correct and without going into any unnecessary detail, I described the generalities of my infidelity, and told her I was sorry.

To my complete amazement, she took my admission and apology very calmly and with seemingly no rancor.

"I know that I'm partially to blame for this happening," she admitted, "and I know why this happened. So you don't need to explain any more. We both know that you were unhappy and why, but I didn't think it would come to this. I love you too much to see our marriage come to an end, so I forgive you. I'll try harder to be a better wife, but you need to promise me that you'll be a more faithful husband."

We happened to be out to dinner at the time, and while we talked of little else for the rest of the evening, Sam's initial reaction summed up the discussion as the evening went on. I promised her in good faith that I would amend my ways and hoped sincerely that when we had our little household back together in our new Oxon Hill, Maryland, home later that month, our being together again would be the difference-maker.

While Joan had apparently tolerated the birth control pill quite well for a couple of years, there were soon reports published indicating that this artificial intrusion on a woman's menstrual cycle with high dosages of hormones could conceivably be the cause of increased occurrences of breast and cervical cancer. Joan had enough problems with her daily battles against diabetes that she didn't need to introduce more potentially fatal problems into her life. But we didn't want to step backward into the world of more mechanical methods of preventing pregnancy, so now it was my turn to provide a solution. I decided that I should get a vasectomy.

"You can't do that," Joan protested. "You're going to live much longer than I will, and you may want to have more children when you remarry. You'll ruin your life if you do that and I beg you not to."

"I'm not sure your logic will hold up very well, dear," I countered. "First of all, you have been in excellent health in recent years, with or without diabetes, and I'm not convinced that I'll outlive you by any means. Second, you're drawing two very iffy conclusions—that I'd want to remarry and that I'd want to have more children if I did. I don't think I can buy either one of those ideas. What I am concerned about is your more immediate risk in continuing with the pill and with the fact that we both know that we're not about to go back to condoms or IUDs. So let me be the judge of the best way for us to face the future, and it's hard to argue against the wisdom of my having a vasectomy."

We discussed the issue at great length over the next month or so, but Sam finally came around to my way of thinking. With a little snip here and a little snip there, our life was about to change—we hoped.

*   *   *

My assignment in the Pentagon[25] was to a newly created small group of officers—a small think tank if your will—who were charged with creating a USAF strategic plan, a look twenty to twenty-five years into the future. I had just recently received an early promotion to major but I was still the most junior officer in the group. It was an exciting and challenging mission and we found ourselves rather deeply involved in the Pentagon's most important issues of the day. The thinking was that it would be difficult to take a prolonged look into the future if we didn't know what was going on in the here and now.

Meanwhile, Joan was hired to teach in the neighborhood elementary school and she accepted the position eagerly. Just about the time that the school bus came to pick up our three children, she would leave to go to her school, and the timing was the same when they all arrived home again each day. The two salaries helped us to afford an active social life, with both her fellow teachers and my fellow toilers in the Pentagon.

The newly developed neighborhood where we had moved was replete with pre-teens the ages of ours and they quickly developed enduring friendships. We were a happy family and although my ten- to twelve-hour workdays were rather long—made more so by the Washington grid-lock commute, we still managed to share activities with our kids. And Joan was true to her word that she would try to be more receptive in our intimate life.

---

[25]   For more detailed coverage of this period of my career, see my earlier book, *Portraits in Brass*, published in 2008.

The combination of a long work week—we often worked Saturdays—plus the many chores inherent in moving into a newly built home, kept me on the straight and narrow. We made it a habit to go out to dinner one or two times each month, just the two of us. And we often entertained at dinner parties in our own home, something that we both enjoyed very much. I also decided to create a rec room in our unfinished basement, and while the kids were too young to be of much physical help, they enjoyed being there and watching what I was doing. All things considered, it was a good time for us.

When my Pentagon tour was about to come to an end in the summer of 1973, my assignment was to go, as a student, to the Industrial College of the Armed Forces, part of the National Defense University. This was a much sought-after plum, a one-year sabbatical that was unparalleled for career enhancement, not to mention the fact that it was also a period to get one's batteries recharged. The best part was that the school is in Washington (Fort McNair) and there'd be no need to move our household and uproot the children once again—a situation that becomes more difficult for them, the older they get. I had planned to take a month's leave before school began in late August and we would all go on a rare vacation together to the New England seashore.

But that came to a screeching halt when I received a call from the Air Staff director of personnel at home one Saturday afternoon. He told me that I had just been selected as the special assistant (speech writer and research assistant) to the newly appointed Chief of Staff of the Air Force (CSAF).[26] I had just recently been promoted to lieutenant colonel, before my peers once again, and this was a sure indication that I was on a fast track to success. All plans were off as I began my new assignment the following Monday morning. The kids were disappointed, Joan was as well, but she fully realized what it might mean to my career. By contrast, I was somewhat ambivalent. It had been a rigorous three and a half years and I was ready for a break. But at the same time it was also a singular honor and challenge. This new assignment also meant at least another

---

[26]   See *Portraits in Brass.*

year at the Pentagon and, hopefully, another shot at senior service college.

If anything, work days became longer, my time with the kids decreased, and while I was vain enough to enjoy the rarified atmosphere of being one of four members of the Chief's personal staff, the family situation changed and not for the better. I think Sam might have felt that she was being neglected. I was around the house less than before; I wasn't as helpful to her as I had been; and we no longer had dinner together as a family each evening. I was getting home too late for that.

When CSAF General George S. Brown left the following summer to become Chairman of the Joint Chiefs of Staff, I was asked if I wanted to go with him in the same capacity or stay in the USAF Chief's office in what would be for me a new position, the assistant executive officer. To my everlasting regret, I chose the latter job.

If I thought the hours were long in the previous year, they were a piece of cake by comparison to the daily schedule kept by the new Chief, General David C. Jones. I was expected to open the office at 0530 each morning, including Saturdays and often Sundays. And I very seldom left the office before 1930 at night. Jones was a confirmed workaholic and expected his staff to be the same. Needless to say, family life became nearly non-existent, and Joan rightfully disliked the change—though she never once uttered a word of complaint. She was more tired trying to hold down two full-time jobs, not to say that I was a bundle of energy either. And our intimacy dwindled to one of its lowest points.

Looking back, I would have to admit that my personal career ambitions had begun to take precedence over most everything else. I saw the possibility of another early promotion on the horizon, which most likely would have meant that I would one day have a good chance to become a general officer. And since this is usually regarded as the pinnacle of a military career, I was neglectful of the more important things in my life: my family, especially Sam. Through no one's fault but mine, we gradually began to drift apart, emotionally.

Around Christmas time of that year, my old boss and mentor from Vandenberg, Colonel John Everhart and his wife, Betty, invited us to a party at their home in Arlington, Virginia. Among the guests were a couple of our approximate age, and I found the woman to be one of the most attractive people I had ever met. Maggie, as I'll call her, had a slender graceful figure, was beautifully dressed, and when I talked to her, I discovered a personality to match her physical attributes. And it soon became apparent that she found me equally attractive. I'm not sure who it was that evening who took the initiative, but we agreed that we would meet for lunch someday.

Because of my demanding schedule, I usually ate lunch at my desk in the office, but the next time the CSAF was on a trip, I hadn't forgotten the agreement and decided that someday was now. I called Maggie at work and we agreed to meet at a small restaurant in DC. It was hardly an assignation and neither of us made any overt move to carry our meeting beyond the platonic condition that it was in at the time. But body English on both our parts made it pretty clear that the initial attraction had gone beyond that stage.

The next time we were hosting a dinner party and developing a guest list, I suggested that Maggie and her husband might make a good addition at the table. Joan remembered them both from the Christmas party and agreed that they would add to the evening and, after a telephone invitation, they accepted. I was seated beside Maggie at the table, and Joan was beside Maggie's husband. As we were cleaning up the dishes after the guests had left, she casually observed, "He was a bit of an ass, I thought, but you certainly didn't find her that way. You didn't have a minute for anyone else the whole evening, and it's easy to see why. She's very attractive, but you'd better be careful. I get the feeling that she finds you that same way and that could be trouble."

I suppose I mumbled some sort of apology or excuse for not being a better host, but passed off the mutual attraction suggestion as not being anything to be concerned about.

As the months passed, I probably had lunch with Maggie one or two more times, but as spring came to an end, I was advised by the Air Staff director of personnel that the coming summer would be a good time for me to leave the Chief's office. He went so far to convince me that he offered me another slot at the Industrial College of the Armed Forces (ICAF), the same senior professional military school that I had been scheduled to attend two years previously. I wisely took his suggestion.

Maggie was a government employee and there were many executive department office buildings within walking distance of Fort McNair. She happened to work at one of them, thereby providing a far greater opportunity to get together for lunch or a drink after work. And we began to take advantage of those opportunities. No deceit was involved at the time—I simply never mentioned the meetings—and the relationship had still not advanced much beyond what it had been for the previous six or eight months. But Joan's warning that my attraction to Maggie "could be trouble" was about to become prescient.

When we were making plans to meet for lunch one day, Maggie suggested that instead of going to one of the little restaurants in the area, why not come to her apartment, which was not terribly far away. Her husband was on a business trip, so it wouldn't be a problem. Needless to say, we didn't have any lunch that day and thus began another period of out and out infidelity on my part.

For many of the same reasons I had used to excuse my behavior six years previously, I began to find a justification for what I was doing. But for the first and only time in my life, I began to think in terms of both Maggie and me divorcing our spouses and marrying one another. And it was not just my thinking alone. She was running the same thoughts through her mind and we discussed the idea and the ramifications in great detail through the end of 1975. Not only was there trouble, we were getting serious about following through with the idea.

There's an old adage that the wife of a philanderer is the last one to know, but that wasn't the case with Sam. Thinking the way that I was, I'm sure that my mind was directly reflected in the way that I interacted with her. And sometime in early January of 1976, she once again confronted me directly with her suspicions that I was seeing another woman. And it didn't take a great deal of deductive reasoning for her to figure out who that woman was.

I admitted once again that her suspicions were correct, but I recall being much more cavalier about it this time. I didn't apologize, in so many words, but I did acknowledge that I had no intention of hurting her. But I added salt to her wound by also admitting that I didn't think our marriage of eighteen years was working out, at least as I saw things.

Her reaction was one of shock and great sadness, though there was certainly an element of anger as well. And who could blame her?

"You promised that it would never come to this," she told me through her tears. "How could you let it come to this without even trying at least to discuss the problems we were having in a calm intelligent way? How could you?"

And I had no answer for her. Instead, I cruelly treated her with silence.

A few days passed, and Sam asked me one morning if I would at least try some counseling before taking any drastic steps. Her cousin, the chaplain who had officiated at our wedding ceremony, was now the chaplain for the Military District of Washington, and ironically lived in base quarters at Fort McNair. She thought he would be a good place to start and we set up a meeting with him there. She had told him in general terms why we wanted to talk to him, but left any details to the time we'd all be together.

He began by saying that he would try to be as unbiased and objective in our discussions as he could be, notwithstanding the fact that Joan was his cousin. "But you know that divorce is frowned on by the Church," he went on, "and I'll have to be perfectly honest and tell you that I'm participating in order to try to save your marriage, not to adjudicate who's right or who's wrong. I want you to succeed in keeping your marriage vows, nothing else."

Father Benson's opening comment came as no surprise to me, and in fact, I would have been surprised if he said anything different. But by this time, my thinking had gone to the point that logic and responsibility by themselves would not convince me. It was an evolving era in which "saving the marriage for the children" had become regarded as quaint and old-fashioned, supplanted by the egocentric idea of "whatever's good for me." And it was pretty clear at the end of the meeting that I had not been convinced and was still bent on my self-aggrandizing course of action.

On the way home, Joan asked me when I was going to move out. It seemed contradictory to her that I would want to remain living with her if I planned to separate and co-habit with someone else. As I look back on the time, I remember being overwhelmed by the finality of the thought that I would move out of "my home"—at least until a fateful decision had been made. It also made me realize that my convictions were nowhere near as firm as I had portrayed them in the meeting we had just left.

When I arrived home from school a couple of nights later, Joan took out the classified ad pages of *The Washington Post* and showed me three circled advertisements for furnished efficiency apartments. Pointing to one of them, she said, "This one sounds the best to me and I'd like you to call right now and go look at it. And if you like what you see, go ahead and make a deposit and we'll discuss the financial support for me and the kids when you get home. I can't live with you like this and I'm not going to either. Now it's time for you to make up your mind one way or the other."

Her matter-of-fact, business-like tone stunned me. Sam is really giving me an ultimatum, isn't she, I thought. And if I go out that door to look at the apartment, I'll be making a very critical decision about our future. I went, I took the apartment, and we decided on all the details that night. We decided not to have a formal separation agreement but to keep things as amicable as possible. Sam trusted me to be good to my word regarding finances and visitations with the children, she told me, even though she had lost all trust in my allegiance to my promises of commitment to her.

Meanwhile, Maggie was going through a comparable process with her husband, the only difference being that they abjured the idea of a separation agreement and went directly to the divorce proceedings. While their divorce would be uncontested—their marriage had been on rocky grounds long before I came along—DC law stipulated that the divorcing couple must live separately for a specific period of time and co-habitation with someone else could be grounds for the judge to disallow the divorce petition. As a consequence, Maggie also rented an efficiency apartment and we maintained separate residences, even though we seldom spent the nights alone. I think that subconsciously I regarded the separate living arrangements as a lack of total commitment to one another, and I was comfortable with that assumption.

Graduation from ICAF occurred in June of 1976. My new assignment from school was to the Supreme Headquarters, Allied

Powers in Europe (SHAPE),[27] the military headquarters of NATO located in Mons, Belgium. I was to be the USAF executive assistant to the Supreme Allied Commander, General Alexander M. Haig, Jr. As Maggie was a government civilian employee, she was eligible for a transfer to SHAPE as long as there was a vacancy in the skill and pay grade for which she was applying. And while there was one opening, she wanted me to go by myself, get the lay of the land, and she would come sometime later—perhaps another indication of lack of certainty on both our parts.

I had taken the three kids, now teenagers, to the Fourth of July celebration on the National Mall—along with Maggie. They seemed unperturbed by the fact that their mother and I were separated and they clearly liked Maggie and enjoyed her company. But teenagers tend to be close-mouthed or inscrutable when they are hurt or upset and perhaps they liked the fact that my new friend treated them like young adults and never told them what to do or how to behave. Underneath, as I was to learn later, their emotions were very conflicted and they probably felt rather insecure.

When I went to say good-bye to the children and Joan, she asked me straight out if I would reconsider the decision that she admittedly had forced me to make. But since I was finished straddling the fence, I told her that I wouldn't and it was perhaps the time and the circumstance to begin new lives for ourselves. I know it hurt her badly to beg, in a sense, and being refused was even worse, and I left home and family far more conflicted myself than I thought I would be.

When I arrived at SHAPE, I found that there were a number of old friends there as well as people whom I had known during my six years at the Pentagon. So there would be no lack of friendly faces. I also had a lot of time to think about the decisions that I had made over the past year. And while I was not inclined to change them in any way, the mere fact that I was rehashing them in my mind indicated some guilt or doubt on my part.

The small group of friends with whom I was closest and felt most comfortable were all married and got together virtually every weekend either to go out to dinner or to entertain frequently in their

---

27   See *Portraits in Brass.*

own homes. They immediately started including me, and to "balance the table," they began inviting the single executive secretary to one of the four-star generals at SHAPE. And while no intent was implicit in their actions, Nellie, as I'll call her, and I came to see one another at times other than by coincidental invitations from our friends. She and I had known one another casually in the Pentagon years before, we had a lot in common with each other, and we clearly enjoyed being together.

When our association became more than friendly, I began to wonder who the hell I was. I had been unfaithful to my wife in favor of being with Maggie. Now I was being unfaithful to Maggie by my newly found liaison with Nellie. Had I so little sense of commitment that the philosophy of the recently popular song lyrics, "If you can't be with the one you love, love the one you're with," had overtaken my better judgment and sense of morality? While I hated to admit it to myself, there was certainly some merit in that question. But I was enjoying my life too much to pay much attention to the almost-stilled voice of conscience inside me.

In early November, I received a phone call from a former neighbor in Maryland—the best friend I had made there. He told me that Danny was having serious problems. He was into marijuana, running around with a bad bunch of kids, skipping school, and getting involved in minor neighborhood vandalism.

"I don't know what you can do about it when you're in Belgium," George told me, "but he's headed for serious trouble and you need to be aware of that. By the way, Joan did not ask me to call you, but at the same time, I'll try to give her as much help for the time being as I can."

I knew that General Haig was going back to Washington in his own airplane the following morning. I immediately went into his office, gave him a very scant outline of the problem, and asked if I could be added to the manifest for the flight back. He agreed readily and told me to take as long as I needed back there and to let him know if there was anything he or Mrs. Haig could do to help.

My next stop was to go to Nellie's office to tell her what I was going to do. In the forty or so steps between my office and hers, I made a decision that I was going back to being the husband and father that I should be. She said she understood and had even thought from time to time that it would come to this some day. She then kissed me on the cheek and said, "Please do what you think is right and when you get back there and the time is right, I want you to tell her about us. I know down deep that you've always loved Joan, and strange as it may sound right now, I also want to be their friend when she and the children arrive."

I didn't have the chance to call Sam before leaving Belgium and tell her I was coming and when we arrived at Andrews AFB, outside of Washington, the next afternoon, I called and asked her to pick me up. She seemed quite surprised to hear my voice, but quickly recovered her aplomb. "Why don't you get a BOQ room at Andrews for tonight and give me a call tomorrow. You told me that we needed to start our own separate lives back in July and I've been trying to do just that. This is completely unexpected to have you re-enter my life again, and I need to do some serious thinking."

I hadn't even told Sam that I wanted to put our family back together and she was reluctant even to see me.

The next day when we met, I told her why I was back—Danny—and told her that the only way I could see to get him back on the straight and narrow was for her and the children to come to Belgium to live. Her first response was to ask me if that was the only reason I wanted to put the family back together again, and then when I seemed to answer that satisfactorily, she told me that she would have to think about it!

My arrogant ego was wounded to the quick. I was of the preconceived notion that all I'd have to do was beckon and she'd come running. And here she was, not showing the slightest bit of enthusiasm and with what appeared to be a very real chance that she'd send me packing.

The next evening, she invited me to come to dinner so that we could talk about the future. Dinner was to be just the two of us, but beforehand I spent time with the kids and had a long frank conversation with Danny. I told him specifically, and the other two later, that if they came to join me, living in a military community overseas was a whole different world than the civilian world they had occupied for the past six years. Behavior that was frowned on but tolerated in their current environment was totally unacceptable over there, and my head would roll, not just theirs, if they got out of line.

Sam began our dinner together with an impish smile and a small toast, "Here's to being a family again [long pause] as long as you agree to the conditions that I've written down for you to sign in *blood*."

I knew now what the results of her hours of contemplation had yielded and her conditions were simply a matter of common sense, protection, and commitment. She was never going to go through the mental agony of being unwanted and cast aside as she had endured for the past year, nor did I wish to put her through that again. She needed to trust me to be faithful to her and treat her with the respect and dignity that she deserved. And she needed me to sincerely want to be with her, not just stay with her because of the children or because I swore that I would.

At the end of a tearful, bittersweet dinner, I swore to her that "we will grow old together" and, as it turned out, we did.

But to show another aspect of her impeccably generous character and deep consideration for others, she told me that I owed Maggie the courtesy of telling her face to face of our decision, and that I should not let the next day go by without seeing her. It went without saying that nothing should go beyond the point of this explanation, and it didn't. Maggie was extremely angry when I told her what had happened, but not for the decision itself, it seemed, but the fact that I had not told her first. I have never understood her thinking on the issue, but as Sam was intuitively well aware, I did feel more honorable for having informed her personally.

*   *   *

The older two children, Christine in particular, did not at all like the idea of being yanked out of the environment in which they had lived for six years—longer by far than any place they had lived. They were both juniors in high school by this time and Danny was in the ninth grade. Christine even went so far as to tell me I should go back to where I had come from and stop messing up their lives—a strong statement, of course, but we recognized it as her frustration over the impending disruption in what was a rather critical point in their lives.

Danny, by contrast, showed no preference either way. He was just sullen and non-communicative—a teenage brat of the first order. Before I headed back to Belgium,[28] I took him aside again and appealed to his better nature to try to atone with his mom for all the problems and heartache he had caused her—which he did reluctantly. I also then tried to generate some enthusiasm in him for straightening out his life and for the adventures that lay ahead. That was going to take a lot more time.

It was just a matter of five weeks before the family arrived at Zaventem IAP in Brussels, just ten days or so before Christmas. Our dog, a Lhasa Apso named Chou-Chou, had come three weeks earlier and was in the capable care of Joyce and Randy Peat, two of our closest friends. The daily New York–Brussels flight arrived at midnight every night after a two-hour stopover in London. And as was the case for most winter days in that area of Europe, it was raw and cold when they arrived with a light mist falling, right on the verge of turning to snow.

As we headed to the parking lot, each of us carrying bags, I looked around me and there was no sign of Chris. I stopped and looked back at the airport exit through the foggy mist and there she stood, slack shouldered and looking absolutely miserable.

I walked back to her, put my arm around her shoulder and said, "C'mon, sweetie. You're tired; it's been a long trip and things will look a lot better after a good night's rest."

She lifted her head toward me, tears running down her face with an expression of abject misery and said four words that I'll never forget, "I hate it here!"

But teens have a very special way of quickly recovering their equilibrium, and the Peat's daughter, Sondra, was wonderfully helpful in making that happen. She was the same age as Scott and

---

[28] There was a great deal to be done—Joan's resignation from her teaching position, a realty contract to sell the house, packing our household goods, shipping her car, etc.—that had to be done before they could move to join me, and Joan did a magnificent job in a short period of time.

Christine, also a junior at SHAPE-American High School, and in no time, Sondra had introduced all three children to most of the others in the high school.

The other families there were also remarkably hospitable and went out of their way to make us welcome. I had done as Nellie suggested earlier and told Joan all about our relationship. She also played a significant part in making us welcome, practically adopting the three kids as her new "niece and nephews." To the exemplary credit of both women, she and Joan liked one another from the time they met, there was never a hint of jealousy or animosity, and they remained friends for the entire time we were there, and for years after.

The NATO military headquarters had only been in Mons, Belgium, for less than a decade by the time we arrived in the mid-'70s. It had formerly been located in Paris, but Charles DeGaulle had evicted both the political and military centers of operations as part of his xenophobic independence movement of the previous decade. Mons had been one of the economic disaster areas of Belgium—one of the major reasons that the Belgian government eagerly sought the NATO relocation—and the infrastructure had not yet developed to the point of fully supporting the influx of people. In addition, we were out of cycle for normal military transfers, which usually take place during the summers, thereby causing the least disruption of families.

Consequently we were faced with a long wait for a home of our own to become available, and we spent our first few months there living in a hotel directly across from SHAPE headquarters. The accommodations were good, all things considered. Joan and I had a small suite while the two boys shared a large room and Christine had her own room. Because of the housing crisis in the area, the government paid for ninety days of public lodging and would extend that for an additional thirty days if circumstances warranted.

The public services were also conducive to making the waiting time as comfortable as possible. The kids were able to walk to school and the teen club, both of which were right on the installation. Public transportation was very well planned and they were also able to use the bus to get around town and visit their friends—not that they could have driven anyway since the minimum driving age in

Belgium at the time was eighteen. Ironically, there was no minimum age to be served alcohol and they and their friends found the Belgian beer to be quite palatable.

I had previously found a very excellent restaurant, which also happened to be within walking distance of our hotel, and Sam and I went there on our very first night out. Belgian cuisine is reputed to be among the best in the world—a reputation that is exceptionally well-deserved—and she thoroughly enjoyed her first experience. But far more important, we both removed all the barriers of communication that had arisen over the previous few years and candidly discussed all the issues between us that had been sublimated, for whatever reasons, in our recent past. I suspect that we closed the restaurant that night, had more than our share of wine, but probably made the most important step ever in assuring that our reunited marriage would last.

It was not long before we found the house that we wished to be ours, but there was one problem: it was already occupied by a U.S. Army colonel and his family. But he had been notified that he was to be given a command—the goal of most ambitious military career officers—they were not to move until early spring. But the place was worth waiting for. It was an eight-bedroom town house on the *peripherique* (the ring road or beltway) around the city of Mons.

There were four bedrooms on the second floor and four more on the third floor, and a feature most unusual for a home that old: a gas-fired central heating system with a separate electrical baseboard system for the third floor. Each room throughout the house had its own gorgeously tiled fireplace though all but one had been sealed off when the central heating was installed. In every respect it was worth the wait ten times over to have such a lovely place.

It was in wonderful condition, with two sitting rooms, a huge dining room with a table that would seat twenty-four, and an office on the ground floor. But the kitchen showed the hundred-year age of the home. It had running water and a stub-up for a gas stove—nothing else, not even a cabinet. It also had an unheated pantry adjacent to the kitchen, which in time past had been used for perishable food storage in winter.

But that was a welcome challenge, not a drawback, as far as Sam was concerned. Within days of our moving in, she had the kitchen furnished with a stove, refrigerator, work tables, and cabinets to store our kitchenware and dishes. Over the next year and a half, we often entertained for a dozen or more guests and, with adequate prior planning, found the limited work spaces and appliances to be more than adequate. She loved the house and in no time had made it into a most comfortable home.

It had been a long time since I had seen Sam so glowing and effervescent. But it didn't need a genius to understand the reasons why. In addition to being mentally and emotionally at peace, she was also in a prolonged period of excellent control of her diabetes and the ogre-like prospect of her becoming pregnant again was gone forever.

Our year and a half in Belgium flew by. One of the reasons was that I had made the firm commitment that spending my time at work and neglecting the family was a thing of the past. I owed it to Sam probably more so than the children, who had reached the age when they began to break away from doing things with their parents and instead devoting their time and attention to their friends. Yes, the chagrin that Christine felt when she first arrived in the country quickly dissipated and all three of the kids soon forgot their connections to Maryland.

Joan and I decided that despite the nearly twenty-year hiatus, we would take up skiing again. We had such a relatively short distance to go to some of the best skiing in the world—the Alps were less than a day's drive away—and all three kids thought they might like to give it a try also. There was even enthusiasm when they discovered that we were going to Austria on a planned trip with their closest friends' parents. It was the start of a series of ski vacations that continued for the rest of our time in Europe.

Joan always loved to tell the story of another short vacation in which I wasn't able to participate. As Mother's Day approached, all three of them told her at dinner a few days before that they had a special gift that they wished to give her. They wanted to take her to Paris for the weekend.

Sam thought that was a fine idea. Her love affair with Paris had begun in the late '50s and, if anything, it was now in full bloom. And besides, Paris was now only a two-hour drive down the autoroute from Mons.

"How are we going to get there?" she asked them.

"Well, we thought you wouldn't mind driving," was the quick rejoinder.

"And where are we going to stay, and who's going to pay for all this?" she playfully questioned, knowing full well that they knew that she'd jump at the chance to go to Paris on a moment's notice.

They told her that they had put aside a little money, but thought she wouldn't mind kicking in the difference—which, of course, she didn't mind at all. I was on a SHAPE business trip to Turkey that weekend—not very good planning on my part—and I admired her courage tremendously for her willingness to drive in that beautiful city. But she did and it turned out to be a delightful weekend, primarily because she did everything the kids wanted to do. And in the process she inculcated a love of the City of Lights in each of them that very nearly matched hers.

On their return to Mons, they had to stop at the France-Belgium border crossing. Sam had bought a few things in Paris—who could resist?—and she wanted to collect back the value added tax of 17 percent on everything she had purchased. When she approached the customs official to make the claim, she addressed him in English, telling him what she wanted to do.

The arrogant little peacock puffed up his feathers and told her, "Madam, you are in France and in France we speak French!"

Sam had been taking French language classes since she arrived in the French-speaking part of Belgium—as she had nearly twenty years previously when we lived in France. However, she always had great difficulty with pronunciation, particularly the rolled "R" and the nasal sounds of many words. But she screwed up her courage and began to try to explain her purpose *en français*. Before she got a full sentence out of her mouth, the agent threw up his hands, covered his ears with both hands and then motioned for her to stop. Within moments, she concluded her business with the extreme Francophile, and left—laughing.

"That'll teach him," she told the kids when she reached the car, still chuckling to herself over her victory. However, it's not unlikely that the customs agent couldn't wait to get home that evening to tell his wife of the fun he had that day with another American.

*   *   *

I had been promoted to colonel during this time and we thought there might be a good chance that our NATO assignment might be terminated at the end of the second year. And the reading of the tea leaves was accurate. But instead of going back to the States or to another base in England or Germany, we headed instead to Athens, where I would become the commander of Hellenikon Air Base and the senior U.S. commander in Greece.

The young lady who had "hated it here" begged to stay the summer in Mons with her new best friends. Both she and Scott had graduated from SHAPE-American High School, and all the close-knit group of friends wanted one more final summer together before they all headed off to college in September. The Peats laughingly agreed that they would take on one more daughter for the summer. In August, Chris joined us in Athens just prior to heading to Germany where she would attend the University of Maryland-Munich Campus. So it was that Joan and I, Scott and Dan (he was too old to be called Danny anymore, he told us) along with Chou-Chou set off on one more adventure.

One of the SHAPE protocol officers with whom we had become friendly, an Italian Army captain, was delighted that we were going to travel by car across France, Switzerland, through the St. Gotthard train tunnel, and into Italy where we would stop briefly in Lake Como and Venice before taking a car ferry to Greece.

"You must let me make the arrangements for your trip," he insisted. "As you know, I'm a northern Italian and I have many close contacts throughout the area. I would be honored to make your journey as pleasant as possible," Antonio told us. Who could pass up an offer like that?

On our first day out, we drove from Mons to Como, Italy, what seems like an incredible distance to Americans who sometimes take two days to cross just one state. But actually, the distance was less than eight hundred kilometers (five hundred miles) and the roads were excellent all the way. The scenery was superb, especially in Switzerland, and we reached the St. Gotthard train tunnel well in advance of our reservations on the train. The tunnel entrance is well over three thousand feet in altitude and the pass—which is impassable for half the year because of snow—rises much higher. The railroad tunnel[29] was built in 1882 and for much of the twentieth century was the longest tunnel in the world at fifteen kilometers (nine miles).

It was a fascinating process as we drove up a ramp to a flatbed railroad car, where the vehicle was chained down. We were told that we must not leave the engine running and could not turn on the interior or exterior car lights during the passage into Airolo in Uri canton, right on the border of Italy. The interior of the tunnel was in total darkness, as of course was the interior of the car, but every once in a while, there would be a brilliant flash of light from the contact with the overhead electrical line that provided power for the train's engines. Chou-Chou was so frightened that he jumped into Joan's lap and left a small wet spot on her skirt.

We emerged from the tunnel less than eight minutes later but the trip somehow seemed much longer than that. We reversed the process when we debarked from the train and were soon driving down the south side of the pass where we would reach Como, our destination for the night.

Antonio didn't disappoint us in the slightest with our first hotel reservation. It was in the Hotel Metropole, a gorgeous five-star hotel on the main piazza, overlooking the waterfront of the beautiful *Lago di Como* (Lake Como). Our room was right in the front center of the building and looked directly out over the piazza and the large marina. I detected a small bit of Italian chicanery when the desk clerk addressed me as *Generale* and the bell captain was personally directing the handling of our luggage. Since I couldn't speak Italian, of course, there was no way I could correct his slight error in my rank—with Sam smiling all the while at that wily Antonio.

On our first night in Italy, of course, the boys wanted—what else—pizza! So we sent them on their way while we sought out a little higher level of cuisine at a small, romantic *trattoria* recommended by the concierge. We were not taking any leave on the way to Greece so the least we could do, we reasoned, was to splurge a little while we were en route.

---

[29] There is now a motor vehicle tunnel that parallels the railway tunnel, but it had not been completed when we made the trip.

During dinner, we talked about Joan's favorite tragic love story, Ernest Hemingway's *A Farewell to Arms*. In the novel (allegedly autobiographical), the heroine was a nurse who Hemingway met recovering from wounds in an Italian Army hospital in Milan when he was an Italian Army ambulance driver in WW I. The nurse became pregnant, Hemingway became a pacifist and deserted, and they escaped by rowing a boat across *Lago di Como* into Switzerland. The book ends when the nurse dies in childbirth, along with the baby, during a raging Alpine thunderstorm.

Joan had also lost two of her own babies with a thunderstorm clearly raging outside the hospital in Germany while she was in labor. Obviously, it made a deep impression on her and she related to that tragedy through most of her life. And here we were in the same little town where the novel and movie had taken place.

But in her inimitable fashion, she didn't become sad or maudlin recalling her own tragedies. Instead she luxuriated in the romance of the beautiful little town and asked to go for a walk on the waterfront after we finished dinner.

As we stood looking out over the marina at the lights shimmering on the surface of the lake, she turned and looked into my eyes and said "Thank you."

Smiling back at her I asked, "What for?"

"For everything that I can think of right now. For marrying me. For always being by my side and supporting me through all the difficulties that I've had over the years. For coming back to me and the children when the reasons we separated were probably as much my fault as they were yours. Just for loving me the way you do, that's what for."

And then she reached up and kissed me softly and sweetly. I've loved Como ever since and I know she did too—even though we never went back again.

Our next stop was Venice, a relatively short drive across the north of Italy where we would eventually catch a sea-going ferry in order to transit the Adriatic Sea and proceed on into Greece. But first we would spend a couple of days in this city of canals that dates back into the eighth century, and was at one time the home, in the Middle Ages, of one of the most powerful city-states of Europe.

But first we needed to take a water taxi out to the island city itself. We told the taxi driver that we wanted to go to the Hotel Monaco, and in classic Italian gesture, he smiled and raised his eyebrows heaven-ward as if to say—I'm impressed. And with good reason. The hotel, like the one the night before, was exactly where we wanted to be, a fact that became obvious when we reached our destination. We docked at a side entrance to the hotel, and when I told the porter my name, he disappeared into the hotel and returned with a nattily dressed gentleman—who later revealed himself to be the manager—and with a radiant smile said, "*Bienvenido, Generale.*" Clearly, it hadn't been a mistake in Como. Antonio had done it again. But this time he outdid himself.

Soon a whole bevy of porters was stacking our bags on a luggage cart, and the manager, himself, escorted us to our room—or rather I should say suite. It was a sitting room with two bedrooms. Our bedroom was quite large, with a luxurious four-poster bed that was adorned with magnificent pillows and shams, and a beautiful quilted spread that appeared to be an antique. And, of course, the draperies, upholstery, and the entire room decor matched perfectly. Both the sitting room and our bedroom had floor-to-ceiling windows that looked directly out on the Grand Canal and the harbor. And while the boys' room was less lavish than ours, it too was a thing of beauty, with two single beds and more than adequate room.

As we got our bearings, we found that we could not have been better located. We were within easy walking distance of Piazza San Marco and its superb basilica. The Bridge of Sighs was a few short steps in the other direction. And the Doge's Palace, another of the magnificent landmarks of Venice, was just a few steps beyond. But happiest of all was the fact that immediately outside the main entrance was a gondola dock with gondoliers ready and eager to take us wherever we wished to go, any time of day or night. Our hotel manager kindly advised us to have the doorman prearrange the fare whenever we wished to book one of the boats. It was excellent advice because ordinarily they would charge whatever the traffic might bear, and coming out of our hotel, we saw huge *lira* signs in the boatmen's eyes"

On our first evening there, all four of us went to a trattoria around the corner from the hotel. We were a bit tired from the journey and a light dinner seemed to appeal to all of us. In the countries north of the Alps, we were in the habit of bringing Chou-Chou with us to restaurants, as did most dog owners. He was always well-behaved and just lay under the table while we ate. But that evening we were to find that the custom did not extend into Italy. The restaurateurs were accustomed to the habits of the northern Europeans but that didn't mean they liked them. So instead of being seated near the open front of the trattoria, we were given a table way in the rear near the entrance to the kitchen.

Not long after we were seated, one of the waiters passed by our table, saw Chou-Chou's nose sticking out between the two boys' seats, and kicked at him—though I don't believe he ever made contact. Many other waiters came and went and the dog remained placid. But the next time the fellow who had threatened him passed, the tiny tiger jumped out from his place beneath the table, growled menacingly, and snapped at his ankle. We thought that the waiter, who was carrying a tray full of dirty dishes, was going to jump out of his skin. He just barely maintained his load of dishes in his eagerness to avoid the marauding predator. Like the waiter before him, Chou-Chou did not make contact with the man's ankle, but he certainly caused him to steer clear of our table for the rest of the evening.

Having learned our lesson the following evening, we left the puppy in our hotel room the next night while we went to a more elegant dinner—while the boys went after pizza again. This time it was the dog that showed his disdain for having been left behind. When we returned to the room, we soon discovered that he had peed right in the middle of our bed—something that he had never done since he was housebroken. I went down to the lobby to explain and apologize profusely to the night manager, but he was completely unfazed. *No problema*, he assured me and sent a maid to change the linens right away. But we wondered at how these hoteliers could be so courteous at a time like that, and what they really thought about us for allowing such a thing to happen.

We touched all the tourist stops in this magnificent city and even crossed the great harbor by gondola to the island of Murano, world-famous for the magnificent glass that is made there We watched the whole process and were enthralled by the skill of the glass blowers. And if I recall, Joan even bought a relatively small decorative piece, just to put on display in our home with all the other mementos that we had been gathering over the years. But now, on the morning of our third day, it was time to leave beautiful Venice and head on to our ultimate destination: Athens.

When we hear the term, ferry, Americans tend to picture a car carrier that crosses the Hudson River like the Weehawken Ferry, which sails between New Jersey and Manhattan. But the one we were taking was an ocean liner with staterooms, dining rooms, etc. The major difference is that this ship had a side ramp on which your car was driven into the hold where it remained for the twenty-four hours we would be en route. Meanwhile, we and the boys were in pleasant, comfortable cabins on the upper decks and had a short overnight cruise from northern italy to western Greece.

The ferry went down the Adriatic to the port of Patras on the northwest coast of the Peloponnesian Peninsula, and from there we would drive across the northern coast of the peninsula to Corinth and then into Attica province on the mainland. We drove through the port city of Piraeus, just south of Athens, and then on to Glyfada, our final destination. Glyfada is a coastal suburb of Athens, the nearest city to Hellenikon Air Base,[30] and also the home of the Bona Vista Hotel, a one-time luxury resort hotel that had been leased for many years by the U.S. government as a transient hotel for Americans arriving in and departing from Greece. The Bona Vista was to be our home for the next six weeks.

*   *   *

Our two years in Greece were one of the best assignments that we had in our career, as well as a wonderful period in our lives, for many reasons. The most important one was that Joan's health remained well under control. Medical technology had developed significantly in the past twenty years, probably spurred by the

---

[30]   Hellenikon Air Base was actually located on the east side of Athens International Airport and shared the area with a Greek air base by the same name. In the preparations for the 2004 Olympic Games in Athens, this airport was closed, the airport was relocated farther to the northeast and the U.S. base was closed completely.

logarithmic growth of the incidence in diabetes as we became a fast food nation. But the two most important of these developments, for Joan at least, were the disposable insulin syringe with its fine gauge needle, and the finger-prick blood testing device that gave accurate up-to-the-moment blood sugar readings. In addition, a fast-acting insulin had been developed which, taken in concert with a long-lasting basal dose of insulin, would now permit much more accurate and immediate control.

In a negative sense, these developments also permitted her to get into some bad habits For so many years, Joan used diet to control how much and what food items she consumed. But now with much finer regulation possible, she could eat whatever she wanted, whenever she wanted, and then "cover" the excess intake with fast-acting regular insulin. And while she didn't abuse the newfound freedom that was offered, this process of covering also resulted in long term weight gain—not huge amounts in a short period of time, but more like a half or three-quarters of a pound each month, which over the course of a few years begins to add up.

We were constantly on the go during this period, entertaining at home, eating out in the local tavernas,[31] and enjoying the remarkable historical sites of this ancient cradle of democracy. We suspected that we could live in Greece for the rest of our lives and never see all of the wonders of just the Athens area, let alone the rest of this remarkable country. Despite my command responsibilities, we had some of the closest friends we ever had any place and were constantly interacting with them.

Shortly before we arrived at Hellenikon, the CIA station chief at the American Embassy, Richard Welch, was assassinated in a drive-by shooting that the Seventeen September Organization[32] claimed as their doing. In a cooperative investigation between the

---

[31]   The taverna is an ancient Greek custom. Evening meals are seldom taken at home but more often at a local eatery where it is usually cheaper to eat than to cook a comparable meal at home.

[32]   The Seventeen September group was named after a police crackdown on student revolutionaries at the Athens Polytechnic University and named for the date of the attack in which a number of students were killed in the rioting. They had a history of extreme violence that lasted for nearly three decades.

State and Defense Departments and the Greek KBI, the internal security organization similar to our FBI, the finding was that the American Ambassador was the number one target of the Seventeen Novembrists and the commander of Hellenikon AB was number two. As a result, both the ambassador and I were assigned armored sedans as staff cars, and were given extensive briefings (including our families) on personal safety and evasive tactics. Further, we were assigned permanent drivers, former Greek commandos, who had been thoroughly trained at the FBI Academy in Quantico, Virginia.

Unfortunately, Christine was still in Belgium when this indoctrination took place, and even though I placed great emphasis with her on being alert to her surroundings when she first arrived, she apparently didn't fathom the gravity of the situation to the extent I had hoped.

She soon got a part-time job as a shampoo girl at the beauty parlor at the Bona Vista Hotel for the remainder of her summer vacation. She took a military shuttle bus from the bottom of our street each day since we were allowed to have only one car in Greece and that was Joan's mode of transportation.

One evening at dinner, Chris very innocently said, "You know, it's funny. Every morning when I go out to get the bus, there's this guy who stands across the street from me and when I get off the bus coming home, he is usually in the same place."

The next morning I reported the incident to our base security police and the embassy chief of security, both of whom informed their counterparts in the Greek security forces. They were waiting when Chris went to the bus later that morning and immediately arrested the lurker. As it turned out, he was a wanted Libyan terrorist who was suspected to have been involved in an attack the previous year. Needless to say, after that episode, I didn't need to try very hard to stress the necessity for vigilance to my family members. And I'll have to admit, it helped me to focus my attention as well.

Perhaps the biggest challenge we had there was the evacuation of U.S. citizens from Iran, an operation that lasted from early November 1978 to mid-February 1979.[33] It was a commitment on

---

[33] See *Portraits in Brass* for detailed coverage of the operation.

the part of the entire base community during which we welcomed literally tens of thousands of refugees from Iran, housed them, fed them, cared for their every need, and then sent them on via daily commercial charter flights to destinations in Europe and throughout the United States. It was a seven-day-per-week operation that went non-stop through the Christmas and New Years holidays. Despite the gigantic logistical challenges, the people of Hellenikon didn't just amaze me but far exceeded the expectations of both the State and Defense Departments.

I have never been prouder of a community than I was during that period of time. There was a mission to perform and all military personnel, their families, and the base civilian employees never gave a thought to duty hours, time off, or recompense. And the sense of teamwork and camaraderie didn't last for just the period of the crisis, but extended from then until well after the time we left. Sam was beside me every day and pitched in just as hard as all the others: feeding and changing diapers of the infants, helping those in an emotional state of shock to recover their equilibrium, and anything else that needed to be done. We always looked back at that time period as one of the proudest moments of our lives together.

But all was not well with those aspects of being in Athens that were beyond our power to control. This was the era of the Carter Administration and budgets for operating and maintaining the base were cut not only into the muscle but a bit of the bone as well. It got so bad the one of my staff directors suggested that we all bring a few rolls of toilet paper from home and donate them to the organizations that needed the supplies the most. Despite the generous thoughts behind the proposal, I told the staff that I would resign my command and commission before we had to resort to that extreme measure.

But those budget shortages didn't seem to bother our senators and congressmen in the slightest. Roughly every other month or so, I would get advance notice of a congressional delegation's (or CODEL, in the parlance of the privileged few) upcoming arrival at Hellenikon. The message would tell me the number of dignitaries who were coming, by whom they would be accompanied—usually a spouse—and what type of support I was required to provide them.

When each CODEL arrived, I would ask the members to take just five minutes before they headed for shopping and sightseeing in Athens to hear a quick briefing on the severe funding shortages we were experiencing and the impact this was having on the morale and welfare of the troops. Of perhaps a dozen such groups that came to the base over those two years, only one delegation leader—Senator Alan K. Simpson of Wyoming—accepted my invitation. Excuses ranged from, "My wife isn't feeling well and we need to get to our hotel," to "We're already late for a scheduled private tour of the Acropolis." Sam was normally there to meet all groups that included spouses, and after each expression of total disinterest, she would simply shake her head in disgust.

Our family also became somewhat smaller during the time we spent in Athens. First, Christine headed off to college in Munich. But in a much different way than most youngsters begin this great new adventure. Joan was, of course, committed to going to Munich with her and getting her settled in her new environment. In shopping for the best airfare she could find, Joan decided they would make an adventure out of the trip and it turned out to be more than they bargained for. They would fly LOT, the Polish national airlines, from Athens to Budapest and from there on to Munich. But a vital consideration in all of this was the fact that the Iron Curtain was still very much a reality and few Americans ever ventured behind it without having a very good reason.

I was fully aware that, as the commander of the base, I was an unquestioned target for Soviet and other Bloc Nations intelligence services. In fact, because of my security clearances, I was unable to travel behind the Iron Curtain. I mentioned this to Joan and she sort of shrugged it off with the attitude that the bad guys might be interested in me but there was no reason that they would be interested in any way in her and Chris. So she even built an eight-hour layover in Budapest, got a visa from the Hungarian Embassy in Athens for the two of them to visit, and planned to use the time to tour this lovely city.

When they landed in Budapest, both she and Chris were shocked and amazed to see soldiers carrying machine guns at port arms in every direction they looked. They seemed very menacing she was to tell me later. A few moments later, when they went through customs, she told the agent that they had arranged a tour of the city and showed him the visa. He demanded that they put their passports into an official looking satchel before he would let them through the gate, and knowing that one never should surrender his or her passport, she demurred. Then you won't get to leave the terminal, she was told. Take your choice!

After a long harangue she was finally assured that the passports would be there waiting for them when they returned, and no one in the city would challenge them to show any documentation, since they were allowed to retain their visas. And in fact, they had a wonderful tour; they saw all of the important sights; they had the most delicious goulash that she ever had, one of Sam's perennial favorites; and finally they headed back to the airport to continue their journey.

But all was not well. As soon as they went through the customs and immigration barrier, a stern, rugged looking uniformed woman took Chris by the arm and told her to accompany her into a nearby room. When Joan started to follow along, totally confused by the sudden threatening action, she was told she wasn't allowed. And though I never saw Sam show any signs of panic at any time in our lives, she said later that she was as close as she had ever been. Christine, who is just about as unflappable as her mother, also told me later that she was "scared, really scared." After questioning everyone who looked official, Joan finally found out what the problem was: Christine was born in Germany, had been naturalized and had an American passport, but obviously there was a "serious irregularity" here.

As time approached for their flight to Munich to depart, Joan's anxiety began to grow. She hadn't seen Chris for well over an hour, didn't know where they had taken her, and was right on the verge of calling the U.S. Embassy for assistance. But at the last minute, Chris was brought out of the room where she had been taken, both were escorted by armed guards as if they were criminals going into exile and were the last to board the plane before it took off.

Sam finally agreed later that it wasn't just me who was targeted by intelligence operatives as this was a clear case of harassment by the Hungarian Communist government. They were just making a point of reminding me, through my family members, that they were in charge and that we shouldn't forget it. Nor was this the last case of Soviet-style harassment we would encounter during our remaining years in Europe.

But the adventure of taking Christine off to college didn't end there. When most of Christine's in-processing had been completed, she was assigned to her dormitory room where she met her new roommates. As subtly as she could, she told her mother that she "couldn't stand" the two girls with whom she had been placed. Joan promised her that she'd try to help her get a room change but first she needed to go to the American Express bank to get some German and American cash for Chris's spending money—before the days of giving your child a credit card when they went away to school.

While waiting in line at the bank, she heard a young lady in front of her say that she didn't care for the assigned roommates she had and that she was looking to change rooms. Joan took the cue and after hearing her chat with her friend for a while, Joan concluded that the young lady appeared to be very personable. She approached her, told her that Chris was also unhappy with her pairing, and the young lady agreed to go back to the dorm area to see if they could work something out.

So when both of the girls each decided that the other would do just fine, Joan decided it was time to return to Athens. She left with a sense of satisfaction that she had come through the experience a whole lot wiser, and was also pleased that Chris would be very satisfied with the new arrangement and get a decent start on her college career.

A week later we received our first letter from Chris, which began, "Nice going, Mom. The second night we were together, Julie hit on me and told me that she was a lesbian. I told her that I wasn't and said that that's the way it was going to stay. I'm pretty sure that she got the message and will look elsewhere for her fun. Actually, she's pretty nice otherwise and everything will be fine."

Though Scott had the ability to get through high school, he was clearly not college material. So he decided to enlist in the Air Force. He took all the placement exams and did fairly well according to the recruiter, and within a couple of weeks, he was off to Lackland AFB, Texas, where he began basic training. In the first recruit photograph he sent home, I discovered that the Air Force had succeeded in doing what I hadn't been able to convince him of since he was in junior high school: he had a very short haircut!

That left just Dan at home, but Sam was entirely too occupied within the base and local Greek communities to suffer from empty nest syndrome. At an embassy reception we attended, she was to learn of a home that was operated by a Greek Orthodox priest who was caring for a group of two dozen abandoned, orphaned, and abused young teenagers. While he had a lot of volunteer help with the social and physical care of the children, he was looking for someone to teach English as part of the school curriculum that he ran. Joan didn't need a second to think about the challenge. She volunteered on the spot.

Greek men in general and Orthodox priests in particular have a well-deserved reputation for being misogynistic. And Father Demetrius was no exception. Early on in her teaching efforts, she discovered that the discipline in the home was excessively rigid and the headmaster was a martinet, particularly as far as the young girls were concerned. It was not long before both the young boys and girls were coming to her outside of class complaining of the treatment they received, particularly the punishments for seemingly innocuous offenses.

Joan spoke to some of our Greek friends about her findings, and the men actually found it rather amusing—at least in the sense that Joan had the naive courage to challenge Father Demetrius, head on.

"He's a king in his own private domain," she was told, "and the last thing you ever want to do is to oppose the 'divine right of kings' as each of these guys thinks he has. The government will never interfere with the internal activities of the church, and the bishops are even worse. They regard themselves above these petty monarchs, but would never involve themselves in issues that they might be or have been guilty of at one time themselves. Unless you can prove that there is something nefarious or harmful going on in that home, no one will listen to you," they concluded.

That spunky little lady still tried though. She addressed various things she disagreed with to the priest from time to time, but her objections went in one of his ears and out the other. At first he laughed at her, telling her that the Greeks didn't spoil and coddle their children the way Americans do, but ultimately he ended up telling her that if she didn't like the way he ran things, she was welcome to leave.

When two teenagers came to the door of our home one day to ask for refuge, that was the last straw for Joan. We didn't take them in because of the international diplomatic ramifications that might ensue, but refusing them nearly broke her heart. She was both sad and fiercely angry, but finally conceded that our Greek friends were right. She hated admitting defeat, but finally ended up terminating her relation with the school in abject frustration. She always looked back at the episode as a failure on her part, even though she was powerless to control or even influence the situation.

There's an old saying that the squeaky wheel is always the one that gets the grease, but there's a downside to that adage as well. The commissary store for the Hellenikon base community was not on the base, as it is on most installations, but instead was in a seedy warehouse region of downtown Athens, often more than an hour's drive through horrendous traffic from where most of our military families lived. The local lore was that the store had been located there by the U.S. Embassy because it was more convenient to the embassy staffers. Another rationale was that there was not enough real estate on the base to site a facility that large, which had some merit. And though there may have been a kernel of truth in each proposition, the fact remained that it was a morale issue for all of the base families.

I became the squeaky wheel for all of the Air Force Commissary Service officials who made staff visits to Hellenikon, and I had a growing list of complaints for every one of the officials who visited the base.[34] When the summer of 1980 rolled around, I anticipated that there might be another transfer in the offing for me since, at my rank, two years in a command position was about the best I could expect. Neither Joan nor I wanted to leave, but we were reconciled to the fact that moving was an inevitability.

But we weren't prepared for the news we received in May of that year. We would be reassigned to Ramstein AB in West Germany—which was fine—and I was to become the commander of the Air

---

[34] See *Portraits in Brass* for more detailed coverage of this issue.

Force Commissary Service—Europe. The wheel had squeaked too loudly, apparently. And I was to become the grease to resolve all the problems I had complained about for two years. So be it! I knew very little about the grocery business, but I did know how to run an organization and to resolve issues that were affecting the morale of the people we served.

* * *

Two years after coming from Belgium to Greece, we reversed direction and returned by ocean-going ferry to Italy. But this time around, we left the port city of Piraeus, traversed the centuries-old Corinth Canal and went to Bari, Italy, a small seaport on the heel of the boot of Italy. This was our opportunity to make up for missing the sights of Italy as we had in 1978, and to just a slight degree, we managed to do a bit of sightseeing as we wended our way up the eastern side of the boot. I suspect that if Sam weren't as anxious to get this move over with as I was, she would have been more emphatic about seeing some of the wonders of Italy. But as it turned out, she was just as eager as I to begin the next phase of our military career. We both agreed years before that a vacation en route to a change of station just threw too much confusion into an already hectic time.

We stopped one night in north central Italy and then went through the famous Brenner Pass into Austria where we spent our second night in a suburb of Innsbruck. Being back in the more ordered and normal life of the Teutonic countries seemed to brighten our spirits. For though we loved our tour of duty and the people of Greece, it did get fairly chaotic at times and it seemed pleasant to experience the more predictable environs of Western Europe.

We were very familiar with Ramstein Air Base, having visited the base frequently on R&R when we lived in France years before. I also had gone fairly often to Ramstein—now the headquarters of the United States Air Forces in Europe (USAFE)—many times for wing and base commanders' meetings during our time at Hellenikon. On one or two occasions, Joan accompanied me on a space-available basis so it was like coming home to her as well.

We had no choice of whether we lived on base or rented in the local German communities. As a commander, I was required to live "close to the flagpole," but Sam had no objection to this arrangement. The senior officer base housing complex was made up of four-plex apartment units and there was one unit available when we arrived—and by now I was of sufficient rank to go to the top of the waiting list.

The housing complex—in fact, the entire array of personnel support facilities—had been constructed by the West German government in the late 1940s as reparations for World War II. They were quite modern at the time of construction, and had been continuously maintained in excellent condition, but they were small compared to the current housing styles back in the States. But with her normal *sans souci* attitude, Joan looked at the glass as half full. She pointed out that we were close to all the personnel support facilities (commissary, Base Exchange, gym, etc.) and the officers' club was even within walking distance. Plus we had very nice neighbors living nearby.

My headquarters was not on Ramstein AB, but was about twelve kilometers away at a satellite location called Einsiedlerhof AB. That meant the need for a second car again, but at Ramstein that was not a challenge. Good quality used cars (Mercedes, BMWs, Opels, etc.) were always available at a self-service on-base used car lot where there was no middle man. You put your car on the lot with your name, asking price and phone number posted in the window, and if someone was interested, he or she would call you.

I bought one of my favorite cars of all time: a six-year-old BMW 2002 that was bright orange with a black top and a pea green racing stripe down the middle of the hood and trunk from front to back. Joan thought I had lost my mind. Not long after I had bought it and registered it, she was in hysterics laughing when I got home.

"Did you know that there is one other car just like yours in the Ramstein-Kaiserslautern area?" she began. "One of the other gals showed it to me on Forty Mark Strasse[35] this afternoon and it's

---

[35] Forty Mark Strasse was the nickname given to the main road between the cities of Landstuhl and Kaiserslautern. In one stretch of the road through a forested area, the prostitutes would park their cars, sit on the hood, and wait for business to come by. The standard cost—German efficiency—was 40 Deutsch Marks (about ten dollars at the time) and thus the name given to the road.

owned by one of the pros who peddles her body out there on the roadside. Be prepared, my dear. You're in for a lot of ribbing over this." And, as usual, she was right. But the car was in wonderful condition and I enjoyed it for the entire time we were there.

Probably more so than in any other position I ever held, Joan was an invaluable helper to me. After all, she did the shopping and would always give me feedback if there were things she found amiss in the commissary and, more important, ideas that would help improve customer service. My area of responsibility extended from Norway in the north to Israel in the south and from Turkey in the east to the Azores in the west.[36] So visiting each commissary at least once each year meant that I spent a great deal of time on the road, a situation that Sam viewed as just a routine part of the job.

But most of my travels were during the week. We spent most weekends together, we took all of the leave that I was authorized, and we traveled extensively. I was also able to apply some proverbial grease to all of the squeaky wheels I had previously identified. In fact, it turned out to be not just a satisfying assignment but another period of time during which our personal lives were very happy and our commitment to one another was greatly strengthened.

But one year into the command, a change occurred that was to affect both my career and our lives considerably. At a Fourth of July reception hosted by the Commander-in-Chief of USAFE, General Charlie Gabriel and his wife, Dottie, the CINC pulled me aside and, after an hour-long conversation, he asked me to become his executive assistant. It was an offer I would neither want to refuse nor even think of doing so. And prudently so, because one year later, General Gabriel was selected to become the new Chief of Staff of the Air Force and we were to return to Washington and the Pentagon with him in the same capacity. As a direct consequence, I was promoted to brigadier general a short while later.

It was most gratifying to be back in the mainstream of Air Force operations again, particularly since, as a non-rated officer,[37] this

---

[36]   See *Portraits in Brass* for more detailed coverage of the challenges and solutions.

[37]   The term, rating, refers to an aeronautical rating—either a pilot or a navigator—and officers who were not rated were generally considered

was assuredly a position for which I was an unlikely candidate. I felt completely comfortable in the job, enjoyed it thoroughly, and developed a close rapport with Charlie Gabriel during our first year together in Germany.

Probably the most notable event that took place there occurred less than two months into the job. On August 31, 1981, the infamous Baader-Meinhof gang of terrorists set off a car bomb directly outside our office, shockingly at the exact time that the general usually arrived at the main entrance to the building. Fortunately, the general was delayed at home that morning, and in addition, fortunately a portion of the car bomb did not detonate. Or I wouldn't be writing about it today.

Throughout our final two years in Europe and the next two years in Washington, Joan continued to show no signs of the normal debilitation that long-time insulin-dependent patients experience. Her eyes showed the normal tendency toward deteriorating vision that most middle age people confront, but no signs of retinopathy, which in many, can eventually lead to blindness. Her heart and kidneys, also victims of the ravages of diabetes, were checked semi-annually and she consistently received a clean bill of health. Moving as frequently as we did, she needed to change physicians from time to time, but her medical records were hand-carried with us so that the continuity of her care could be assured. Wherever we went in the 1970s and 1980s, the doctors were quite impressed with her excellent physical condition, could find no particular explanation for the consistently good reports, but universally agreed on their advice to her.

"Whatever it is that you're doing, it's the right thing, so keep it up!"

During our two years back in Washington, Charlie Gabriel was of the conviction that the traditional twelve- to fourteen-hour days, six-day weeks experienced by Pentagon staff officers were not only unproductive—and in some ways counterproductive—but also had

---

to be unqualified to hold certain positions that allegedly required operational experience. Fortunately, this age-old shibboleth has essentially disappeared in the intervening years.

a deleterious affect on the family lives of those officers. So he put an end to it, by decree. He insisted that all Air Staff officers take the leave that they had accumulated—including me—even though he didn't do a very good job of following his own dictates.

As a matter of fact, we were in Switzerland skiing in early December of 1982 when he called me at my hotel at 0300 in the morning to tell me, happily, that I had been promoted to brigadier general—again, a rare happening for a non-rated officer.[38]   Of all the times I had been awakened in the middle of the night for official business, none was ever more welcomed or appreciated than that one. Sam was so excited that she went around to all of our friends' rooms, woke them up, and convened a spontaneous promotion party in the hotel bar. None of the other couples complained either.

Actually, that was far from the only ski trip we took while we were in Europe as well as Washington. Sam was not what one could call a natural athlete, but she loved sports, both as a spectator and a participant. She had been the head cheerleader at her high school in Medford, Massachusetts—though the chauvinistic male classmates at Boston College wanted no females to cheer the Eagles on. She knew the rules and the nuances of most of the major sports and loved to go to games with me and watch them on television. But the more she learned and practiced, skiing became her favorite participatory sport and she became almost as avid about skiing as I was.

Most of our vacations took place in the winter throughout the late 1970s and early 1980s and that generally meant that we were off to the slopes rather than a sunny tropical clime. She began every ski vacation by taking at least one day of lessons and while she'd never become a downhill racer, or even close to it, her skill, confidence, and love for the sport increased. And that, after all, is the reason all of us enjoy sports.

After a very challenging, enjoyable, and most certainly rewarding two years in Washington, Charlie Gabriel decided that I had better move on if I were to avoid being labeled as a one-trick pony. And

---

[38]   At the time, less than 5 percent of the USAF general officers, exclusive of the professional generals (doctors, lawyers, etc.) were non-rated—roughly the same proportion as when I was commissioned twenty-four years earlier.

once again, he challenged the shibboleth that had perennially limited operational positions to rated officers, pilots almost exclusively, and we were assigned to Tokyo where I became the Vice Commander of Fifth Air Force, the operational command over all of the USAF units in Japan and Korea.[39]

We lived in wonderful general officer quarters, built by the Japanese government, on Yokota AB, which was twenty-five kilometers west of downtown Tokyo. The home was superbly laid out for entertaining, a command responsibility that both of us enjoyed, and we did a great deal of it. Not only that, we had an official social schedule that kept us busy—almost too busy—nearly five or six nights each week. There were the usual base functions that are common in overseas locations. As part of the country team, we were included as the U.S. Embassy interacted socially and extensively with the Japanese government officialdom, and we were usually on most guest lists for the social activities hosted by various elements of the Japanese Defense establishment.

The other senior officers' wives and Joan soon found to their chagrin that this constant social whirl was causing them to put on some extra, unwanted weight. "Diet and exercise," the most effective weight-control devices ever developed, soon became their mantra. They got together to plan low-calorie menus for the few evenings we were able to dine at home, and more important, they formed a walking club that met every morning at 0800, rain or shine, to walk briskly along various routes on the base. All but one of the seven members of their club were smokers, Joan included. It was far more common to find smokers among the older female populace in those days, but their vigorous pace soon demonstrated to all of them that smoking had succeeded in causing a serious impact on their respiratory system.

But Sam discovered more bad news than that. After no more that a half mile or so, her calves began to ache and eventually, with a little more walking, they would cramp badly enough that she had to sit down and massage them until the pain went away. She concluded, logically I thought, that this was simply a reaction to her

---

[39]   That command arrangement changed in the last half of the 1980s when 5th AF command was limited to Japan and a newly re-created 7th AF took command and control responsibility for forces in Korea.

lack of sufficient exercise in the recent past, and it would dissipate in time. Unfortunately, this was not to be the case. Instead, as we were to learn a few years later, these cramps were the first signs of one of the ravages of diabetes: peripheral artery disease.

I had tried endlessly to get Sam to quit smoking—I had stopped in 1972 after having the habit for twenty years—but she could never motivate herself sufficiently to stop. One day, she was listening to a broadcast of *Good Morning America* when Dr. Tim Johnson, the long-time ABC News medical consultant, was asked about leg cramps while exercising. His reply made a deep impression on Joan. He said that "sometimes just something as simple as quitting smoking will make the pain go away." And while there was nothing simple about quitting in Joan's mind, it was the first impressionable evidence she had that it really was hazardous—even to her. It was to take another year for her to take the big step, but in the interim, she cut back on cigarettes and continually assured me that she was going to stop "when the time is right."

Skiing continued to be our primary pursuit for leisure activity, and the sport had become very popular as the Japanese economy blossomed. We skied at Sapporo where the Winter Olympics had been held in 1972, and Nagano where the games would later be held in 1998, along with most of the other major resorts. Ski areas were crowded because of the newfound popularity of the sport. But each of our trips turned out to be most unusual and unique—primarily, I suppose, because of the Japanese penchant for developing their own traditions, rather than to copy the way the resorts were run in Europe and the United States. We even had old and dear friends come from the States to join us on a couple of the ski trips, a factor that made the trips even more enjoyable.

We returned from our assignment in Japan and all the exciting travels we had there in the summer of 1986. My assignment was again to Wright-Patterson AFB near Dayton where I was to become the Commandant (the equivalent of the president) of the Air Force Institute of Technology (AFIT). I was privileged to receive my graduate degree through the auspices of AFIT twenty years previously and now I was going to be in charge of the vast scope of the entire university.[40]

It was a distinct change of pace from the exotica of living and socializing in Japan, but the pace and my travels to the many civilian institutions were equally challenging. I enjoyed the assignment tremendously, and once again was able to achieve a number of goals that I had set for the institution when I first arrived there.

One of the couples who had visited us for a skiing holiday in Japan, Susan Christensen and David Cannan, urged us to join them in December of 1986 for a full week of a ski school at Taos, New Mexico. At the time, and to a large extent still today, the Taos ski school had a superb reputation and it was an opportunity that we chose not to pass up. The accommodations were hardly what we had been accustomed to in Europe and Japan, with bunk beds in the rooms and barely enough room to hang up damp ski clothing. But the food was excellent, the camaraderie among the students was close, and most important, the school fully met our expectations.

In particular, Sam made a quantum leap forward in her ability. She was skiing far less tentatively, with much more confidence than ever before. And she was thrilled by her newly developed breakthrough.

When we arrived back at Dayton, she began to talk about another week of skiing—soon. She certainly didn't want her confidence to wane, but more significantly, her enthusiasm had increased a great deal as well. So over the Christmas holiday, we began to talk about another trip in the next month or so. I had accumulated plenty of leave time, and my January schedule was sufficiently flexible that I could take another week toward the end of the month. And this time, we thought that, in contrast to roughing it the way we had done at Taos, we'd do it up right and lean toward first-class

---

[40] AFIT had roughly six hundred resident students at the Wright-Paterson campus, most of whom were studying for advanced degrees in science, engineering, and logistics management. But there were an additional 2,400 students at civilian institutions literally all over the world. Again, most were in advance degree programs, but these also included medical residencies, law degrees, and even the Rhodes and Fulbright scholars who were under AFIT's administrative purview.

accommodations. We had become believers in the aphorism that it only costs a little more to go first class.

We had just about decided that we'd try Jackson Hole, Wyoming, a place we had never been before. But it was always more fun to go with other couples who were old friends and ski buddies. So I called Tom Anderson, who with his wife, Carol, had been frequent skiing companions in Europe, to see if they might be interested in joining us.

"As a matter of fact," Tom told me, "we already have reservations for that week at Steamboat Springs in Colorado, and my brother, Bill, and his wife, Betty, are going with us. Why don't you join us? It's a great area and the more the merrier. Let me know if you want to come with us and I'll just add you to the reservations I have."

It took us about three minutes to agree. We had never been to Steamboat either, so why not?

Sam hadn't forgotten a thing from our week at Taos and I was amazed at how well she was skiing. Usually when we skied together, I would go down the slope for four hundred to five hundred yards and then just wait there, seemingly interminably at times, while Sam slowly and very cautiously wended her way down to join me. Then, of course, there was another wait while she caught her breath. It wasn't a lot of fun for me. She knew it too, so much of the time she'd insist that I ski independently of her with the other guys while she went with some of the other women in the group who skied at her pace.

But it quickly became apparent that those days were gone. When I'd stop and look back up the hill for her, I'd find instead that she was pulling to a stop, just seconds behind me. I was delighted, but she was even more thrilled. I can ski with *you* now, her broad grin seemed to be saying, and I really like the new me.

Steamboat, at the time, had a mid-mountain lodge with a cafeteria type of dining room as most ski areas do, but it also had a private dining room with white napery, good glassware and flatware, and most important, a decent menu with table service. And since we had decided that this was going to be an up-scale vacation, we all chose to eat there at lunch time.

In the many years we had skied in Europe, we became used to the European tradition of wine with our lunch, and that day was to be no exception. A couple of bottles of decent wine were ordered while we pondered our luncheon choices. And when the waiter began to fill our glasses, Joan demurred saying that she'd prefer a diet cola. The other five of us at the table expressed amazement, since Joan enjoyed a glass of wine as much as any of us, and I guess she thought she needed to explain her choice.

"I had such a wonderful morning," she told us, "that I don't want to do anything to spoil things this afternoon. I'm thirsty so I would just as soon diet drink cola today."

Not that she needed to justify her choice—I think someone at the table commented that that meant all the more for us, which engendered a friendly chuckle around the table. We might have spent close to two hours over lunch, all were well-fed, but I could sense that Joan was anxious to get back out on the mountain. So I took the hint and we finished up and headed out for an afternoon of more excellent skiing.

What happened on that afternoon was to make a momentous change in the rest of our lives.

Chapter 3
Growing Old Together

The slope descended rather gently just outside the restaurant and continued down, at ever increasing steepness, for about a half mile until it reached the triple chairlift at the bottom of a depression. As was usually the case, I led off and I thought I saw Sam begin her descent out of the corner of my eye as I passed her. Since she had readily kept up with me during the morning, I maintained a moderate speed but did not look back, sure that she was close behind me.

After going about halfway down toward the lift, I pulled over to the side of the slope and stopped to wait for Sam to catch up. But I didn't see her anywhere and began to wonder if she might have left something in the restaurant and gone back to get it or if perhaps she had fallen. Very soon thereafter, I saw Carol Anderson coming down the slope quite rapidly, and as soon as she saw me, she edged across toward me and stopped.

"Joan fell up near the top. I don't know what happened, but she looks like she is hurt. You'd better come on back up because she didn't look like she was going to get up very quickly."

We both took off our skis and began to walk back up the side of the trail toward where we saw a small crowd start to gather. We also saw the ski patrol arrive and they had an evacuation sled used to take injured skiers off the mountain. As we finally arrived at where the accident had taken place, it was indeed Joan, and Tom Anderson was there as well, assisting the ski patrol as best he could.

I identified myself to the ski patrollers, and dropped down on one knee beside her where she was now in the sled and being belted in for the trip to the base of the mountain. She was obviously in severe pain and grimaced at the slightest movement as they tried to make her comfortable and secure. The head of the rescue team said the he feared she had fractured her tibial plateau, and they would be taking her to the local hospital as soon as they could. They had already radioed for an ambulance, and it was clear to me from their demeanor that they didn't consider this to be a routine accident.

When we reached the chairlift at the bottom of the hill, the patrol had to lash the sled across the three-seat chair so that we could go back up over the ridge in front of us and then proceed down the slope on the other side to the first aid hut at the base. Sam and the sled that she was on went on the chair in front of us, alone— apparently the only way that they could get her where she needed to go—and though I was frightened to see her strapped down on the chair by herself, it was obviously the only way that it could be done. And having watched them so far, I fully trusted their judgment and abilities. I followed along on the same chair with the two patrollers and we reached the dismount area without any problems.

In the next five or six minutes, I got a look at a darker side of the American character, which irritated me considerably. As we went down the face of the mountain, skier after skier couldn't resist coming over right beside the sled to gawk at Joan, with many of them spraying snow over her face and the blanket that covered her as they came as close as possible to get a good look. I quickly shifted positions from behind the sled to the side from which the gawkers were coming, warning them away with my ski pole when some even tried to get between me and the sled. It was not a pretty scene, by any means, but her rescuers soon had us safely down the mountain where we went directly to the ambulance that was waiting there. They took my skis and poles into the first aid hut and told me to get into the ambulance with her.

When we arrived at the local hospital, there were a number of people waiting, some with an arm in a sling, others with bloody scrapes on their faces where they had taken a nose-dive into the snow—known as a face-plant among skiers. But apparently the ski patrol were experienced enough to triage patients before they arrived at the hospital, and Joan was taken directly into x-ray within moments of our arrival.

Not long after, a very young doctor asked me to come into the treatment room where Joan had been taken. Somehow or other, he knew that I was an Air Force general—probably from the ID card that I had to show at the entrance to confirm that I had military insurance coverage—and he told me that he had been an Air Force Academy graduate, had gotten out of the U.S. Air Force because he wanted to go to medical school, and that he had just finished his orthopedic residency.

He asked me to come over to where Joan's x-rays were hung on a reading light, and proceeded to show me the mess that had been made of her right leg. The patrollers were correct when they diagnosed a crushed tibial plateau but the pictures also revealed that she had a spiral fracture that extended more than halfway down the tibia.

"I'll be brutally frank with you, General," he began. "Your wife has sustained a very severe injury, and the associated complications are way beyond the capabilities of this hospital and beyond my level of expertise by a long way. She needs to get to a major hospital for care. The only recourse I can see right now is to put her leg in an old-fashioned plaster cast in order to keep it immobilized. I've already given her a pain medication and I'll need to admit her to the hospital overnight to be sure that the leg doesn't swell too much. I'm sorry that I can't do any better than that but this break is the worst I've seen, and it's bad enough that it might even necessitate an amputation."

We had flown into Steamboat Springs on American Airlines, but in order to get Joan to immediate proper medical attention, we would have to go out on the next morning's flight on a space-available basis. Our return reservations were still five days off and all of the flights in and out of Steamboat were fully booked. I spent that evening debating my options and trying to determine the best course of action. One thought I had—and which I wish I had pursued—was to rent a car and drive from Steamboat to Denver where Fitzsimmons Army Hospital was located. But I rejected that idea because I was concerned that she would have to remain in Denver for a long time after surgery while I would be back in Dayton.

My final decision was to take a chance on getting space on the morning AA flight, a decision that caused untold misery and pain for Joan. There were two flights out that morning and we did not get on the first one. But the American Airlines station manager realized that Joan's condition was quite serious and he made a courageous decision. He would declare the flight overbooked, offer a reward of some sort to two people who would voluntarily give up their seats, and get Joan on the outbound flight. It was going to Dallas where we could connect to a second flight to Cincinnati—after a five-hour wait in the Dallas terminal. There seemed to be no choice but to take that flight, but I finally made the one wise decision of the day. I called the hospital commander at Wright-Patterson and asked him to send an ambulance to the airport in Cincinnati to bring her back home.

She was given oral pain medication for the flights with directions to take one tablet every four hours. But the pain became so intense that she was taking a tablet every hour and a half by the time we reached home base at 2300 that night. Sam's courage and resolve were inspirational throughout the horrible day, and by the time she was in a hospital bed with the cast removed, she collapsed from exhaustion.

The chief orthopedist at the Wright-Patterson USAF General Hospital was waiting for us when we arrived. He also took x-rays, of course, and confirmed the young doctor's estimate of the severity of her injury. He told me that he needed to wait for at least thirty-six hours before he could operate in order to allow the swelling to decrease and for Joan to stabilize after such a severely traumatic experience. And he recommended that I go home and get some rest. He was going to induce sleep for Joan and I would also need to prepare myself for the grueling couple of days that lie ahead.

And grueling they were, for Joan most certainly, and for the doctors who worked on her. The chief surgeon estimated that her surgery would last a good three to four hours when he briefed us on what he planned to do. When I kissed her as she was being wheeled into the operating room a day and a half later, she told me that she was going to be fine and that I shouldn't worry. It brought back so many unhappy memories of the many times that she had disappeared through operating room doors, telling me the same thing, only to have her heart broken when she lost yet another baby.

I was afraid to leave the surgical waiting room lest someone needed to get hold of me for a decision that needed to be made—or worse. The idea of a possible amputation was constantly in the back of my mind as the time stretched into four, then five, and then six hours that she was in the OR. When the surgeon finally came out, he looked frazzled and exhausted, and wore an expression that wasn't very reassuring that the surgery had been a great success.

He told me that he nearly came out three hours before to ask my permission to amputate. But that was such an extreme alternative that he wanted to do all within his skill to save the leg and return Joan to as nearly normal a life as he could. I thanked him and asked for his prognosis of how things went.

"Only time will tell," was as definitive as he could get. Then he went on to say that her tibial plateau was so badly crushed that the bone looked "like coarse-grained cream of wheat." He went on to say that he had taken nearly a cup of bone from both sides of her pelvis in order to rebuild the top of her tibia. The bone fragments were held together by a considerable number of screws, as was the spiral fracture lower down in her tibia.

"The borrow area where I harvested the bone will be very painful for at least two weeks," he went on, "but something else that I have to do may even make her forget that pain. I've put her on a machine that will continually bend her knee nearly ninety degrees and then straighten it out again for up to twenty-three hours each day. It will cycle about two times each minute and it's somewhat like being on a bicycle on your back, except the 'pedal' will be driving her motion, not the other way around. It will be exceptionally painful but it's the only way that I can assure that the knee joint will remain functional while it's healing."

When I reached her room, it was clear that the surgeon had not exaggerated. Despite still having residual affects from the anesthetic that had been administered during surgery, as well as having an IV port inserted in her arm that dripped additional pain medication, the poor love appeared to be in agony. I explained to her why she had to be hooked up to the contraption and her first question was, naturally, for how long?

When I told her that it would be on almost constantly for over two weeks, a look of total defeat crossed her face. She closed her eyes, still wearing a pained expression. But within minutes she opened them again, and with a changed visage to one of teeth-grinding resolve, she said that she could endure the pain as long as she didn't have to lose the leg. Once again, her indomitable spirit came to the fore and the gritty determination not to give up took precedence over the pain that would continue to persist for weeks.

I visited Sam in the morning before I went to work, at noon, and then again, spent the evenings with her day after day for close to a month. She clearly showed that the exercising device was still causing her agony every day. She often commented how much she looked forward to having it turned off for that one hour each day, and even more so, the day when it could be removed entirely. That, it turned out would be a gradual process, with longer and more frequent break times after the first two weeks. But even though she had apparently been successful in keeping the joint limber, the pain was still intense no matter how much time she had to be on the horrible machine, as she called it. And she called it many other names that weren't quite as nice.

It was a happy day when the machine was removed from the bottom of her hospital bed over three weeks after the surgery. She was advised that she still needed to bend the knee on her own as frequently as possible, and she faithfully did as she was told. Soon she was sitting up in a chair beside the bed for more hours than she was in the bed, and she was getting eager to go home—and I was equally eager to have her there.

Our wonderful old base quarters were three-story brick buildings that had been built as a WPA (Works Progress Administration) project back in the mid-1930s as part of FDR's recovery program from the Great Depression. While they were well designed and built to last forever, the rooms were small and, of course, little natural light came through the small windows. The bedrooms were on the second floor, and it was impossible for Sam to ascend the steep, narrow staircase to the bedroom. So we turned the living room into a bedroom, using a convertible sofa that we happened to have bought a couple of years previously.

Dan had come back home when we moved there in order to continue his education, majoring in hospitality management at Sinclair College in Dayton. As had become a custom of the times— and a decided contrast to his parents when we were somewhat older than he—he had a girlfriend and they occupied a dormer room on the third floor. It turned out to be fortuitous as Joan was able to have some company and care during the daytime, and both he and Kristi were helpful around the house

The doctor did not want to put her into a cast because it would tend to negate all the pain and effort that had gone into maintaining flexibility in her knee joint. As a compromise, he put her into a brace that provided support for her lower leg while still offering fore and aft movement of her knee. But she was rigidly prohibited from putting any weight on the leg. The general belief was that an injury like the one she sustained would take up to two months to heal, and with her diabetic condition, it would likely take at least one month more than that.

Joan was ecstatic to be home, and even though she continued to experience a lot of pain, she had mastered the use of crutches and she was increasingly mobile as the days and weeks passed. If Sam ever hated anything in her entire life—and I'm being presumptuous using the term because the word wasn't part of her vocabulary—it was being in the hospital. And her feelings were hardly self-centered. Perhaps more than anything, she disliked the fact that I found it necessary to spend so much of my time with her. She also disliked being a "burden" to anyone, to use her terminology, and that applied to hospital staff, doctors, and anyone else involved in her care.

So being home was vitally important to her. She still was chronically concerned over the burden that it placed on me, but I was much happier having her where I could take care of her rather than spending time idly in an oppressive hospital room. And there was very little disagreement when she viewed things from that perspective.

But all was not going well as far as her healing was concerned. Starting the sixth week after the accident, we made weekly visits to the orthopedic surgeon. X-rays were taken and the level of healing was evaluated. To the amazement of most everyone involved in her care, the tibial plateau—the most critical element of her injury—

was showing signs of robust healing, but the more common element of the injury, the fracture of the tibia itself, showed little to no indication of knitting. It was clear that we were in for a long siege.

For obvious reasons, I had taken over all of the household chores, in particular the cooking and cleaning—though Dan and Kristi helped a great deal. It was hardly a struggle to do the cooking since I had been handy in the kitchen since I was a youngster, and in fact, usually did the bulk of the meal preparation when we had guests for dinner. Once again, Sam fretted over the fact that she was "not doing her share" and she found this to be very frustrating. But my concerns were hardly with being the cook and bottle washer. I was much more concerned over the long-term impact of this accident.

So one evening while we were eating, I brought up the idea that had obviously never entered her mind. I told her that I was strongly considering submitting my request to retire from the USAF so that we could settle down some place more conducive to her temporary disability.

Sam was both shocked and disbelieving. She began by saying that she wouldn't hear of it; that she was becoming more independent every day; that she certainly was able to live in the house we were in for as long as I remained in my current position; and that I still had more promotions and challenging jobs upcoming. It was certainly not a decision that should be based on her situation, she asserted.

And she was probably right or at least partially so. But I wasn't all that optimistic about my chances of further advancement and, in fact, had been quietly inquiring about potential second career opportunities that might be available to us. I had just recently been approached by a search committee seeking a new president for a large university in northern Ohio, and had been told, in essence, that the job was mine if I wanted it. But I was more intrigued by a conversation with my old boss, Charlie Gabriel. He told me that he and Donald Hicks, a senior Northrop Corporation executive and former Assistant Secretary of Defense, were putting together a small engineering and management consulting firm. Charlie thought it would be a good second career for me.

And though Sam and I were reluctant to end the only career we had ever known in over thirty years of marriage, we finally decided that we would embark on a business career. The offices were to open in northern Virginia, we would return to the Washington DC area, which both Joan and I loved, and I would immediately get a 50 percent increase over my military salary—plus my retirement pension would begin immediately.

My retirement was a bittersweet affair, managed very well by the AFIT staff. I was deeply touched by the great number of family members from the East Coast who came to celebrate the end of my military career with me. The resident students and senior staff had a formal parade and passing of the colors, a relatively rare occurrence in a service that does very little marching (although we fly in formation very smartly). My boss, Lieutenant General Truman Spangrud, the commander of Air University, gave a very flattering speech that rang of regret that I was leaving the Air Force "so early."

I had developed a close friendship with General Earl O'Loughlin, the commander of Air Force Logistics Command, also at Wright-Patterson, who also honored me by his presence. He gave me an interesting outlook on the future in our private conversation just moments before the formalities began.

"Right now, you're a brigadier general to just about everyone here today, but tomorrow you become just 'general'—primarily because no one in civilian life really knows the difference any more." Interestingly, he was basically right.

Seven months after her accident, Joan's tibia was still far from healed but she had become very agile on her crutches and got around quite well. She was in the first row of the VIP section of the audience along with the O'Loughlins and I don't think she ever looked as radiant to me as she did that day. As dependable as daybreak and dusk, she had completely reoriented her thinking to the future and was excitedly anticipating our imminent return to the city she loved—almost as much as Paris.

And on September 1, 1987, I entered the retired roles of the U.S. Air Force and we prepared for the next phase of our lives.

*   *   *

Our move to the DC area was going to be well-organized, we had decided, and there was no longer a need to get into a house right away as was usually the case when it was a military move. We had our whole future in front of us and time to make choices that were geared toward living in one location for an extended duration. Our primary household goods were all in storage awaiting the ultimate decision, but we had sent a separate shipment that would provide us with all we needed temporarily.

Our family was all grown and on their own by now, so we thought that a nice house and a yard was no longer necessary and our first venture into unknown territory was going to be apartment living. Why not? There were lots of advantages, particularly from the maintenance and upkeep standpoint, and the up-scale building that we chose was on a high hill in Arlington, Virginia, with a marvelous view of downtown Washington and its many well-recognized monuments. However, in keeping with our effort to make the right decision for the long term, we began by renting, rather than buying a condominium.

And that was a wise decision as it turned out. It was not long before we discovered that the apartment was somewhat limiting. Even though our rental included a small storage locker on the same floor, it would eventually be far too small to contain all of the treasures we had accumulated over the years of our travels. We also found that even though this particular unit was generously sized, we began to feel a little too enclosed after a while.

One evening we hosted Tom and Carol Anderson for dinner. They too had retired from the Air Force, lived very close by in Arlington and knew the area far better than we did. During the course of conversation during dinner, Joan expressed her lack of total satisfaction with our arrangement, a comment that spurred Carol's imagination.

"Have you seen the townhouses down on the far side of Arlington Ridge Road?" she asked. "They are relatively new and they're gorgeous. There are some retired generals and admirals living there. I know of at least one senator and a couple of congressmen who have bought there as well. I think the places probably cost mega-bucks, but they might be worth looking at if you want a compromise between an apartment and a house with a yard."

Joan told her she had considered a townhouse when we were moving back, but with her leg still far from healed, she needed a place all on one floor because she couldn't handle stairs very well.

Carol handled that problem in just a few sentences when she told us that, as far as she knew, all of the three-story townhouses had elevators installed or at least a space where an elevator could be installed. You would have thought that Carol was getting a finder's fee, she was so convincing, and we determined right then that there would certainly be no harm in looking.

And we did, just a few days later. The one vacant place we were shown by the realtor was beautiful and, indeed, had an elevator already installed. We both were convinced with just one showing. The top floor was pretty much devoted to a huge master bedroom/sitting room combination with a gas-fired fireplace, large walk-in closets, and a master bath with a shower, bidet—or foot-washer as Joan jokingly called it—and whirlpool tub. There was also a smaller guest bedroom and bath on the same floor. The middle floor was devoted to a very ample eat-in kitchen with top-of-the-line appliances; a dining room that was adequate to contain our twelve-place dining room table; plus a large living room with another fireplace and an enclosed brick patio off the living room. The ground floor consisted of the one-car garage, a very large recreation room, an office, and a lower-level patio with a brick stairway leading up to the ground-level patio above.

The construction and the materials that went into the entire unit were of top quality. We needed no sales pitch. This was the place we had come to imagine in our minds' eyes as being just perfect for our needs. But Carol had been correct. They did cost "mega-bucks" at least in terms of our accustomed income from military years. But when we did the math that evening, we concluded that it might require a bit of belt-tightening, but we could afford the anticipated costs. So we made an offer the next day.

During the time we lived in this wonderful home, I became more and more obsessed with finding a cure for Joan's broken leg. She had developed the ability to get around quite well, but without her ever thinking of complaining, I knew that she experienced chronic pain. She had been able to master the ability to drive the car again, and I had assured myself that she was able to do so safely. The new brace that she had received just prior to leaving Ohio was able to take up most of her weight with a pressure pad on the lower side of her knee as well as with the portion of it that encased her thigh. She was then able to put partial weight on the foot itself—a factor the doctors thought might promote healing of the bone—and she would even take a few steps without the crutches from time to time.

She was assigned to a young orthopedic surgeon—an USAF major who had recently completed his residency—when we began using the Malcolm Grow Medical Center at Andrews AFB for our medical care. We were enthused by his interest and approach during our initial appointments and concluded that he had recently been exposed to many new theories and techniques during his residency, a conclusion that proved to be correct. He proposed a variety of potential sources for remedying the situation, many of which we eventually tried. He offered a referral to a doctor in San Francisco who proposed more surgery on the leg, but without much of a convincing argument that this would result in any surety of healing. Another doctor who we visited was a micro-surgeon in New Orleans who would enhance the blood supply to the affected area in the hopes that this might have a positive result.

And the young major himself performed surgery on the leg. He removed the large screws from her tibial plateau, which had healed, and put new plates on the broken tibia. He then placed her in a straight-leg cast for nearly fourteen months. The cast was replaced and x-rays taken every six weeks during that period, but to no avail.

At relatively the same time period, a delightful movie called *Driving Miss Daisy,* starring Jessica Tandy and Morgan Freeman, became quite popular. And since Sam was unable to sit in the passenger seat of the car because of the cast, she dubbed herself Miss Daisy and I became her driver. She would slide across the rear seat, pulling the cast along the seat as she went, and then buckle herself in at a bit of an angle as we went wherever we needed to go. Her sense of humor always remained keen despite the awkwardness, inconvenience, and discomfort that were always with her.

We dearly loved the home we had purchased in Arlington. We entertained frequently. We traveled and led as normal a life as possible, considering Joan's limitations. And it would have been quite idyllic except for one thing: I was not happy in the second career that I had chosen for myself.[41] Charlie Gabriel became disenchanted a lot sooner than I had and left the company less than three years after it was formed. I was to follow suit not long thereafter.

One of the first consequences of doing this was that we realized that we could no longer afford our dream home unless I got a job in which the salary was commensurate with what I had been making. And unless I were to accept employment with an aerospace or defense firm or took a position as a civil servant, which I chose not to do, it would ultimately mean that we must relocate. And while we were going to have to move anyway, we concluded that the whole world was open to us when we relocated.

We started addressing the future with a brainstorming session over a bottle of wine one evening and we came up with some very reasonable prospects. We tried to be non-judgmental as the ideas were tossed out. The ancillary considerations could be addressed later on, but first we needed to think of how we would really enjoy spending the rest of our working lives together.

I told Joan that one of the great loves of both our lives was wine— not just drinking it with our evening meals as we had ever since we lived in France when we were in our 20s. We were also intrigued with growing the right grapes, the process of turning the fruit into a delicious food and beverage, as well as the social gratification of marketing the product to other wine-lovers. We rarely passed up a tour of a winery whenever the opportunity presented itself.

"If I had my choice of what I did, I would go to the University of California at Davis for a year of concentrated study in oenology, after which I would find employment somewhere in the wine production business," was my contribution to our future.

Sam thought that sounded intriguing but she didn't think she wanted to live in California, thought that we couldn't afford a year of college while having only my retirement pay to live on, and so on.

"Uh-uh, we weren't going to be judgmental, remember?" I cautioned her. "We'll cross those bridges when the time comes, but first, tell me what you would like to do."

---

[41]   See my first Book, *The Loving Room*, published in 2001 for further detail.

"If you're going to allow anything to be thrown out right now, I know exactly what I'd love to do and have thought about for years. Given a choice of anything in the world, I would love to own a little small elegant hotel or country inn where we could entertain the way we've been doing for so many years—without getting paid for it. We're both good cooks. We've talked before many times about owning a small restaurant, and I think that having a small inn that served gourmet meals would be even better than that."

"Okay," I responded, "let's both do some research into what it takes for these ideas to become a reality and then we can start assessing the pros and cons of each one. And if it turns out that either or both of these ideas are impractical or unattainable, then we'll go back to the drawing board again."

It wasn't three days later that I came home and Sam greeted me with a huge grin on her face. "You need to take next Thursday and Friday off. I found a couple who own an inn on the coast of Maine—he's an Annapolis graduate a few years after you—and I spent about an hour on the phone with her this afternoon. They recommended that if we were really interested in being innkeepers, we had to attend a seminar on the topic first. I called the people that they suggested as the best source of information, and they're hosting one of their quarterly seminars next Thursday through Sunday in the Poconos. And I've made reservations for us!"

Well, I had said we needed to research our choices and Sam had certainly done that. But then when she told me that 80 percent of those who attend these seminars are convinced that innkeeping is not for them, I was convinced that the seminar might be very worthwhile. It seemed harmless enough and if those who were conducting the seminar were honest enough to tell both the good and the bad about the avocation—and it sounded like they were—it would be worth the education if nothing else.

The seminar was conducted by a fellow from Vermont named Bill Oates and his wife, Heide, and it was very well done, presenting both the positive and negative sides of the business. Bill spent a great amount of time on the financial portion of the business and did not paint a very bright picture of the profit and loss aspects. Heide was a psychologist and put heavy emphasis on the negative impact that the profession often has on a husband-and-wife team operating an inn. But at the end of the four days, Joan was more enthusiastic than ever. And while I was hardly as enamored of the idea as she was, I thought it was certainly a feasible alternative. And if it would make her happy, then I certainly owed her that at the very least.

On the drive back to Virginia that Sunday afternoon, I said to Sam. "I'll tell you what. If you've really got your heart set on it, I'll be willing to give it a try. You essentially gave up your professional career to follow me around the world. You've been the most devoted wife and the best military partner that I could ever imagine through all those years. And you've earned the right to make the final choice on what our next big step in life is going to be. Now all we have to do is to figure out how we're going to get the financing and where we're going to do this."

But the most important consideration by far, to me at least, was the fact that Sam's leg was still broken and there was no one who had been able to project when, if ever, it was going to heal. I mentioned this to her in the context that she's not going to be sitting around if we buy an inn. In spite of the romanticism that most prospective innkeepers attach to the business, there is a huge amount of work that needs to be done and that means being on one's feet for a good part of the time. And our recently completed seminar certainly confirmed this reality.

But with her ever-present optimism, Sam quickly put that question to bed. "I am going to get this leg to heal one way or the other, and I feel sure it will happen in the near future. And even if it doesn't, I've been very mobile lately and will continue to improve as time goes by."

So the rest of the way, Sam sat there taking notes on a pad of paper resting on her knee while we both came up with ideas that should be followed up if we were to make a success of such a venture. And the biggest obstacles, we both agreed, were, first, where the financing was going to come from and, second, how would Sam handle such a challenge when she was still hobbling around on a broken right shin bone. Both of those considerations had bold question marks beside them at the top of the page of her notes.

Bill Oates, the seminar leader, happened to be an inn broker in addition to conducting his tutorials on the business. As part of the seminar package, he offered to keep former attendees aware of properties that were becoming available, and to facilitate his offer, he had those who were interested further to fill out a questionnaire about their individual desires. He also pointedly told us that this service was to be at no extra cost to us. His fees would be paid by the sellers.

So it was not long after that when we started to receive information on properties that might fit in with our ideas for our innkeeping career. We followed up on a lot of them in various areas nearby to where we lived. We visited inns in the hunt country and the wine region of Virginia and also the shore resorts of Maryland and Delaware. In fact, most of our weekends in early spring of 1991 were spent on the road looking at inns that were for sale. (We were later to learn that *every* inn is for sale—it's always just a matter of price.) But none that we saw fit our image of what we were looking for.

Finally, Oates sent us a bit farther afield with a referral to an inn in Lenox, Massachusetts, the summer home of the Boston Symphony Orchestra at world-renowned Tanglewood. I had already written a lengthy business plan, with emphasis on the need to have a destination—an attraction that brought guests to the area around the property, not for the property by itself. And Lenox certainly exceeded this criterion in many ways. But the property to which he referred us was not at all to our liking.

Wisely, Joan had contacted a realtor in Lenox well before we visited there to have her on the lookout for an alternate in the event that the place we were coming to see didn't pan out. The realtor, a very nice woman named Barbara Kolodkin, had once been an innkeeper herself and she fully grasped our goals and was well prepared to assist us.

And by the end of the second day we were in Lenox, she brought us to the place that met our criteria almost perfectly—The Birchwood Inn.[42] And on June 28, 1991, with financing arrangements made and contracts signed, we became the owners. Our first guests arrived four hours later.

---

[42]   See *The Loving Room* for much more detail on Lenox, the inn, and the process that we went through to purchase it.

I have rarely seen Sam more enthusiastic and proud as she was that day. She finally had a nine-thousand-square-foot ten-bedroom "doll house" to decorate along with a carriage house that had two suites. And she was intent on making it the most exclusive, well-patronized inn in the region. Fortunately, when Dan learned of our intentions, he offered himself—and his education and experience in the hospitality industry—to join us as a partner in the business.

We were soon to realize that, in our enchantment with the appearance and location of the Birchwood, we were too eager to buy the property and had overlooked two key factors: it was seriously in need of major maintenance and repair, and the business had become moribund from lack of marketing. We would need to build up both aspects before any dreams could become a reality.

That summer, the high season of the year while Tanglewood was in session, the owners of the other twenty inns in Lenox were most considerate of us by sending overflow guests to us, enough so that we stayed fully occupied on the weekends at least. But I don't think any of the three of us had ever worked so hard or such long hours in our lives.

When we first took over the business the local newspaper, the *Berkshire Eagle*, had a large headline in their business section that read, "Air Force General Buys Birchwood Inn." For the next three years, while we were transitioning the property into a break-even enterprise, Sam and I dreaded the prospect that the same business section was one day going to headline an article that declared, "Air Force General Declares Bankruptcy." It was that close.

Shortly after we were settled in the inn and finally knew what we were doing, two of our old friends from the White Wine Working Group (WWWG) and active duty days, Chris and Tom House, came from their home in California to spend a few days with us. During their visit they showed us a series of pictures of a ski lodge they had just purchased at Mammoth Lakes, California, home of the world famous Mammoth Mountain ski area. When we finished seeing all the pictures and exclaiming about the beauty of their new winter home, Chris made one of those once-in-a-lifetime proposals.

"You folks are going to work yourselves to death if you don't get an occasional break from this routine you're in. And since we always enjoyed socializing and our ski trips together when we were in Belgium, we thought we should have an annual WWWG reunion each year at Mammoth. We've got plenty of room for five couples to come each year and, chances are, not everyone will make it. What do you folks think? Do you think you could break away for a couple of weeks each winter to do this?"

Chris's announcement *cum* proposal was like a cool wind on a hot summer day, a life preserver to a ship-wrecked sailor and a pardon for a wrongly accused prisoner all in one. You bet we can break away for a couple of weeks each year, we told her. Sure enough, the reunions began the following year and have continued each year ever since, usually at the end of February. And they still continue to this day, fifteen years later.

Obviously, Joan's skiing career had come to a sudden end four years previously, but she participated in the reunions with the same enthusiasm as that of the skiers. She stayed at the lodge most of the time but the gourmet meals, excellent wines, laughter, retelling of old experiences that we had, and the general camaraderie that we shared for so many years have made the annual get-together a treasured tradition and a highlight of the year for all of us.

Before we left Washington to buy the inn, we had asked Joan's orthopedist at Andrews AFB if he could recommend a skilled physician in our new area for the follow-on care of Joan's still-broken leg. While he knew no one at the time, he promised he would keep looking and come up with someone who he thought might be of help.

And he kept that promise with a call to us in October of that year. He said that he had just come from an orthopedic convention a few days previously and had brought with him a documented case history of all Joan had endured. He had talked to a number of more experienced physicians than he, given them copies of his documentation, and asked for a call back if there might be some hope that he or she could offer.

"I just received a call from one of the very best orthopedic doctors in the world," he reported to us. "His name is Jesse Jupiter and he's the head of the ortho department at Harvard Medical School and the chief orthopod at Massachusetts General Hospital in Boston. He's in heavy demand because of his skill and his advanced research in the field, and it's almost impossible to get an appointment with him. But he told me that he is very intrigued by your case and thinks he can help. He's expecting to hear from you," he concluded excitedly and gave us the number of his office. He ended by asking us to please keep him informed of any progress that might be made.

Needless to say, I was on the phone minutes later seeking an appointment for Sam with Dr. Jupiter. And true to his word, his receptionist was expecting the call and asked us to come to Mass General the following week to see him.

With all of the trips that we had made around the country to see highly recommended, eminent physicians in their field—all to no avail—we were not as optimistic as perhaps we would have been a few years before. But with Jesse Jupiter's sterling credentials, it was hard not to become hopeful once again as we headed to Boston the following Monday.

First thing after we checked in, Joan was sent to have new x-rays taken and then we waited for more than an hour in a waiting room that was crowded with people who were quite obviously in as bad or worse shape than Joan. When it was her turn, we went to a tiny examining room and soon thereafter, the great man entered—along with four residents who made the room so crowded that I needed to step outside and observe from the doorway.

Dr. Jupiter slipped the first x-ray into the viewing screen, studied it for not more than a minute or two, and then casually proclaimed, "I can fix that!"

He then turned to his four residents and went through point by point what he intended to do while they each nodded sagely to each step of his tutorial. Then he turned to Joan—ignoring me as if I weren't even there, a quality that I admired in him—and with a kind, engaging smile on his face he told her, "I've been working on a new technique with a Soviet physician for about two years that is tailor-made for this fracture. And I know from reading your case history that you're more than a little anxious to get on with your life—on two good legs. So if you agree, I'll fit you in for surgery right after Thanksgiving and we'll have you back on your feet shortly after the new year."

And Jesse Jupiter's brusque comment—that almost seemed like a boast—was fulfilled just exactly as he had predicted. In fact, after he completed the surgery and was about to discharge Joan from the hospital two days later, he said there was no real reason why we had to come back in six weeks; he was certain that the leg would be healed. But if it would give us a little better feeling of assurance, then we should come on back.

By mid-January, Sam was out of the walking cast she had worn, was fitted with a temporary brace that would keep her foot and knee in alignment, and was putting more and more weight on the foot as each day passed. To say that we were ecstatic would have been an understatement. From January of 1987 to January of 1992, she had had surgery on six separate occasions—including this most recent one; she had numerous solutions proposed, many of which involved surgery, but none of which ever worked out; and had spent a total of twenty-six months, off and on, in straight-leg casts.

She endured five years of often severe pain, experimentation, physical limitations, and disappointment, a sad history that had finally come to an end. She had been healed and Miss Daisy would be back in the front seat again. But throughout the terrible ordeal, I never once heard her complain, never saw her manifest any signs of depression or anger, and she was always convinced that one day she would recover. The power of positive thinking was once again proven to be an irrepressible adjunct to good medical practice. And needless to say, the name of Jesse Jupiter was enshrined in our private hall of heroes.

One other "best happenings" of not just the period of our ownership of the inn but of our entire married life occurred nearly halfway through our time there. Our thirty-something confirmed bachelor son found the love of his life, Anne Marie Marshall, a lovely and talented young English lass who had grown up in Southampton. Their courtship and marriage might fill a whole chapter, but suffice it to say that both Joan and I were delighted with the union and Anne was warmly welcomed into our home and family.

Our eight years of owning the Birchwood Inn were hardly uneventful. They were punctuated by hard work, long hours, little time off, and a mixture of joyous occasions and an occasional bad experience. Once Joan was back on her feet again, she worked almost tirelessly in her unflagging determination to make a success of the Birchwood Inn. Unfortunately, it was too often at the expense of her own health and well-being.

Breakfast and lunch, for example, were eaten on the run. Usually we would have a portion of the breakfast that was served to the guests, but instead of sitting down to eat, she would take an occasional bite in between trips to the dining room to see to the needs of the guests. And not unexpectedly, this led to bad habits in Joan's care of her diabetes. It took us nearly two and a half years—thanks to the arrival of Anne into our family—before we started eating dinner together in the evening after the guests had been taken care of. And equally important, we had become much more civil, taking our meal at a table in the dining room that we closed off for the meal.

Joan's old knowledge that she could cover any amount of food intake with short-acting insulin led to weight gain on her part, with some unneeded help from the Department of Agriculture. In the early '90s, the department released a food pyramid that was designed to aid Americans in selecting healthy eating habits. Unfortunately, the pyramid has since been assessed as being badly out of proportion in favor of starches, grains, and other carbohydrates. This was all that Joan needed. She had been a carbohydrate lover for her entire life, and of all the carbs, there was none that she liked better than pasta.

As a consequence, we began to consume pasta three to four evening meals each week. Since I did the cooking, I tried to make the dinners as close to the guidance as possible, having pasta mixed with fresh vegetables and shellfish that had been lightly sautéed in virgin olive oil, for example.

The original food pyramid guidance turned out to be wrong after further research was done. It was later discovered that all carbohydrates are not equal. particularly for diabetics, and only those with a low glycemic index are the ones that should be consumed in the proportions that had been advertised. And pasta was not one of those. As might be expected, all of us, not just Joan, began to gain weight—not good for anyone but a dangerous long-term trend for a diabetic.

Joan also neglected her diabetic control in the other direction as well. At times she would become so busy that she didn't take the time to eat—after she had taken her large morning dose of insulin. This neglect often resulted in a hypoglycemic reaction—often termed an insulin reaction—where her blood sugar was too low and she would get dizzy, muddled in her thinking, a bit belligerent, and unable to do much of anything until the blood sugar level was raised to normal again.

In all of the nearly forty years that Joan had been insulin dependent, she never had an insulin reaction that she couldn't take care of, usually by herself. But while we were at the inn, she had to be hospitalized once because she was rendered unconscious and unable to assist in her recovery. The only solution was to administer a highly concentrated dosage of carbohydrates intravenously. It goes without saying that both weight gain and frequent insulin reactions were injurious to her long-term health. Both Dan and I had to lecture her from time to time to the effect that her well-being was far more important than the comfort of the guests and we expected her to take care of her own needs first and foremost. In time, she did.

While we didn't share the same qualitative opinions of our years as innkeepers, all four of us shared many of the same conclusions. The profession hardly deserved the aura of romanticism that surrounded innkeeping in the eyes of non-innkeepers. The work was hard, much too hard for the rewards that ensued. The majority of guests were warm, friendly people we were proud to host in our home. The few who were not nice to the extreme of being obnoxious were hardly representative of our clientele as a whole, but certainly left the most lasting impressions. And the financial bottom line to be gained from the long hours and total financial commitment was not commensurate with the payback—at least in my judgment.

But the one area in which we agreed wholeheartedly was the unifying affect that the Birchwood Inn had on our families during our period of ownership. Joan's family was relatively small by comparison to mine but when we made a head count we discovered that, between us, we had well over one hundred close relatives—brothers, sisters, parents, nephews, nieces, along with their spouses—living in the New England area. Each Thanksgiving that we were in Lenox, we closed the inn for five days and invited all to come to celebrate the holiday weekend with us. As many as sixty came in different years and we never had fewer than forty, often represented by as many as four separate generations.

These were glorious days with cousins who had never met before sharing the joys that only close family ties can bring. Everyone pitched in to help so the workload was considerably diminished for us and that portion of it that Sam and I had was pure pleasure and an act of love. From the very first Thanksgiving we were together, the family members decided that it would be an ideal time to decorate the inn, inside and out, for the coming Christmas holidays, a decision that became a wonderful family tradition for most of the 1990s. But the most important aspect of it was the wonderful sense of kinship that came from all who were able to participate. Young and old still recall those days with a feeling of wonder, nostalgia, and, finally, regret that ultimately, those days had to come to an end.

At about the fifth or sixth year of owning and operating the inn, the toll of the hard work and long hours on Joan's health began to become apparent to me. And when I suggested that perhaps it was time to put the inn on the market and begin our second retirement, surprisingly, she offered no objection. The lore of the industry was that it took about two full years after an inn was put on the market until the property was actually turned over to the new owners. That lore proved to be true in our case as well, and on February 16, 1999, just a few months short of eight years in the business, we signed the papers, left the Birchwood Inn, left Massachusetts, and headed for Colorado where we intended to spend the rest of our lives.

*   *   *

Back when we first decided to sell the Birchwood Inn, we made up our minds that we really didn't want to stay in Lenox or Massachusetts. So we drew up a list of places that would appeal to us for retirement, each with a different set of reasons why we might like to live there, but all of which included access to good health care for Joan. The locations included Asheville, North Carolina; San Antonio; the Albuquerque-Santa Fe area of New Mexico; Colorado Springs; and the Seattle-Vancouver, BC, area in the northwest. Joan suggested that we take a long weekend from time to time and visit each one in order to get a better feel for the region.

We planned to visit them in the order I've mentioned, and in each area, Joan contacted a realtor, in advance, to act as our guide. She gave no promise that we'd actually settle down in that location, but did promise that we would contract with the person who helped if we selected his or her area as our "final resting place," as we termed it to our friends and family.

The third place we visited was Colorado Springs and after the second day there, Joan announced, "We can stop looking. This place has to be one of the most beautiful areas anywhere we've ever been, and it has the nicest weather of anyplace in the United States. This is where I want to spend the rest of my days."

Although this had been Joan's first time in the Springs, as it's affectionately known by the residents, I had been there a few times in order to give speeches to the Air Force Academy cadets. She had no argument from me. I couldn't have been happier with her choice.

We both actually let out a short cheer as we crossed the Massachusetts border on our way west. It took a while, but we finally realized that the ancient mariner's albatross had been lifted from around our necks for all time and we were free to begin the rest of our lives. We were quite a sight traveling down the highways in a rented Penske truck with a trailer on the back carrying our Nissan Maxima. We left most of our household goods in storage as we intended to take a short-term rental of an apartment for a few months while we looked for the perfect, final home for ourselves.

The trip was mostly routine and the cab of the truck was surprisingly comfortable and well-appointed. We ran into occasional snow squalls—it wasn't the best time of year to make a cross-country trek—and we actually lost the drive shaft off a relatively new truck just south of Des Moines. Thanks to a kind Iowa state trooper, we were rescued by a rental company tow truck and brought back to Des Moines where our whole load needed to be transferred to another truck. But that day's delay was something that we took in stride. After all, we had no commitments and our time was our own to do with as we wished.

Our final day consisted of only about four hours of driving and we entered our newly adopted state well before noon—with the sun shining brightly and the temperature in the mid-60s in

February. And here we thought we'd be up to our armpits in snow. Our intention when we arrived in Colorado Springs was to take a day or so to rest up and relax. But once we were settled in the visiting officer quarters (VOQ) at the U.S. Air Force Academy, Sam was far too restless to waste time. So we went out after lunch and started looking at small rental apartments. And by 1700 that same afternoon, we had signed a three-month lease on a very comfortable two-bedroom unit that included access to a fitness center, our own private garage, and many other nice amenities

Once again, Sam was wise enough to make arrangements with a realtor and in this case it was a retired U.S. Army colonel, a chaplain, eponymously named Peter Lent. How could one fail to trust a real estate agent who seemed to be destined from christening to be a man of the cloth?

We had long before set out the main criteria for the home we'd be looking for. In fact, we would have liked to replicate the townhouse that we had owned in Arlington, Virginia, and in Colorado Springs, a home like that would be far less expensive than the one we once owned. I didn't care for yard or home maintenance after the years at the inn and a townhouse or patio home would be an excellent way of get out from under what I regarded as an onerous chore.

We also decided that we needed to look for a home where we could live on only one floor, thinking of the fact we were now both near sixty-five years of age and there would inevitably come a day when stairs might well pose a difficult challenge. That meant a home with everything—master bedroom, kitchen, dining room, family room, laundry, and so on—easily accessible without resorting to stairs.

It took a day or so to unload the truck into the little apartment and unpack all that we had brought with us. But bright and early the very next morning, Sam left with Peter Lent to pursue her favorite hobby: house hunting. While we were living in the VOQ, we had visited with a classmate, a close friend at the Naval Academy and fellow Air Force retiree, Roger Williamson and his lovely wife, Elaine. With their advice we debated over what part of this sprawling, fast-growing city we wished to live in. And we decided that the northwest, close to the academy, best suited our needs. So that's where Sam and Peter began.

They were not the least bit laggardly in their quest for our new home and they averaged looking at ten or twelve properties each day for that entire week. On the weekend, Joan told me that she had selected the three places she liked the best, and she wanted me to go look at them that day. I had found her judgment to be impeccable on each of the many moves that we had made in the past forty-two years, so I had no doubt when we set out that morning that I would like each of them—and she did too—and my judgment would be critical in the place we would live in, probably for the rest of our lives.

I don't think that she intentionally stacked the deck, but the third place we looked at was clearly my preference, and I told her so. She smiled knowingly and told me it was her preference also. But before we went into any negotiations to purchase the property, she also wanted me to look at some model homes in a new area that was under development. The price was considerably higher for the model—well beyond our means in my judgment (but not in hers). But perhaps one of the key factors in her set of criteria was the view. "Why live in a home in Colorado that doesn't have a stellar view of the mountains?" she had often told me. But the lot that she had picked out on which to build was surrounded by trees, and when I pointed that out to her, that possibility came to an end.

By contrast, the home that we both liked very much had a spectacular view of Pikes Peak from the front windows, seemingly close enough to reach out and touch America's best know promontory. It was a five-bedroom, four-thousand-square-foot house with a three-car garage. The house was on three levels with a half-acre yard that was less than five years old. And in consonance with our principal specification, the master bedroom and all the daily living facilities were contained on one floor. One of the bedrooms on the top floor had been converted to an office. The home was also in a lovely neighborhood.

"I know that a large yard is not what you wanted, but all of the townhouses that I have seen are nowhere near as nice as the one we owned before and they seem way overpriced to me. If we can get this for the price that Peter thinks it will sell for, we can afford to have the yard maintenance done by a landscaper. I really love the place, and if you agree, I think we should make an offer."

So within two weeks of arriving in Colorado, we had found our home, completed the negotiations, and had a signed contract. And we still had two and a half months to go on our apartment lease.

A few days later, with the prior agreement of the owners, we went back to the house to do some measurements and get a more accurate sense of where our furnishings would best fit. I was standing by the bar that separated the kitchen from the family room, talking to the lady of the house. As I glanced out the window, I thought to myself that I hadn't noticed the large statue of a mule deer buck with a huge set of antlers that was right beside the patio. And the reason became apparent when the buck moved a few moments later and bounded to the rear of the property toward the large park behind us. It suddenly became obvious we were going to have four-legged neighbors as well as bipedal ones. And we were to learn that bears, and occasionally mountain lions, would become our uninvited guests as well.

During our conversation with the current owner, she asked if we had any objection to delaying the closing on the house for six to eight weeks, as something had come up to delay the completion of the home they were building in the Denver area. I nearly hugged her when she asked. It would work out perfectly and in the interim, we would have the time and the ability to become better acquainted with our new home state—especially to find the easiest routes to the ski areas.

Our best friends during the eight years we had owned our inn were Joy and Scotty Farrelly, the owners of the Cliffwood Inn, which was just down the street from us. They were also the owners of a small house in Santa Fe, which was their getaway to sanity when the inn business permitted. We had stayed with them the night before we left to come west and they made us promise that we would come to stay with them for a few days in Santa Fe after we got acclimated to Colorado. They had planned to close their inn for the better part of March and recharge their batteries there. We were welcome to come and stay with them as long as we could. And what could be better? We had time on our hands and Santa Fe was just a five-hour drive from the Springs, so we accepted their invitation.

Despite the fact that it had only been a few weeks since we left Lenox, our reunion was an excited one. We spent the rest of that first day talking about all the things that had occurred since last we were together, with special emphasis on how much we enjoyed Colorado Springs and the lovely new home we were purchasing. Joan was tired from the drive and we chose to go to bed in their guest room fairly early.

After we settled down for the night, I noticed that Joan seemed a bit fitful and I asked her if she was alright. She passed off her restlessness as probably just a little indigestion, so I got her a couple of Tums to see if that would settle her stomach. I'm not really sure who fell asleep first, but I do know that it was hours later when Sam awakened me.

She told me that she had terrible abdominal pains and they seemed to be getting worse. When she showed me the location of the pain—right below her rib cage—it was clear that it was not appendicitis but it was also clear that the pain was increasing in intensity. After fifteen minutes or so, I was getting more concerned, had fully awakened, and I told her that it would be a good idea if I took her to the hospital emergency room.

Her dislike for hospitals prompted a quick refusal, but seemingly seconds later, the intensity of the pain increased to the point that she changed her mind about waiting it out until morning. I quickly woke our hosts to find out where the nearest hospital was located while Joan prepared to leave. Moments later we were on our way to St. Vincent Regional Medical Center, arriving there just after 0300. The emergency room physician examined her carefully, gave her a small amount of liquid to drink that he said would ease her pain somewhat, and told us that he believed that the problem stemmed from her gall bladder and he needed to do some tests to determine if she had gall stones or if some other problem existed.

By 0500, after the tests were completed, he told us that it appeared to him that the gall bladder would have to be removed, but he wanted to wait until the chief of surgery came to the hospital in another hour to confirm his diagnosis and to determine the best course of action to take. And by 0630, Joan was on her way to the operating room where the gall bladder would be removed, fortunately by a minimally invasive laparoscopic procedure, rather than having to cut her open.

By noon, Joan was sufficiently recovered from this emergency procedure that Joy and Scotty were able to come to visit. Joan had already begun to tell anyone who would listen that she was certainly well enough to go home—or at least back to the Farrelly's house. Our plans for touring and dining in and about the Santa Fe area came to an abrupt halt, but at least Joan was alright and said she was quite comfortable—though watching her when she moved, it was clear that she still had quite a bit of residual pain. But by this time in our lives together, I knew that she would sooner cut out her tongue before she would complain about her discomfort.

Two days after her surgery, we retraced our steps back to Colorado Springs with Joan bolstered by pillows in the front seat beside me.

The extra time we had to prepare for our move into our new home was an unexpected but much appreciated respite while she recovered her strength, and when we finally closed on the mortgage in mid-May and received the keys to our new home, Sam was well prepared to get us settled—for the twenty-ninth time in the forty-two years we had been married. She was unquestionably a pro in doing so as she was in many other endeavors that punctuated our world-wide odyssey, which had finally come to an end.

One evening at dinner before we left Lenox, we were pondering the problem of getting both of our cars out to Colorado. I had just about decided that I was going to have to contract with one of the agencies that does this sort of thing and then I would tow the other car behind the truck that we would rent to take our personal things out of the Birchwood Inn.

As I was speaking, I saw Anne and Dan exchange glances and a brief nod from one to the other and Dan said, "We'll be glad to take your Subaru out there for you. Anne wants to see the country outside of New England, and there isn't a better way than to take a leisurely drive and stop when we want and see the sights."

Problem solved! Paying their expenses to make the trip and then fly back home would be markedly less expensive than to contract to have it done. And Anne would get her opportunity to see more of the States.

They were both greatly enthused when they came back from their trip over the beauty and climate of Colorado and immediately volunteered to come back out to help us move into our new home when the time came. And they did exactly that in mid-May when the household goods that we hadn't seen for eight years finally showed up at 1315 Golden Hills Road. They stayed for the entire week, unpacking boxes, moving furniture into place, and doing all the other chores that come with a major household move.

At the end of the week, we had a celebratory dinner together the night before they were headed back to Lenox. Out of the blue, Dan posed the question, "What would you think if we gave up our jobs and moved out here to Colorado Springs?"

They went on to say that their two trips to Colorado—even though they had been here less than ten days all told—was all they needed to convince them that this was where they wanted to live. Joan was overcome with joy and we spent the rest of the evening making plans for how and when this could be carried out. They would, of course, live with us until they found jobs and got their feet on the ground; they would get all the help they needed, when the time came, from the realtor who had helped us with out house hunting; and I would come back to drive the rental van load of their household goods—far less than we had because they had just been married a short time—out to Colorado while they took the northern route so that Anne could see even more of this great country of ours.

And five months later, they had cleared up all the loose ends of their lives in New England and were the newest Coloradans to come here and settle. In retrospect, it was the most fortuitous decision that could have been made.

*   *   *

Joan had gained too much weight while we were at the inn and one of the first vows she made after we were settled in our new home was to lose weight and get control of her health. That included joining a spa and fitness center and using the facilities at least three times per week. She had previously found that swimming had been excellent exercise when we lived in Virginia, so she began by going to water aerobics classes. Soon thereafter, she expanded her activities to using the aerobic equipment and the weight machines in the fitness center. She was far from becoming a female body builder, but her efforts were serious and she began to show some very positive results after just a few months.

We also began to develop a circle of new friends, aided by our old friends, Elaine and Roger Williamson, and life took on a very rosy glow as the weeks and months passed. About the same time, we became interested in volunteer work with the local public library district through which we became English tutors for newly arrived immigrants and we also began hosting conversational English group meetings for new arrivals to our country who had a basic fluency in the language but needed help with pronunciation and comprehension.

Life was good in Colorado. Retirement came at a perfect time in our lives—I had turned sixty-five and Sam would follow me to that magic age a few months later. And I don't think we'd ever been happier.

One day in August of 2000, we were driving home from "the club" as we had become accustomed to calling the fitness center, and Sam told me that she had a sore throat. I asked her how bad it was and whether she had any other symptoms of a cold coming on. She said that it was nothing to worry about—probably the fact that we still weren't quite used to the exceptionally low humidity that typified the high desert climate of our new home.

Over the next few months, she would mention periodically that the sore throat would come and go, but when I suggested that it might be worthwhile to have a doctor check it out, she laughed the notion off saying that it was just a minor discomfort and it always went away pretty quickly.

One Saturday night in late October, we hosted another couple with whom we had become friendly for a quiet dinner at our home. This was one of Sam's favorite things to do and she enjoyed setting a lovely table, which our guests always commented on. It was a fairly early evening when the guests left and we decided to clean up the mess that usually occurs from one of these occasions so we wouldn't have to face it in the morning.

As we were climbing into bed, she told me, "I've had that same sore throat all evening and it just doesn't seem to go away the way it has before."

I asked her if it hurt when she swallowed and she said that it didn't. I looked in her throat to see if there was any inflammation and saw none. So then I asked her to show me exactly where the pain of her sore throat was, and she pointed more to the side of her neck rather than the area where one might expect a sore throat to manifest itself.

"I tell you what, Sam, if that doesn't go away pretty quickly, I'm going to take you to the emergency room, and even if it does go away tonight, you're going to go to the hospital first thing Monday morning. That 'sore throat' of yours is not a sore throat, and it's been around far too long, so it's time to find out what's causing the pain."

Ordinarily, Joan would object whenever I mentioned going to see a doctor, but this time she just remained silent. And about two hours later she awakened me to say that the pain had worsened and maybe it was time to go to the emergency room right now.

When we arrived at the Air Force Academy Hospital ER, there was obviously an emergency already going on and the young sergeant who normally screened the new arrivals told us that he'd be with us in a few minutes after he assisted with the on-going crisis that had just occurred. About twenty minutes later, after the patient was placed in an ambulance for transfer to one of the large city hospitals that was better equipped to handle major problems, he finally turned his attention to us.

When we told him what Joan's problem was—and by this time the pain had extended into her chest—the poor guy fell all over himself apologizing for the delay. He immediately recognized what we had been missing for months: Sam was having a myocardial infarction, or in plain English, a heart attack.

The doctor immediately drew blood to determine if the tell-tale enzymes were present but he didn't wait until the lab report came back. They immediately established an intravenous port and began to administer blood thinners to prevent the further advancement of the blockage of Joan's coronary arteries. Moments later, after reviewing the lab data, he came to us and said that what he had done thus far was not adequate and we had a choice to make.

"I need to administer a super clot buster but it isn't just something that I can do lightly. This drug can very possibly kill you,

Mrs. Toner, because it's very potent. But I'm very concerned that you could well not survive this heart attack if I don't take drastic measures. In all honesty, if you and I were to change places, I would give you permission to administer the drug. I'm not a cardiologist, but I've had enough ER experience to know that you're in very critical condition."

Sam looked at me for just the blink of an eye, and without any further hesitation, told him to give her the clot buster. Within the next few days we were to learn that this action saved her life.

The ER staff closely monitored her for the next twenty minutes or so until an ambulance arrived to take her to Memorial Hospital in downtown Colorado Springs.[43] I was gratified by the exceptional care and compassion that all the medical people showed at the ER and during the transfer. The Memorial Hospital emergency staff were alert and ready for Joan when we arrived.

The cardiologist on duty quickly appraised the situation and sat down with me to get more details of Joan's general health situation and the onset of her symptoms. He was, of course, very interested in her diabetic condition and how well it was being managed. He then told me that she was in no immediate danger, she would be closely monitored, and they would perform a few tests to determine the gravity of the situation. He also recommended that I go home to get some rest as nothing of any consequence would be done until the next morning.

When I arrived back at the hospital, they told me that they were just then preparing Joan to do an angiogram to determine the precise location of the blockages in her coronary arteries and the degree to which they were blocked. And after waiting for what seemed to be the entire morning, a doctor came to me in the waiting room.

---

[43]   The Air Force Academy Hospital exists primarily to provide health care for the cadets, staff, and faculty of the academy, and it does not have the complete array of capabilities that one finds in a general hospital.   Since the establishment of the academy in the 1950s, the hospital has maintained a close working relationship with the two general hospitals in the city—Penrose St. Francis Hospital is the other—and they routinely accept all cases that are beyond the capabilities of the AFA Hospital

"Your wife has had a very serious heart attack," Dr. James Albert told me, "and if the doctor at the Air Force Academy hadn't taken the prompt action that he did, I'm afraid she wouldn't be here for us to have this conversation. Virtually all her primary coronary arteries have severe blockages, some up to nearly 99 percent. She's a tough lady to have gone so long before this occurred and then to survive when it did. She needs to have a multiple bypass operation, and we always like to do those as soon as possible. But based on the seriousness of her condition, we've elected to wait until Monday morning, first thing, because I want the full complement of the OR available and the complete facilities of the hospital to be staffed before we do this. It's not going to be easy, but it's the only hope we have."

He then told me that Joan would be in the acute coronary care unit until then and she would be monitored very closely at all times. He also told me that I should plan to stay with her as much as I could in the interim and to encourage her as much as possible. He made it completely clear that this was a crucial juncture in our lives and I needed to be prepared for any eventuality. Thank God that Anne and Dan were here with us.

When Monday morning arrived, I was in her room well before the time for her open-heart surgery and, though she had been given sedatives throughout the previous twenty-four hours, she was fully lucid and we talked for most of the time while I held her hand. As was typical of her approach to life, she didn't skirt the issue at all but began telling me what she expected of me if she didn't survive. She didn't want any heroic measures to keep her alive, saying she'd rather be dead than become a vegetative burden on me for years to come. She wanted me to put her death behind me as quickly as I could and get on with life without her. She wanted me to find someone new to be with and, perhaps, marry, because she knew that loneliness would be particularly hard for me, and she told me repeatedly that she loved me and how happy she had been for our whole life together.

Finally, the time came and Anne, Dan, and I accompanied her down to the operating theater where I was allowed to come into the preparation area for a last few minutes with her. Despite the tubing and other obstructions, she reached up and pulled my face down to hers.

"I don't think I'm going to make it through this," she confided in me, "but I want you to remember that I've always loved you since the first time I kissed you and, no matter what, never a day went by that I stopped loving you. And I always will; you are everything to me."

I tried to chide her gently into believing that hers were just the apprehensions that come with such a critical event in her life and that she was going to get this ordeal over with and be better than she had been in years. But I had to choke back tears when I said this because I knew that there was a very real possibility that she might be right and that this was the last time I would ever be with her. As the nurses and technicians wheeled her into operating room, the head OR nurse came over to me and squeezed my hand.

"Don't worry," she told me. "We're going to take real good care of her." But the look of deep concern in her eyes was not terribly reassuring.

Moments later, I joined Anne and Dan in the surgical waiting room, and the long wait began. Minutes seemed like hours and Joan's final words to me kept coming back to remind of what a fragile position she was in. We had been told that the procedure would probably take three hours, but when three and then four hours passed, the level of concern increased accordingly.

Finally, I saw the chief OR nurse coming around the corner heading straight for us. The concerned look on her face was very disconcerting and I knew instantly that the news was not good.

"Your wife is still in the operating room," she began, "and I'm afraid we've run into some serious problems. Dr. Albert has done five separate bypasses but as he completed the final one and we were shifting her from the heart-lung machine, we were unable to get her heart restarted. It's not something we run into very often, but then on the other hand, it doesn't mean that we've lost her either."

She then took both of my hands into hers and continued, "I'm sorry to be the bearer of such bad news but keeping you in the dark just makes things more difficult for you the longer you wait. We're going to start undoing each bypass one by one and doing it over again to see if there's a solution by doing that. I promise you that we're doing the absolute best we can. But if you are a praying person, it's time to pray even harder."

And with a final squeeze of my hands, she turned and started back to the OR. Anne and Dan were standing nearby and heard what was said. Anne took me by the hand and we returned to where we had been seated, and I completely broke down sobbing. I can't ever recall feeling so completely devastated. Even though the attending physicians had cautioned me that Joan was in very serious condition, I never allowed myself to even contemplate the possibility that she might not survive. And here that possibility was staring me boldly in the face.

In time, I recovered my composure and the wait began again. But time no longer mattered as it had before because I was completely preoccupied with facing the alternative that Sam might actually die. What would I possibly do? How could I face the future without her?

Finally, Dr. Albert came from the same direction that his nurse had come previously. His expression was blank and he looked like he was physically exhausted. And he had every good reason to look that way as Joan had been in surgery for nearly seven hours by this time. He shook his head from side to side as if he couldn't believe what he had just been through with Joan, but his first words were reassuring.

"It was one of the toughest fights I've been in, but we finally finished and sewed her back up. She's on a respirator but, thank God, her heart's beating on its own. She's been through a terribly difficult ordeal and she's obviously a strong, determined woman to come through this the way she has."

He then went on to tell me that she was in for a long recovery as he had to harvest many more veins from her legs than normal in order to redo each of the five bypasses. She was in recovery at the present time, he went on, and it probably would be at least an hour before she would return to the CCU. He also pointed out that she had been very heavily sedated because of the length of the procedure and it might be from six to ten hours before she'd awaken. He concluded by telling us that she was far from being out of the woods and that the first twenty-four hours would be critical.

"If she makes it through to this time tomorrow, you can begin to relax a little, but it's going to be a tough struggle ahead for her."

When we went up to the CCU, the charge nurse asked us to remain in the waiting room until they got Joan settled in her bed. When I finally was allowed into her room, I was shocked beyond belief. Her face and arms were so swollen with edema that she looked like a blow-up doll. Her face was so puffed that her head appeared like a balloon that had been inflated and eyebrows and nostrils had been painted on, with a respirator tube projected upward where her mouth should be. It was hard to believe that there was a human being lying in the bed, let alone that it was my dear Sam.

The nurse who was with her told me not to be real concerned about the way she looked. Many patients have a similar appearance after a long bout of surgery, she told me, and she was getting a large dose of an IV diuretic that would gradually reduce the swelling over the next few days. That couldn't occur quickly enough for me.

I told Anne and Dan that they needed to go home, get a good meal, and plan on going to work in the morning. I was going to remain by Mom's bedside for the night and I promised them that if there was any sign of problems, I would call them right away. I also asked them to call Christine and Scott and let them know that the first crisis was passed. I prayed, at the same time, that the next twenty-four hours would be crisis-free.

Around 1900, the normal shift change time, a male nurse came into the room and relieved the woman who had been with Joan from the moment she returned from the recovery room. He took a seat on the other side of her bed and introduced himself, telling me that Joan would be his only patient for the entire period of the shift, a revelation that reinforced my conclusion that she was in very critical condition.

I soon learned that Bill was a retired U. S. Air Force lieutenant colonel who had no connection to the medical field during the twenty years he had served on active duty. But he had always had a secret desire to be a doctor for all those years, and though he figured that he was too old to begin the dozen or so years of study to become a physician, he could still satisfy his goals to an extent by becoming a nurse. So he had gone to nursing school immediately after he retired and here he was caring for my wife during the first, critical moments after her surgery. And that brief conversation began my education on heart disease and the proper care of coronary patients.

The night passed slowly, but our sporadic conversation helped to fill the time. We talked a lot about our respective military careers, but I doubt that our conversation ever had my complete attention, and I rarely took my eyes off Joan for more than a few seconds at a time, hoping against hope to see some signs of life.

As the clock approached midnight, and after having sat all day in the surgical waiting room, like St. Peter in the Garden of Gethsemane, I found myself nodding off from time to time. Bill smiled over at me and commented on the fact that I must be quite tired if I could doze off in the very uncomfortable straight chair on which I was seated. He then suggested that I put my head down on the bed beside Joan and get a bit of a cat-nap, assuring me that he would wake me if there were any change.

Finally, at about 0300 the next morning, Joan began to stir slightly. At first it was just a slight moan that was music to my ears. As the minutes ticked by, slight hand movements began and her eyelids flickered from time to time. That small indication of life in her terribly distorted body gave me hope that the crisis was over—even though I was fully aware that these signs were just indicative of the fact that her anesthesia was wearing off, not that she was suddenly out of danger and on the road to recovery.

The next hours and days became a blur to me, though I remember distinctly the thrill that I felt when she finally opened her eyes near dawn and looked over at me. Her expression was initially one of fear, punctuated by disorientation, but there was a brief sign of recognition and a hint of growing security when we held eye contact with one another. No glance that I can ever recall, before or since, ever held greater meaning than that one. I knew from that moment forward that she was determined to recover.

Over the next few days, the "air" went out of the balloon and her facial features and her distended body gradually resumed its old familiar look. The dreaded respirator had been removed—Joan was claustrophobic and the large tube down her throat frightened her—and she had regained her full cardio-pulmonary capability.

Even though she didn't complain, she was in considerable pain, not just from the chest area that had been opened down the full length of the sternum and then wired back together again. The borrow area from which the veins had been harvested for the bypasses was an equal source of discomfort. I was stunned the first time I saw her legs. She had incisions on the inside of both legs from her crotch all the way to her ankles—incisions that were secured by metal staples every half inch of the way from top to bottom. But she had made it through the crisis period and was courageously determined to regain her health as quickly as possible.

To begin her fourth day in the CCU, another very positive indicator came when she was transferred from there to the coronary care ward nearby. She had begun to sit up in bed, she was eating a little each meal, and her diabetes was under reasonable control. The CCU was like being in the operating room all the time with all the technical equipment that surrounded her, so the change to a regular room was therapeutic for her, especially with her ability to look out on the mountains that she loved so dearly.

Since Sam had never had any coronary difficulties in the past, we did not have a cardiologist to provide for her care. A constant procession of different staff doctors would come by her room for morning rounds and occasionally throughout the day. As it turned out, the cardiologists were all associates from the same service, so it was a relief to learn that at least they could share Joan's status information on their internal computer network. But neither of us was enamored of seeing different faces, different personalities and demeanors, and different bedside manners day after day.

Finally, on her fourth day on the ward, a week after her surgery, yet another new doctor came in to visit with Joan. He introduced himself as Paul Sherry—an act of courtesy that not every physician had thought to offer—and he seemed to be well versed on Joan's case. He examined her more thoroughly than anyone else had done previously, and we both liked the sense of technical competence that he exuded, and even more, his tender compassion that caused him to stand out immediately in our minds.

At the end of his examination, he asked us if we had any problems with the care that she had been receiving. I didn't have to think twice and immediately told him that I was concerned about the team approach by the cardiologists we had seen previously. He smiled broadly when I said that and his first response came as somewhat of a surprise to both of us.

"To be perfectly honest, I don't like that either. I don't think a patient receives the best care possible if the doctors that she sees are changing all the time." And then he went on to say, "Your case, Mrs. Toner, is one of the most interesting and complex that I've seen in some time. You're a diabetic, which complicates your situation. You could easily have succumbed to the severity of the MI that you just had. And you have made a remarkable recovery from a very protracted and difficult surgical procedure not very long ago. I think you need to have greater consistency in the care you receive, so I'd like to suggest to you that I take you on as my private patient—that I'll be your cardiologist full-time and you won't see anyone else except on a rare occasion when it might become necessary."

If Joan had been able to get out of bed, I think she would have hugged him. And with just a hint of a tear of gratitude in her eyes, she told him, "I'd like that very much. Thank you!"

Paul stayed in the room for another twenty minutes or so, partly to get greater insight into Joan's background, and partly to examine her even further. When he was looking at the array of staples on the inside of her legs, he asked her how long she had been insulin dependent. When she told him that it was over forty years, he raised his eyebrows.

"You're in amazingly good condition for that long a duration. You even have all your fingers and toes!" he commented. And then went on to ask more detail regarding the scar tissue on her right leg from the ski injury that had occurred a decade before.

As he was about to leave Joan's room, he seemed to hesitate slightly, and then asked me to accompany him. We went to a small break room on the ward and had a brief discussion about Joan's situation, with emphasis on the part that I would play in, first, her recovery, and later in her long-term care. He suggested that I might like him to give me technical articles and data on subjects related to her condition, an offer that I eagerly accepted. Finally, he mentioned that he heard I was a retired USAF general and went on to tell me that he was an Air Force Academy graduate, had gone to medical school through the auspices of the U. S. Air Force, and had been a military physician until he retired a few years previously.

Then with a broad, infectious grin, he said, "I think we're going to have a very long association with one another, so we probably should decide how that association will be conducted. We can go by 'doctor' and 'general' if you want, but I'd prefer that you call me Paul."

I put out my hand and told him that I'd prefer to be called Dick, and accompanied by a warm, firm handshake, a very deep and meaningful friendship was born. Suffice it to say that Paul's offer to be her private cardiologist and our acceptance was the singularly most important decision that Sam and I ever made with respect to her health care.

Early that afternoon, a pert, attractive, forty-ish blond woman came into Joan's room, wearing a white smock that might have indicated another doctor coming to see her. But the mystery was quickly dispelled when she smiled brightly and announced, "Hi, I'm Patti. I'm Dr. Sherry's nurse-assistant and I understand that we'll be seeing quite a lot of each other in the future. Dr. Sherry is so pleased that you've entrusted your care to him and I can assure you that you will receive the best care possible. Dr. Sherry is a wonderful physician but an even finer human being and I think you'll come to like and respect him as much as I do."

No truer words could have been spoken. The only addition that I would make to that would be that we also came to love and respect Patti Friesen as well. She was and is a woman of great compassion and accessibility who has become more like a member of our family than a medical professional we might see from time to time. She has been very dear to both Joan and me.

After roughly ten days, Paul asked Joan if she thought she was able to go home, and she very eagerly agreed that would be the best medicine she could imagine. Our daughter, Christine, God bless her, had come from Florida to help out with this difficult transition, as she has regularly ever since. And Paul had previously ascertained my agreement that we could handle this. To back it up, he gave me his card, which contained his office, cell, and home phone numbers with instructions to call him any time of day or night if need be. (Patti later gave me all her phone numbers, as well, with the same admonition to call first and worry later about whether it was the right thing to do.) How many medical professionals do you find in this day and age who would ever do such a thing?

Sam was delighted to be home and she was somewhat mobile—I had been walking her around the corridors of the ward five or six times per day for the preceding week—so she adapted to home life rather quickly. Anne, Christine, and Dan were a huge help and we spent each evening together cheering her on and marveling at her amazing willpower and bravery. Paul, Patti, and the wonderful coronary ward nurses had given me extensive preparation in her care, and I felt complete confidence in monitoring her progress. But I had overlooked one important thing.

Shortly after we had her settled in at home, just the two of us were in our bedroom—Joan resting in bed after a long day while I was reading in a chair beside her. Seemingly out of nowhere she spoke some rather shocking words to me.

"You have kidded me about my survival after my telling you that I wouldn't. But I actually did die during the operation."

She then went on to tell me that she had had what is commonly referred to as an out-of-body experience and she was convinced that, at that point in time, she had actually passed away.

"I don't know how long I had been under anesthesia since you're never aware of time or anything else under a general. But suddenly, I was fully awake and I seemed to be floating in the air way above the operating room. The light that surrounded me was bright and white, and I was struck by the fact that everything in the operating room was pure white—despite the fact that I knew that the whole staff had on colored scrubs when we entered. Only the faces were their natural color.

"I could see them working over me and hear them talking just as if I were right down there among them, and while there was no indication of panic in anyone's voice, they were very anxious because they couldn't get my heart to beat on its own. The conversation was very disciplined and terse, but it seemed apparent that they weren't going to give up on me. I heard Dr. Albert tell the head nurse to go out and tell you that things didn't look good but they were doing their best to save me.

"When she left the OR, I seemed to rise a bit higher up into the air and I hovered over her on the way to the waiting room and when she took both your hands in hers to talk to you. Just like the OR, everything was a brilliant white except for people's faces. I saw the nurse talk to you and then return toward the OR. I know exactly where the waiting room is in the hospital even though I've never been there so that's what makes the whole experience so eerie. When you went back to sit down with the kids, I heard you tell them what had been said, and then I watched as Anne pulled you toward her and put her arms around you while you sobbed.

"I know all this is very hard to believe, and I would be very skeptical if you told me the same story. But it happened, just the way I've told you, and I think that's a pretty strong indication that I'm going to get through this."

Needless to say, I was stupefied listening to what she had to tell me. I then asked her if she remembered anything else.

"I just recall the end of the experience—I'm not going to call it a dream because I know it happened. After I watched you for a few more moments, I started to rise up into the air higher and higher and the white glow got brighter and brighter. So much so that it hurt my eyes to look at it. Then very slowly, the brightness began to fade and I just seemed to fall asleep naturally, into the state that is normal for being under anesthesia. I don't remember anything else until I slowly became conscious with you by my side in the CCU."

I suspect that there are many learned explanations for what occurred, and I've discovered since then that a great deal of research has gone into attempting to explain what is taking place when an experience such as this occurs. But I have never chosen to question or doubt that this actually occurred, and Joan was simply telling me exactly what had imprinted itself on her mind.

It wasn't but days later that Sam asked me to come into the bathroom where she was washing and pointed to the wounds on her legs. They were fiery red and the heat of the surface of her skin was a sure indication that the wounds where the veins had been taken were highly inflamed and possibly infected. I called Dr. Albert's office to report this and was asked to bring her in right away.

Because diabetics are notoriously slow healers, we had been told that Joan should probably plan on waiting at least four weeks before the staples were removed from the wounds. And even though we were a few days short of that time frame, the physician's assistant who was on duty in the office determined that because of her diabetes, she was probably having an allergic reaction to the staples themselves and it was time for them to be removed.

He told Joan that she would only feel a "pinch" as he extracted each staple, but I don't think he took into account the fact that they were already hypersensitive because of the swelling and inflammation, and I could see her eyes glistening with tears as each of the eighty-plus pieces of metal were removed. It wasn't that she was about to cry; it was the severity of the pain that she choked back as each one was pulled. I thought she was going to break the bones in my hand, she was squeezing it so hard, but she never once cried out or complained. In reality, use of a topical anesthetic had clearly been called for.

When the PA completed the task, he placed an antibiotic salve on the wounds, wrapped the legs lightly in gauze, and let us go. After we got into the car, Sam sighed and said, "Wow, that really hurt but my legs feel better already."

Progress continued rapidly for the next few days, but on the evening of the day we drove Christine to the airport so that she could return to her Florida home and family, the first of many setbacks occurred. We were sitting in the family room watching the news on television when Sam told me she had been having chest pains for the past hour or so. At first she thought they were just some discomfort that came with the healing of her sternum and rib cage. But she said they had started to become a little more severe in the past hour.

I had accepted her stoicism with regard to the "sore throat" that she had previously, but I wasn't going to make that same mistake again. And I went to the telephone and called 911. She told me that she thought I might be a bit overly cautious, but I was hearing none of it this time. Moments later, the fire and rescue squad were at our door and they, too, didn't think that it was a situation that deserved a wait-and-see approach Less than a half hour later, Joan was back on the coronary care ward, Patti had been notified, and Paul Sherry was en route to the hospital.

I was anxious that somehow I had missed something or had not taken adequate care of her, but Paul soon disabused me of that notion. A series of tests quickly confirmed that Paul's initial impressions were correct and she was experiencing an episode of congestive heart failure (CHF), a condition in which a build-up of fluid around her already-weakened heart was putting pressure on the heart muscle and preventing it from providing an adequate blood supply to her cardio-pulmonary system and thus causing chest pain or angina.

Paul immediately began an intravenous regimen of diuretics to bring down the fluid build-up and thus reduce the fluid pressure on her heart. But it was not going to be a simple process of simply reducing this particular surplus of fluid in her system; he needed time to balance out all of the medications she was receiving—including oral diuretics—and that balancing process was going to take time. We needed to plan on at least a week in the hospital, he told us. While it was primarily a process of attaining the proper balance, the drugs she was being administered were so potent that Joan would need to be monitored continually while this process took place.

Sam's father had died a few years previously of congestive heart failure but neither of us was particularly conversant about the disease. But now it was time to learn in depth, and Paul would eventually bring me enough articles to fill a small textbook on this facet of heart disease alone. I would sit with Joan in her hospital room for hours, with the articles in my lap and a medical dictionary borrowed from the nurse's station by my side. And when I thought I had grasped certain aspects of what I was reading, I'd try to explain them to Sam in terms that were not as technical. In between my studies, I would "nag" her into going for longer and longer walks every hour or so, or bathing her, changing her bed, and doing other little chores to free up the hard working staff of the ward.

On the day before Thanksgiving, Paul came in for his morning visit and he seemed to have something on his mind. Finally, he said that he had told us just a short time before that he didn't like the musical-chairs style of patient care and had asked us if he could be Joan's exclusive physician.

"But already, I'm reneging on the mutual pledge because I'm leaving this afternoon to go away with my aged mother and my wife and children for the Thanksgiving weekend. I'm sorry to do this to you, but my mother is getting along in years and while she's still with us, I want to make the most of the holiday periods with her."

He then went on to tell us where he was going, who would be replacing him from his service over the weekend, apologizing profusely all the while for going back on his pledge. Neither of us, of course, felt in any way that he was doing anything of the sort and tried to reassure him that he was doing the right thing, and we would make exactly the same choice if the situation were reversed.

Anne and Dan busied themselves that night putting together a minimalist turkey dinner for the holiday and, truth be known, none of us really felt in a very celebratory mood with the focus of our family in the hospital. But toward noontime the kids brought in a nicely laid out plate with turkey, mashed potatoes, a little stuffing, green beans, cranberry sauce, and gravy—all Mom's favorites—and after it was warmed in the unit microwave, she was able to pick at the meal a little. But it just wasn't our traditional Thanksgiving and none of us felt the least bit festive.

About 1500 that afternoon, Paul Sherry walked into the room and wished us both a happy Thanksgiving. Joan responded to his sentiments but then asked him what in the world he was doing in the hospital on this holiday afternoon. He was supposed to be away for the long weekend.

"Well, to be perfectly honest, I've not been in much of a holiday frame of mind as I've been very concerned about you. So rather than be bad company for my family and spoil their holiday, I decided to come back home and check to see how you were doing."

Not that the colleague who was standing in for him couldn't do the same thing for him in a brief telephone conversation. And with that, he pulled up a chair and sat on the opposite side of her bed from me and spent the next three or four hours with his prize patient. We talked a lot about Sam's condition and her prospects of recovery, but we talked of other more personal things, all of us opening up our lives and families in a wonderful, heart-warming conversation.

But it wasn't just that afternoon that this dedicated man spent with Joan and me. He was back the following day for a similar amount of time and then again on Saturday morning he came into the hospital for another check on her progress. As he was leaving, he almost apologetically told us that he wouldn't be in on Sunday. He felt much more confident that Joan was reaching full stability, so he was going back to join his family and bring them back home the next day.

That weekend, Paul Sherry elevated himself in our judgment to somewhere between an ordinary mortal and sainthood. It was the singularly most profound example of professional dedication and selfless devotion that either of us had ever witnessed—and probably will never see the equal of again.

The process of obtaining the correct balance of the many medications she was taking daily took much longer than anticipated and she remained in the hospital for nearly three weeks. During that time, she had a series of coronary catheterizations,[44] and stents were emplaced in two of her coronary arteries.

As if these difficulties were not enough, we were to discover that Joan had developed sores on both of her feet, caused by a combination of poor peripheral artery circulation and pressure spots on her toes and her heels. These sores eventually led to gangrene in some of the toes, and a series of five separate operations to amputate four of her toes over the next three years. Paul Sherry believed that perhaps he had jinxed Joan just weeks before when he commented on the fact that she still had all her fingers and toes despite being an insulin-dependent diabetic for so many years.

Sam also endured two separate operations during which a stent was placed in her left femoral artery—one of the large main arteries from the aorta extending from the abdomen down into both legs to provide blood supply to the extremities—as well as a bypass installed in the femoral artery of her right leg. Here was yet another problem that had to be monitored and dealt with as needed: peripheral artery disease. While Joan had managed to avoid virtually all of the hazards of diabetes for an amazingly long period of time, it was clear that the grace period was over. However, her eyes and kidneys were still

---

[44]   A coronary catheterization is a procedure by which a small tube is introduced into the femoral artery in the leg and moved through vascular system to the heart where the physician can monitor heart functions, such as blood flow, blockages, etc. It is also the basis of taking x-rays of the coronary arteries (angiogram) or introducing a balloon to open blockages (angioplasty) or to emplace stents into partially blocked arteries.

in excellent functional order, so that was a way of looking at the glass being half full—as Sam always seemed to manage to do.

After enduring all of the ravages of the disease, seemingly crammed into a period of less than two months, Joan finally came back home again and we set off down the road to her recovery. She had been walking frequently and regularly in the hospital, so we continued at home as well. In addition, she began a thrice weekly cardiac rehabilitation program that was provided by Memorial Hospital. The rehab nurses were excellent and they did a superb job of encouraging without overextending their patients. Joan showed rapid progress and soon seemed to be back nearly to normal, though the wounds on her legs, feet, and chest would still be a long time healing.

My description of what Joan had to face during the waning days of 2000 and early the following year all seem rather clinical when related in the fashion and the order I have just done. But the problems she overcame involved a considerable amount of emotional and psychological trauma as well. There were more than a few days when we were fearful that she would not be able to survive, and despite his positive attitude and encouragement, Paul Sherry was above all an honest and straightforward man. And he told me on more than one occasion that Joan was in danger of succumbing to all that was afflicting her. And despite our no longer being active participants in our religion, Joan was asked by the Catholic hospital chaplain if she wished to receive Extreme Unction, the final blessings and prayers of the Catholic Church when death seemed imminent. She accepted the offer, and not for the last time, in her on-going battle for survival.

Yet, as was to be her hallmark over the next eight years, Sam survived this confrontation with the Grim Reaper and was soon eager to get on with her life. In mid-February, we invited Christine and Mike, along with our two grandchildren, Daniel and Colleen, to come to Breckenridge for a week-long ski vacation, a tradition that continued every year thereafter. We had been concerned about the altitude at Breckenridge—the village is at 9,600 feet and the condo that we rented is at 10,000 feet—so we tested that out in the summer and learned in advance that Joan, despite her cardio-pulmonary difficulties, was able to tolerate the altitude better than our flatlander kids from Florida. An amazing woman, to say the least.

We missed the WWWG reunion at Mammoth in 2001 for obvious reasons, but our annual hosts, Tom and Chris House, thought that we should make up for that with a summertime visit. Joan was feeling well enough for a long car journey, so we drove to Mammoth where we celebrated the Fourth of July holiday, went from there for a tour of nearby Yosemite National Park, and then on to spend another relaxing, wonderful week with the Houses at their summer—actually, primary—home in Carmel, California. From there, we visited my old Naval Academy roommate and his wife, Bill and Jean Murphy, at their home near Sacramento.

After wending our way back home by way of Utah and Wyoming, Joan was in wonderful health and eager for more travel at the first opportunity. She was indefatigable. But the good health was not to continue uninterrupted.

On October 12, 2001, Joan awoke with chest pains (angina) in the early morning. She had been prescribed Nitrostat, a commercial version of the sublingual old standby, nitroglycerine, which has been used for decades to reduce the effect of angina. Though Joan very rarely used the Nitrostat, we had been told that if two doses were insufficient to relieve the pain, then that was a clear signal we needed to head to the hospital. I made a quick call to Patti before we left the house and there was a bed in the coronary care ward waiting for Sam when we arrived at Memorial Hospital.

She was no sooner wired up to the telemonitoring device than Paul and Patti came into the room. After a quick physical exam, he said the there was some arrhythmia but he didn't think that there was anything critical at this juncture. But he ordered the appropriate blood tests and scheduled another heart catheterization for the first thing next morning. Joan's chest pain soon abated and she seemed quite comfortable, sitting up in a chair in her room.

The blood tests soon revealed that there was an indication of a mild heart attack and Paul made the decision to go ahead with the catheterization procedure the next morning to determine the extent of damage to the heart muscles, if any. The result was the proverbial good news and bad news. First, and most important, there was no sign of any damage to the heart itself. Unfortunately,

Dr. Sherry also discovered that three of the five bypasses that had been constructed the previous year had collapsed or were no longer functioning because of occlusions. In addition, one of the stents that had been inserted in one of her coronary arteries was also occluded. But, remarkably, he also found evidence that small, new coronary arteries had been spontaneously generated and were providing some blood supply to the left ventricle.

"You're one in a million, Joan," he told her. "With all those occlusions and collapsed bypasses, you should have been in a huge amount of pain, completely out of breath, and barely able to function. But you seem to be doing very well. Then, on top of all that, to find that new arteries are picking up some of the role of those that you've lost is not just rare, it's amazing. It must be that you have a very skilled guardian angel looking over you or all the good care that this guy is giving you," he concluded, nodding his head toward me.

Joan smiled and agreed that both were working on her behalf, "And you're the guardian angel," she told him.

Paul saw no reason that Joan needed to remain in the hospital, and after the mandatory six-hour wait, flat on one's back with a pressure pack on the incision where the catheter had been inserted into the femoral artery in her groin, he would leave orders for her to be discharged and we could go home. If only the first heart attack had been that uneventful.

I'm not sure about the Thanksgiving holiday, or whether heart attacks are like earthquakes where after-shocks are common, but just five weeks after the most recent attack, Joan was back in the hospital again. We had a wonderful Thanksgiving dinner with family and friends. Joan had seemed to be in excellent spirits and energetic throughout the day. But as we were preparing for bed that evening, I saw her go to her nightstand where she kept a small bottle of Nitrostat and take one.

"You're having chest pains again, aren't you!" I demanded.

"They're not that bad, and they'll go away," she countered.

But my antennae were up to the max and I had her sit down while we saw whether she was right or not. Sure enough we were back in the hospital that very night with Patti Friesen once again having cleared her admission in advance and having a bed waiting for her in the coronary care ward. Fortunately, this heart attack was much like the most recent one. Again she was catheterized; no appreciable damage was found to the heart itself; but this time there was an opportunity to possibly clear some of the occlusive buildup in one of the main arteries and an angioplasty[45] was conducted.

This procedure apparently was effective, as Joan's condition improved rapidly and she was released to return home. Joan had now experienced three myocardial infarctions in just a little over a year. She had open-heart surgery following the first one, and it was nearly six months before she recovered from that initial crisis. The next two were, fortunately, far less critical and she quickly rebounded from each one. She would have been inhuman if she did not experience some amount of depression and anxiety, but each time she rebounded with amazing speed and her attitude had essentially been very positive, and she was fully willing to continue her inspirational fight for survival.

But the worst was yet to come. Unlike the old adage, this time things didn't necessarily come in threes. For it was only six weeks later on January 6 that yet another MI occurred and this one required emergency ambulance service to bring her to the hospital, where she was immediately sent to the CCU.

After a very brief examination, the degree of seriousness became very apparent to me as Dr. Sherry asked me to leave the room—something he never had done before when performing a sensitive procedure—as he was going to insert a Swan-Ganz catheter[46] into Joan's pulmonary artery. Catheters for angiographies

---

[45]   In an angioplasty, the catheter is tipped with a small balloon, which is inflated when it is properly positioned at the point of the blockage. Then the balloon is inflated, pressing the occlusive material (plaque) back against the arterial wall and thus opening the artery to greater blood flow.

[46]   The Swan-Ganz catheter is named for its inventors and is also known as a pulmonary artery catheter. It is normally inserted into the patient's pulmonary artery in the neck and is threaded directly into the heart with multiple sensors in the various heart chambers. The pulmonary artery catheter allows direct, simultaneous measurement of pressures in the right atrium, right ventricle, pulmonary artery, and the filling pressure ("wedge" pressure) of the left atrium (National Institute of Health, online medical dictionary).

are introduced into a large vein or artery, often in the groin, where the blood pressure is less and, therefore, the procedure is less risky. However this catheterization was to be in a major artery in Joan's neck where pressures are higher and the risk can unquestionably be life threatening.

Paul explained this to us both before beginning, but he felt that it was imperative to insert the catheter if he were to determine precisely where the problems existed and, perhaps, develop a strategy to effectuate some improvement in her condition. He also told me privately that without such an intervention, he didn't believe that Joan could survive.   When I saw the blood-soaked sheets being removed following his successful placement of the catheter, it became very apparent why Paul chose not to have me present.

When Sam awoke from the mild sedation that preceded the procedure, she was groggy and nauseous but seemed otherwise in good spirits. The second-by-second data was recorded and Paul, as well as other colleagues of his, spent a great amount of effort analyzing the data and discussing their conclusions. Privately, he told me that he and the others saw very little possibility of saving her unless some major intervention was undertaken—by which he meant that the principal hope was another open-heart bypass operation, or in the technical terminology, a CABG (pronounced as an acronym "cabbage") or a Coronary Artery Bypass Graft.

That evening, I sat with Sam, and for a while Anne and Dan joined us, to discuss what her views were toward undergoing the same procedure she had been through just fourteen months before.

"They're going to have to guarantee me a whole lot of years ahead of me to live, and a lot easier time than I had last time, in order for me to agree to go through that again," she told us. "I'm sorry, dear, I know you want to do everything possible to keep me alive and I love you for that. But if I don't have a life that's worth living, and I'm nothing but a burden on you and the family, there's no reason for me to be alive. I hope you'll understand and support me when decision-making time comes, and from what Paul said when he left, that's going to be early tomorrow morning."

And that was exactly correct. At 0700 the next morning, a group of four doctors came into Joan's room: Dr. Albert, the cardiac surgeon who had performed her previous surgery, one of his colleagues, Paul

Sherry, and one of his partners at Parkside Cardiology Associates. They had met previously, discussed her case at great length, and reached the same conclusion that Paul had hinted at the evening before.

Joan told them at the outset that her mind was a little fuzzy from all the medications she had been taking and that she appreciated their courtesy in addressing their concerns directly to her. But she felt that she would be better served if I represented her in the discussion that was about to take place. All agreed, of course.

After I confirmed that they had come to recommend another CABG and they admitted that this was correct, I came directly to the point. "If we were to do nothing, and I were to take Joan home as she is now, how long do you think she will survive?"

They looked from one to another as if they were reluctant to answer, but finally Paul replied that the consensus was that Joan would probably be gone in six weeks to two months.

I then asked them how long they thought her life could or would be extended if she were to have the surgery.

Once again, they conveyed a sense of reluctance to answer, but Paul spoke up to say that they thought that she'd have at least six months before she would succumb.

"I know that you're all committed to saving lives and Joan and I appreciate that you want to do everything you possibly can to keep her alive. But I also know that Joan's experience following the last bypass surgery she had was miserable. And when you trade off two months of relatively quiet existence against six months of pain and misery, it isn't worth it to Joan, and as much as I want her to be with me forever, I don't want to see her go through that again. We decided last night that we respectfully decline, and Joan just wants to go home for her final days."

Then I turned to Sam and asked her if that's what she wished me to say. With a strong voice and a look of absolute conviction on her face she told them this was exactly what she wanted. Then the other three doctors each shook Joan's and my hand and, with heads bowed, quietly filed out of the room. They seemed to know that this would be her answer—and we suspected that Paul had already briefed them to that effect—and there was no point in further argument. The following quotation from Dr. Sherry's notes, transcribed on February 1, 2002, tell the story from his perspective.

Joan had a very difficult time with coronary disease from diabetes. She is a non-candidate for another CABG for a number of reasons. The first and foremost reason is that she simply does not desire to go through another difficult heart surgery. She also states that she does not wish to pursue another coronary intervention, as the last one was very difficult for her. She developed cardiogenic shock on the cath lab table and had intractable severe vomiting. She asked me today if it would be possible to just take pain medications at home and ride out any other heart attacks that might occur.

I informed the patient that it would be perfectly appropriate to take pain medication if she gets into a severe chest pain syndrome again. I certainly understand that she is exhausted with the number of coronary and peripheral vascular procedures that have been done. Her long term prognosis is poor and she knows this. I explained to her and her husband that the major goals would be to enjoy what remaining quality of life she has at home. I have given her a prescription for intravenous Demerol and intravenous Phenergan should she get into severe chest pain syndrome at home. She really would prefer to not have to be admitted to the hospital should these problems develop.

I can readily imagine how difficult it was for Paul to dictate these words. No person could have tried any harder to save Joan from this apparent fate than he had, and I detected a note of defeat in the way he expressed himself while composing these words.

Paul also told me that he originally thought Joan should be admitted to a hospice center, but after seeing how determined she was to go home, he had changed his mind. However, before we left the hospital, he would arrange for a home hospice nurse to visit Joan at least three times each week.

There was work to be done before Sam was to be released from the hospital. Much of it was training me in the details of her care.

She needed to have a PICC[47] line installed first and then I needed to learn how to keep the entry area sterile by changing the dressing that protected it, once weekly. I was also instructed on how to administer the pain medications, how to monitor her fluid retention, and was given fairly wide latitude in judging what should and should not be done for her continuing care. My extensive education undertaken by Dr. Sherry was going to be put to the test. At the same time, I also assured Dr. Sherry and Patti that I would immediately report any changes that occurred or actions I had taken.

The first days at home were frightening to say the least. While neither of us actually articulated our fears, the prospect of her dying in her sleep or going into the agonizing constrictions of a massive heart attack were foremost in both of our minds. Sam spent much of the first days at home in our bed, and when I didn't have any pressing chores to take care of, I would sit by her side of the bed reading a book and usually holding her hand. It was like the certainty of catastrophe was imminent but if we tried very hard to ignore it, it might just go away.

On her second evening home, she seemed to be dozing, but suddenly opened her eyes, and without any preliminary comment, asked me to get a legal pad of paper and a pen. For about the next half hour, she sat nearly upright in the bed, with a bolster to support her back and the pad of paper on her knee. Occasionally she jotted something down and then spent some time looking at the ceiling, obviously deep in thought. I had no idea what she was doing, but figured I'd find out in due time, so I became engrossed once again in the book I was reading. Finally, she handed me the pad, and I was surprised to see that it just contained two lists of names on either side of the page. As I glanced at it briefly, I recognized the names, but it made no sense to me otherwise. So finally, I just asked her, "What's this?"

---

[47]   A PICC line is a peripherally inserted central catheter, a small plastic tubing that (in Joan's case) was inserted in her upper arm just above the bend in her elbow. It is threaded through the venous system until the other end is emplaced directly into the heart. It is used for intravenous administration of drugs as well as for drawing blood for testing.

With utter sincerity on her face and especially in her eyes, she informed me, "I know that I don't have long to live but I also know that the loneliness of your living alone for long will be disastrous for you. You are not a loner and I know that the best way to prevent that is for you to get married again soon after I'm gone. So I've made out a list for you to help you decide who you're going to marry next. The column on the left contains the names of the women you should marry, in the order that I recommend The column on the right contains the names of the women who I don't want you to marry because they would all bring more problems to the union than happiness. Call it intuition, but I just don't think any of them are right for you."

As I looked at the left column, I couldn't believe my eyes. The first person on the list was a woman who almost became a nun many years before, and still had never been married even though she was nearing seventy years old. Number two was a much younger woman who was married, and when I questioned Sam on that, she replied matter-of-factly, "She won't be in a little while!"

As I looked down both columns, I didn't have the heart to tell her that the only women who were listed there who could interest me in the slightest were the ones in the no-no column. But I merely thanked her for her help, trying all the while to stifle impolite laughter. As time passed following that evening, and Joan's health stabilized once again, we had a number of laughs over "the list," but I know deep down that she was never more sincere in her life than she was that evening.

The hospice nurse was a very nice and a highly skilled woman. She was both compassionate and considerate in treating Joan, and was also concerned about how I was doing in the hour-to-hour care I was providing. She had watched me change the dressing on the PICC line, had seen me flush the line with heparin, as is periodically necessary, and would ask me a number of "what if" questions related to Joan's care.

Finally, at the end of the second week of her coming, she told us she was required to submit a report at the end of each week, which concluded with her recommendation as to whether further hospice care was warranted.

"I hate to admit it," she told Joan, "but I'm not doing a single thing for you that your husband isn't fully capable of doing. And, more important, he's very well attuned to your condition and is skilled at noticing any changes. So unless you have any strong objections, I'm going to recommend that home hospice care for you be suspended. Certainly, if things should change for the worse, all you need to do is call and I or one of my colleagues will return with regular visits."

She then gave me the phone number of an office in Denver, which provided all the specialized supplies that were needed for Joan's continuing care and told us they would respond over night with replacement dressings, medications, or anything else that was needed.

Quite candidly, I felt comfortable performing the various tasks that were incidental to Sam's care with the nurse watching me, but I felt a little nervous when it became apparent I was to be on my own from here on out. Then I realized that every time in my career that a supervisor thought I was ready for greater responsibility, I was nervous but had always risen to the challenge. This time, however, I was out of my element and Sam's life was literally at stake. But as the days went by, my confidence grew and far better yet, Joan was hardly appearing like someone who was living on borrowed time. Our weekly visits to Dr. Sherry's office confirmed this fact, and Paul's disbelief at her progress put a strong exclamation point on her improvement. She was becoming known in his office as the Miracle Woman.

One night sometime later, Joan sensed that I was briefly awake in the wee hours of the morning. I had probably gotten up to go to the bathroom.

"Did something wake you up other than the need to go?" she asked. When I told her that nothing had and asked her the reason for the question, she began to relate another eerie tale that, to this day, I have absolutely no reason to doubt.

She said that minutes before I had gotten up, she had been awakened by a very bright white light coming from the bathroom, the entrance to which was directly beside my side of the bed.

"I lifted my head to see if you were in there, but I couldn't understand why the light was so brilliant. When I saw that you were still beside me and looked beyond where you were lying, I saw a young man standing in the doorway and he was looking right at both of us. He was dressed all in white and it seemed like he was wearing a flowing robe of some sort. His hair was almost white it was so blond and he had a short goatee or a full blond beard, I'm not sure which. When I lifted my head up, he smiled at me and I was frightened to death. I started to wake you but I was afraid that he would attack you if I did. Then he just kept smiling and nodding his head as if he agreed with something or he was offering his approval.

"I'm not sure how long he stood there as we stared into each other's eyes but I had a sense of serenity come over me and I was no longer afraid that he was there to do either of us any harm. Just about that time, he began to rise up into the air very slowly. And as he went higher, the brightness of the light began to fade. Then suddenly he disappeared through the ceiling and the light went out completely.

"That no sooner happened then you started to stir and got up to go to the bathroom. That's why I asked you if you had heard something. I've been wide awake ever since I saw the bright light so I know what I saw was not a dream."

With that, I turned on the light and there was no question that Sam, somewhat notorious for waking rather slowly in the morning, was indeed wide awake. She told me that the person she saw was not like any preconception that she had of what Jesus looked like and was not about to conclude that she had been visited by the Lord.

Once again, I suspect that, if a psychologist were consulted, this event might be classified as mild hysteria brought on by the psychological trauma of the diagnosis she had recently experienced. But as I had concluded after her out-of-body experience while undergoing open heart surgery, I was convinced that Sam was relating exactly what she had seen and I was not about to try to dissuade her from what she believed to have been real.

In attempting to analyze what had happened that night, we could only conclude that she had possibly seen a guardian angel— without wings—who was simply assuring her that she was going to survive this traumatic period. And whether or not that was a correct or believable analysis, we know with complete certainty from that day on that Joan's health improved remarkably and she outlived, by far, the dire predictions that had been made by a team of skilled physicians. Her eponym, the Miracle Woman, seemed more and more to have been justifiably anointed.

We had a weekly appointment with Dr. Sherry for the first four weeks after Joan was allowed to go home from the hospital and at each one, he would break out in a smile after examining her. Finally, at the end of the fourth week, he suggested that she could wait for a full two weeks before returning. When we did, he didn't simply smile; he broke out in a broad grin and even had the hint of a tear in his eye.

"I can't believe how good you look and how well everything checks out," he began. "I guess you knew a lot more about who you are and what your abilities are than we did, but right now, rather than slowly deteriorating as we predicted you would, you're in much better shape than you were on the day you were released from the hospital. I have no other explanation for it than the fact that your determination and will to live have overwhelmed what medical science dictated should happen to you. And maybe the great care this guy gives you has made a big difference as well," he concluded, nodding toward me.

Then he paused noticeably, looking quite pensive before he continued on. "Is there something that you'd like to do more than anything else that you can think of right now?"

Sam didn't hesitate for an instant. "I'd like to go back to France, to see Paris once more and to visit the dear friends we had when we lived in Alsace just after we were first married."

Paul seemed slightly surprised by the answer, but immediately replied, "Then go ahead and do it—but do it quickly!"

She didn't need a second invitation. Before the early evening, she had made flight reservations for us from Colorado Springs to Paris, train reservations to Strasbourg where our friends live, and had begun to make out her packing list for the trip. Meanwhile, I had made lodging reservations for us at the Cercle National des Armées, the French officers' club in Paris, where I am an associate member, and had called our French friends, Jacques and Liliane Wehr, to assure that they would be home for our visit. What a miraculous turn of events, indeed.

Before we headed off to France, I asked Patti to check with Paul to see just how confident he was that Joan could survive such a trip. She told me that he wouldn't have agreed to it if he didn't think she were capable of handling it. But just to be on the safe side, I should pack a separate bag with all the special medications that I had been using over the previous month and a half. And despite the fact that none of the IV pain medications had been used, I should certainly bring along the morphine-based drugs to ease Joan's pain in the event things became dire. All Sam's special meds, wound and PICC line dressings, and the painkillers constituted virtually the entire contents of my carry-on bag when we began our journey a few days later.

It never occurred to me that the security checks now in effect at the airport might conceivably cause us some amount of difficulty. I probably should have gotten a letter signed by Paul to indicate that these items were needed for a potential emergency. But then I also realized that we had flown since the 9/11 attack changed all that and each time we had her diabetic equipment, including syringes, in our carry-on bag. And besides, it was too late to do anything about it by that time. In reality, it proved to be no problem on the way to Europe but returning was a different story.

When we were going through the security check at Charles DeGaulle International Airport on our way home, the x-ray equipment found something suspicious, so my carry-on had to be examined by a security inspector. He kept digging and digging through the bag, moving some of the contents on to the table, while shoving others out of the way. Finally, he drew back triumphantly, as if he had found the "missing link," and held up the offending item between his thumb and forefinger. It was a corkscrew!

He told me in French that he would have to confiscate it, and I replied, also in French, that it looked like there would be no wine drunk by us tonight in the States. He gave me that marvelous Gallic shrug and the out-thrust of his lower lip and replied, "*Quelle domage!* [too bad!]," and I think he meant it sincerely. It just seemed so ironic that I had thousands of dollars worth of narcotics that were pushed aside and ignored in order to confiscate that threatening corkscrew. It must have been an easy time for smuggling drugs.

Our visits to both Paris and to our friends' home in Illkirch-Graffenstaden, a suburb of Strasbourg, could not have been more wonderful. Sam got to see the Paris she loved so much, even though it was primarily by taxi, rather than the wonderful, leisurely walks along the Champs-Elysées we had taken there so many times before. But we still stopped at favorite sidewalk cafes for a glass of wine; we still ate onion soup with Beaujolais rosé wine at the Au Pied de Cochon restaurant in the old central market district of Les Halles; and we still managed a half day at the Musée d'Orsay, the old train station that has been converted into a magnificent impressionist art museum. It was Sam's Paris and it was so wonderful to see the joy in her eyes and the swelling of her spirit as each day passed.

In Strasbourg, however, we got down to business and began her physical therapy program in earnest. Jacques and Liliane live in a delightful neighborhood of lovely detached homes, all beautifully maintained and landscaped, and, most important, on completely flat terrain. Each morning and each afternoon, Sam and I went out for a walk. It was admittedly short (about one hundred meters) and slow at first and we made frequent pauses for her to rest. But on each successive day, the walk became a little longer, the pace picked up a little, and the pauses became fewer. Sam didn't particularly like to walk and I know that she was having some amount of pain, but she was also reinforced by her growing strength and duration each day. By the end of our ten days with the Wehrs, she was walking over seven hundred meters (close to a half mile), all the way to the canal that led to the Rhein River and back. France had clearly been the best medicine possible for her.

On our final night in Paris on our way home, with the specter still clearly in mind that this would be our last time together in the City of Lights, I decided it was time for a dinner we would never forget. I selected Restaurant Les Ambassadeurs at Hôtel de Crillon on the Place de Concorde, for both the superb quality of the food and wine as well as the amazing architecture of the restaurant itself. The dining room is two stories in height and features elegant gold marble columns throughout, with matching walls made of the same marble, gorgeous crystal chandeliers, and contrasting maroon drapes and table settings. It is the epitome of old-world luxury and has a reputation for excellence to match.

When we were seated at our table, Sam looked around and with her typical practicality, stage whispered to me, "My God, how much is this going to cost?"

I told her not to worry about it; we could afford it. And the dinner was everything I hoped it would be. The wait staff was superb. They recognized that this was a very special occasion, even though they had no idea what we were actually celebrating. They greatly appreciated that I spoke French to them—and I appreciated the fact that I still could. It just seemed to make it that much more romantic. We lingered for nearly three hours over four small, superb courses and finished with espresso and cognac—each of which was refilled. But this time, nearly forty-five years after her first trip to Paris, my now elegant, sophisticated, lovely wife never even considered putting a sugar cube in the cognac.

The entire evening had been like a dream sequence, as if we were totally alone in this most elegant ambience, with only the occasional fade-in, fade-out interruption of the waiters and sommelier. As we clinked our cognac glasses for the final time that evening, she leaned toward me, and looked directly in my eyes with her enigmatic smile and told me, "We both know why you insisted on doing this tonight and I want you to know that I love you dearly and appreciate it very much. It's been truly memorable."

With every conceivable emotion racing around in my mind, not the least of it being fear that this was the end of a most important chapter in our lives together, the only thing that came to mind to say was, "You're worth it, love. And I just wish we had done it when we arrived also."

And so, with what we both thought was our farewell tour of our beloved Paris, our trip to France came to an end.

*   *   *

On our next appointment with Dr. Sherry, he was even more surprised and pleased than he had been before we left. He expected that the trip would have taken the starch completely out of Joan, but yet she looked better than she had in months. And she felt better too. As we walked through the nurses' station, which was in a centrally located quadrangle with corridors going in every direction toward the treatment rooms, seemingly all the doctors and nurses, Paul's colleagues at Parkside Cardiology, emerged from every direction to shake Joan's hand and tell her how pleased they were with her progress. Not a few people commented on their belief that she truly was a miracle woman.

As the weeks and months rolled on and Sam became stronger and stronger, we were at a total loss to determine why she had not only outlived all expectations, but even more important was that she was hardly a bed-ridden invalid as was the general expectation. It was not an unreasonable conclusion that the trip to France had played a part in her recovery—as, of course, did the ideal mix of medications devised by Dr. Sherry, and a prudent diet and regular exercise. But more than anything, we were both buoyed by the avalanche of prayers and good wishes showered on her from literally every corner of the globe. Sam logically figured that if her health had improved so dramatically from that one trip to France, it should improve even more if we did more traveling. Thus began a series of at least three trips each year, many of which lasted more than three weeks in duration.

But first there was a "minor" coronary artery problem and Joan entered the hospital in April for another heart catheterization and the implanting of more stents in her coronary arteries. Sam acted as if it were the equivalent of getting her teeth cleaned—it was a little uncomfortable for a while but she felt better once it had been done. She treated each of these problems as if they were merely annoying gnats that she wanted to put behind her so she could get on with the more important things in life.

Just two months later, in June to be precise, one of my nieces, Elaine Sullivan, and her husband, Jerry, had planned a family reunion at their home in Sharon, Massachusetts. This had been their periodic gift to the Toner family-at-large ever since we had begun the tradition of reunions at the Birchwood Inn over a decade before. However, not even I thought that Joan would be up to the trip back east so soon after we had been to France and so soon after the catheterization. But she absolutely insisted on our going. "I wouldn't miss it for the world," she told me, and I had no way of arguing with her that she couldn't. She was blooming with good health, at least considering all she had been through.

Once again, she seemed to thrive on the travel and the excitement of going somewhere we never thought she could. And this was to set a pattern for the next four years. It seemed that each time we returned from a trip, Joan would begin planning for the next one. The old adage that the planning and getting there is half the fun of vacations was unquestionably true in Joan's case. After resisting for years, she even became proficient in the use of a computer, sending off emails and surfing the Internet simply to facilitate her planning efforts.

So it came as no surprise to me when she presented me with a detailed itinerary for Anne, Dan, and the two of us to make a driving trip to the Grand Canyon in late August. None of us had ever seen this most magnificent of natural wonders, and it just made good sense that we shouldn't miss the opportunity. Her planning was totally complete and impeccably done, and having been a professional planner for part of my Air Force career, that's a high compliment. To no one's surprise, the trip went off perfectly and we had a wonderful time together—even though it snowed there in late August that year.

From the end of 2002 through 2007, we began every year the same way. Christine, Mike, and their family would come every January for a week of skiing at Breckenridge, Colorado. And the last week in February we went to Mammoth, California, for the WWWG ski reunion, sometimes flying to Reno and renting a car and on a couple of occasions taking a leisurely two-day drive across Utah and Nevada. Yet again, each trip was a tonic for her. But these were just the appetizers. The main courses were always planned for later in each year.

In April of 2003, we took our first in a series of cruises. We flew to England where we boarded a Norwegian Cruise Line ship for a cruise to various Baltic Sea ports, including St. Petersburg, Russia, for the three hundredth anniversary of the founding of that magnificent city by Peter the Great. Sam's trip planning was briefly interrupted by the need for an infected toe to be amputated, followed by thirty consecutive days of two-hour hyperbaric chamber treatments to save the toes she had left. But that was not about to stop her.

In August, we boarded a Holland-America Lines ship in San Francisco, visited ports in Mexico and Costa Rica, traversed the Panama Canal to the Atlantic, visited Caribbean ports, and then came up the East Coast of the States to debark in Boston. The whole concept of cruises truly appealed to her as she was able to do as much or as little as she wanted while still relaxing and seeing and doing things we'd never done before.

We finished off the year with a trip to Florida in November to visit with Christine, Mike, and our grandchildren, Dan and Colleen. Sam loved her privacy and also never wanted to cause any inconvenience to others. So on this visit, and subsequent ones, we always stayed at the VOQ at Patrick AFB, which was literally minutes away from the Moody home in Merritt Island.

The year 2004 was the only year since we sold the inn and moved to Colorado that Joan didn't have a major medical problem requiring hospitalization. But whether or not a hospital stay was necessary, Sam always had a trip or two in her hip pocket and was ready to roll at a moment's notice. So naturally we were on the go for much of the year.

Perhaps the best of all was a trip via a canal hotel barge in May in the Burgundy region of France. We met Jacques and Liliane at the barge in Dijon, along with the fifteen other fellow passengers, and embarked on one of the nicest weeks we've ever shared. Accommodations were a little tight, as one might expect on a barge, but all we did was sleep in the cabin and the rest of the time it was pure fun with a delightful group of old and new friends.

We had arrived in and departed from Paris on our round-trip to France, having taken the TGV, or bullet train, to and from there to Dijon. While we were both inwardly surprised and delighted that our previous visit to Paris was not, in fact, our *adieu* to our favorite city, neither of us commented directly on the fact, perhaps in a subconscious fear that it might jinx the possibility of returning ever again.

We were in the market for a new car that summer so we took advantage of an offer by Volvo to send us to the factory in Gothenburg, Sweden, to take delivery on a new Volvo XC-70. The idea of Volvo, SAS, and the Swedish tourist board paying our transportation was sufficient inducement to buy a car we wanted anyway, but when they were going to pay for part of our stay in that lovely country, it was an offer we couldn't refuse. And to top that off, after we toured southern Sweden for a week, we returned the car to the factory and six weeks later it was delivered to us in Colorado Springs. All this, and the price was considerably lower than we would have paid off the showroom floor. We just wished later that we had stayed longer and seen more of the Scandinavian countries while we had the opportunity.

In August, Sam, Anne, and Dan had a surprise seventieth birthday party for me, which was truly a surprise. I had no inkling of all the planning going on behind my back. Sam always complained that she never could get away with anything because I was constantly alert to what was going on around me. But they certainly fooled me on this occasion. Dozens of old friends and family members came from all over the country to attend and I was shocked when I saw them all gathered in the dining room of the Air Force Academy officer's club—after being lured there under false pretenses by our friends, Elaine and Roger Williamson. To top off the four-day weekend, Dan and I both made a sky-dive from 14,000 feet to the amazement (and fear, for some) of those who were there. Joan wasn't especially enamored of that event, but she easily integrated it with all the other events, to no one's surprise.

It only seemed fair that the following February I lured Joan to a surprise birthday party for her. We were invited to go to Omaha, allegedly just to visit our friends, Karen and Tom Gensler, but it was actually to celebrate her reaching three score and ten. As someone later mentioned, who in the world would go to Omaha in mid-winter if it weren't for a very special occasion? All our children were there, plus Joan's cousin, Bill McCormack, and his wife, Jeanne, came from Boston to help celebrate. Karen and Tom hosted a marvelous dinner that rivaled the best restaurants in the world in elegance, ambience, and culinary artistry. It had been ages since I'd seen Sam enjoy herself as much as she did that weekend. It was one more memorable time to lock into our treasure chest.

Cruising was once again part of our agenda, and in late spring of 2005 we sailed from Fort Lauderdale across the Atlantic and then made a number of port visits in the Azores, Spain, Monaco, and Italy as Holland-America was repositioning a its newest ship,

MS *Westerdam*, for Mediterranean summer cruises. We had a very comfortable small suite with a balcony, but there's not all that much to see when one is at sea for five days. This adventure sure beat the socks off my previous Atlantic crossings courtesy of a U.S. Navy cruiser and destroyer.

In August we had another family reunion in Washington and Annapolis when my Naval Academy class did me the great honor of representing them with an after-dinner speech to the USNA class of 2007. Our class is fifty years senior to theirs, and we had adopted the class of 2007, as part of the academy's "Link in the Chain" program, when they entered the academy as plebes. The occasion was their Commitment Dinner at which the midshipmen signed on for at least seven more years of service. Sam was the most beautiful I had seen her in ages that evening, and it was a thrill to show her off before over one thousand two hundred future naval officers.

Sam was getting more and more daring in her trip planning and our most adventurous cruise yet was to take place in the spring of 2006. Days before we were to leave home, Sam received a call from the cruise line asking her if she'd like to upgrade our accommodations to a captain's suite for a very small increase in cost and she jumped at the chance. It was to turn out to be a superb decision. Our trip began in Valparaiso, Chile, and we headed south, stopping at various Chilean ports and sailing right up to the glaciers in the Patagonian fjords.

We then rounded the Horn with a somewhat stormy passage through the straits of Magellan. In our luxury accommodations aboard a small Norwegian Cruise Lines ship we gained only a slight appreciation for the intrepid mariners who went through these same waters in tiny sailing ships centuries ago. Our journey then took us from the Straits to the Falkland Islands and then up the coast of Argentina. Our final port call was in Montevideo, Uruguay, and we left the ship in Buenos Aires from where we flew back home after a few days of sightseeing there.

We got home just in time to go to Boston for another family reunion hosted by the Sullivans at their home in Sharon, Massachusetts. This also was a family send-off for Anne and Dan as they were moving to England where they would become managers of a restaurant and traditional English pub, a goal in life they had aspired to for years. To say we missed them after they left is a grave understatement.

Unfortunately, the run of good health and lack of hospitalization Joan had enjoyed came crashing down soon after our return from Boston. Somewhere along the way, she developed a staph aureus infection between the bone and steel plate in her right tibia, a seemingly non-threatening event that turned out to be anything but.

After a lengthy process of trying to rid her of the infection with IV antibiotics, the decision was made that the plate Dr. Jupiter had emplaced fourteen years before needed to be removed. This would entail major surgery, of course, but Sam yet again accepted her fate stoically. As an orthopedic procedure, we both recognized that pain and a long rehabilitation process would ensue, but never gave a thought to the possibility that it would become life threatening. Unfortunately, she lost a lot of blood and whole blood transfusions were necessary, resulting in a severe hemolytic[48] reaction.

It was essential that the red blood cells being destroyed be replaced by additional transfusions that were properly typed and matched to her own blood. Consequently, she was placed on an oncology ward with a full-time hematologist on staff to monitor her recovery. During the week she had spent there, Joan received the last rites of the Catholic Church for the second time.

Immediately prior to the operation, I suggested to the orthopedic surgeon that I thought it would be wise to place her leg in a cast since the plate had been the basis for support for many years and once it was removed, her tibia would be significantly weakened. I was also concerned that there were eighteen screws in her leg holding the plate in place, and when they were removed, the holes left behind would further weaken the bone.

---

[48] In the hemolytic reaction that Joan suffered, the transfused blood apparently contained antibodies that did not match those in her system and these antibodies in turn began to attack her red blood cells causing them to burst and very rapidly bring on a severe immuno-reaction which, if not recognized immediately, could have resulted in death.

The doctor insisted that a cast was not necessary as x-rays of the tibia showed that it had completely healed over the years. He said he planned to put a brace on her leg similar to a walking cast and it would provide sufficient support for whatever weakness was caused in her surgery.

During her week in the oncology ward, Joan gradually recovered from the reaction, and was ready to take her first steps with the new brace in place following the plate removal. She said her initial steps were surprisingly comfortable but suddenly she winced with severe pain. When the surgeon came later that day—a Friday afternoon to be more precise—he insisted that it was normal pain and the more she walked, the more comfortable she would be. His prediction couldn't have been more wrong!

Joan tried on a few occasions to test out his theory, but finally, as her pain became more intense, she told me that it was beyond what she could tolerate and felt that she had broken her tibia once more. When the operating physician's colleague who had the weekend duty came by to see Joan on Saturday morning, I insisted he order an x-ray of the leg, and after he tested the lower leg by moving it with his hands—and saw Joan's reaction—he agreed with her surmise that the tibia was broken again.

A portable x-ray machine was brought into her room, the diagnosis was confirmed, and moments later a cast crew assisted the doctor in resetting her leg in a hip-to-toe cast. Before he left, I told him that his fellow orthopedist had declined to put the cast on, had been the cause of undoing literally decades of therapy, and as emphatically as I could, I told him that I would never again let that man near my wife. He accepted my tirade gracefully, knowing full well that I had every reason to be irate.

He went on to tell me that this new break was going to be a significant challenge and he only knew of one person who was up to the challenge. Another of his colleagues, Dr. Rick Meinig, had recently completed a residency in trauma surgery and he was quite certain that Meinig could handle the problem. He also assured me that the doctor who had bungled the post-surgical care would be taken off her case and I wouldn't have to deal with him ever again.

Rick Meinig was indeed the person who could get Joan to walk once more, but it was going to be a long, difficult and near-disastrous series of events before we reached that point. And we were back again where Miss Daisy rode in the back seat everywhere we went. The process of removing her cast, taking x-rays, discovering that little to no healing had taken place, and then placing Joan back in a cast again, continued monthly through early August. Finally, Dr. Meinig came to the conclusion that further attempts to gain a natural knitting of the bone would just lead to further failures.

For the first time, I heard Sam suggest that perhaps it was time to amputate her leg at the knee so that she could spend her effort on rehabilitation and adjustment to a prosthesis rather than stay on a yo-yo of experimentation. She was clearly being worn out by the repeated failures and the emotional drain they were causing. But Rick Meinig had one more arrow in his quiver and convinced Joan that this was certain to work. He proposed putting a titanium rod—or nail as he referred to it—into the full length of her tibia. This would provide rigid stability to the bone, the healing would take place around the nail, and with just a little more physical therapy, she'd be as good as new again.

When we discussed this with Paul Sherry, he was reluctant to put his stamp of approval on it, but at the same time he recognized that something had to be done and even an amputation—the last resort so to speak—would involve major surgery. He was at a loss for how her heart had held out as long as it had and deeply concerned that we were reaching the full limit of its capacity to endure. Yet, he reluctantly agreed that there was no other viable option.

In early December, the date was set for the "insertion of the nail" and in an effort to select Joan's optimum physical condition for surgery, the actual date was determined at essentially the last minute. She was to be fit into the operating room schedule and this, unfortunately, meant a late-afternoon time. The surgery was envisioned as an outpatient procedure, meaning that there was a slight possibility she could be released to go home soon after her time in the recovery room. But Joan was hardly an ordinary patient, and the prospects of this happening were slim to none in our judgment.

The procedure went off quite well and within the expected duration Dr. Meinig had forecast. When he emerged from the OR, he seemed quite pleased and told me that Joan had tolerated the procedure very well; he was quite confident that this was the fix they had been searching for. He went on to report that she was in the recovery room, he'd feel much better if she remained over night, and that I would be informed where she was to be taken after recovering from the anesthetic.

The information I was given a half hour later, however, was far from optimistic. Instead of being transferred to a surgical ward, she was being moved to the intensive care unit (ICU). I went there immediately and as soon as I saw Sam, it was clear that things were not good. She was extremely pale, very nauseous, and was having difficulty breathing.

By this time, it was getting on well into the evening and it was clear that not only was she not going home soon, it was imperative that I spend the night in the ICU with her. As time went by, Sam kept slipping in and out of consciousness and we did little except hold hands. Not long after midnight, one of the staff nurses came into the room, hurriedly, and it was obvious from her urgency that the telemetry at the nurses' station had indicated some sort of emergency. Shortly thereafter, the ICU physician, who happened to be an anesthesiologist, was at her bedside and the concern on his face was evident.

Prior to the surgery, Rick Meinig was mindful of the hemolytic reaction Joan had suffered at the end of August and he had her blood typed and matched and had ordered two matching units of whole blood to be available in the event of need. I mentioned that to the attending physician and asked him if Joan had been transfused. He told me she had and his primary concern was that she was having another similar reaction. He then told me he was going to insert an internal jugular vein catheter and I was welcome to stay. But if that would be a problem for me to watch, I'd better leave because they would have their hands full with Joan. I elected to stay.

Moments later, I felt a hand on my back and turned to see that Paul Sherry had entered the tiny room. He must have made an earlier inquiry into her status and had come immediately when he found out that she was in ICU, having no doubt been told that she was in critical condition. Joan's alluding to him previously as her guardian angel seemed to take on much more substantive meaning. I certainly felt very much relieved to have him there even though I wasn't sure what he could do. He had a brief exchange of information with the attending physician and apparently offered to help in any way he could.

When everything that could be done was taking place, I happened to look at my watch and saw that it was 0300. For some unknown reason, I marked that down in my mind and also happened to notice that there were two doctors and four nurses in the room with me, all working feverishly to help her through the battle. I knew that Sam was in very serious condition but didn't realize how serious until Paul came over to me a short while later, put a very comforting hand on my shoulder and said, "I'm sorry to tell you this, but I don't think were going to be able to save her this time."

Having been awake for nearly twenty-four hours straight at this time, I don't think the full impact of what he said registered with me. For some reason, I mentally disagreed. This wasn't even thinkable. I had seen Sam rally from the depths too many times in the past six years to believe she wouldn't do so again. Had that not been the prevalent thought at the time, I'm not sure how I might have reacted, but in fact, I didn't react at all.

The room Joan had been placed in was more like a closet than anything else, but as the charge nurse explained to me later, it was the only bed on the unit open when she had been brought in the evening before. But by dawn, her indomitable spirit apparently took control and she began to stabilize—not that she was out of danger by any means, but at least her condition was no longer worsening. And early in the morning, Sam was moved to a room that was larger and had a window so that at least she had natural light even though she could see very little from her bed.

I was told that her red blood cell count was extremely low and she was, in fact, in the throes of another hemolytic reaction—but this time, no one knew exactly why. She was also experiencing hypovolemic shock,[49] which complicated matters considerably. Both units of blood had been used during the surgery but her periodic blood tests still indicated that she was dangerously anemic and

---

[49]   Hypovolemic shock is a condition whereby the body has lost a considerable amount of fluid, usually blood, which decreases the ability for the blood to circulate to the vital organs (National Institutes of Health, online medical encyclopedia).

would need considerably more transfusions—of the correct match to hers—and an appeal was sent out to the blood center in Denver for two more units. Unfortunately, because of a very low-level communication error, it would be two days before the blood arrived. And it was only through another remarkable show of strength and determination that Joan was able to hang on.

Still later that first morning, the Catholic chaplain came in to see her and for the third time in less than four years, she received the last rites of the Catholic Church. What affect that might have had will never be known, but in talking to Sam over the next few days, it was clear she had been buoyed by the prayers said for her and had no intention of dying just then.

After nearly a week, and two more units of whole blood, Joan was discharged to go home directly from the ICU. In the interim, she had tested out her new leg briefly, putting just a small amount of weight on it as Dr. Meinig had directed. She was understandably weak but insisted that I bring her crutches from home so that she could at least go from the bed to a chair when she wanted. She repeatedly told me that I wasn't getting enough rest, that I shouldn't be spending so much time with her in the hospital, and that she was going to be fine. Clearly, the Miracle Woman had survived despite the pessimistic expectations, and she was going to recover once more.

Christmas had always been Sam's favorite holiday since she was a small child and whether or not she was able to participate actively in putting out the annual decorations she was certainly going to direct the procedure from her command post in the family room. Anne and Dan had come back from England for the holiday and they were an immense help in getting everything just right for the season. And the combination of the seasonal euphoria that she always experienced and having two of her kids back home worked its magic day by day.

We had a quiet New Year's Eve, for obvious reasons, but when we were drinking a champagne toast to her recovery and the fact that she had lived to see a new year, she began to laugh. "You didn't think I could possible die when our golden year is coming up, did you?"

She was referring to the fact that 2007 was to be the fiftieth anniversary of our wedding as well as the fiftieth anniversary of my graduation from the Naval Academy. She had lots of trip planning to do. Sam had been too ill to return to Boston College the previous fall to celebrate the fiftieth anniversary of her graduation, so she was determined that she was going to have a dual celebration of both occasions when mine came around. What an incredible spirit and outlook on life she had!

*   *   *

In an act of recovery that baffles me to this day, Joan was well enough and able to keep our annual date with the Moody family for our ski vacation at Breckenridge. And by the end of February, she was still using crutches but putting full weight on her leg when we returned to Mammoth Mountain for the annual WWWG reunion. I had spoken sparingly about the details of what Joan had been through just two months previously and our friends were aghast when they learned the full story. They agreed that it was miraculous she had once again survived, let alone made it to the reunion.

The focus of Joan's attention quickly shifted after this to planning for our fiftieth anniversary. We had decided earlier that we wanted to celebrate with our far-flung children and their spouses and thought it would be nice if some very close friends were part of it as well. And after much discussion, and with most pleasant memories of our hotel barge trip on the canals of Burgundy, we decided to repeat that for our anniversary.

Europe had unusually hot summers the previous two years, so we did our cruising in May rather than July, our actual anniversary month. Our initial plan was to rent a hotel barge and take our family and many friends with us for a week. Unfortunately, the cost was prohibitive so we settled for two forty-eight-foot cabin cruisers, designed for canal operation, and did our own self-drive tour of the canals. All of our children and their spouses were able to join us. And since we were in France and since Jacques and Liliane Wehr had been with us two years before, we asked them to join us as well. Finally, Karen and Tom Gensler had once said, after hearing about our original canal cruise, that they would join us if we ever did it again. So they filled out the crew of the two boats—with us old geezers on one boat and the younger generation on the other.

It couldn't have been a more wonderful time. The weather was perfect, the boats were very comfortable, and the towns we visited were wonderfully hospitable. And, of course, the food and wine were superb. The memories from that week will last forever. Each time we get together with our former crew members, the stories are retold and the laughs resound again. It couldn't have been a better choice of how to celebrate this singular event.

So, naturally, since we had gone on the cruise two months before our actual anniversary date, we had to celebrate again when the actual date came. This time it was just the two of us, and we went back to one of our favorite places, the old-world Sonnenalp Hotel in Vail. Summer in the mountains was almost as glorious as in winter. We thoroughly enjoyed our three days there of pampering and I had never seen Sam look so radiant. How absolutely remarkable. Her unique ability to keep focused on the future and maintain a positive attitude never ceased to amaze me.

Our second golden anniversary, as noted earlier, was my fiftieth reunion at the Naval Academy, which was in Annapolis at the end of October. We had a record bunch of grizzled old alums show up for the five-day weekend—nearly one thousand counting spouses and other family members. Once again, I had the singular honor of serving as master of ceremonies for the reunion banquet and the feedback was wonderful. As one of my best friend's wife told me, "I didn't know whether to laugh or cry, but I loved every minute of it!" Many of my classmates knew of the severe trials that had plagued Joan over the previous years and were astounded to see her looking so beautiful and so full of life and joy.

*   *   *

Chapter 4

Finally Exhausted

At the end of the reunion of the WWWG in February of 2007, we had a farewell luncheon together at one of our favorite restaurants in Mammoth Lakes. Someone in the group mentioned that, two of our members, Chris House and Tom Anderson, were going to join most of the rest of us and enter their seventies at the end of January 2008. It became instantly clear that that occasion would be yet another cause for celebration, and various ideas were tossed around. The final decision was made right there at the table. Instead of coming to Mammoth, we would meet again in 2008 at Wengen, Switzerland—a delightful Alpine ski village we had visited together nearly thirty years before.

After a year of careful, joint planning—completely executed on our part by Sam—in late January of 2008, we met at the combined airport and train station in Zurich. And after two changes of trains and some deft maneuvering with Joan—who needed a wheelchair because of her lack of endurance—we arrived nearly twenty-four hours after our departure and got settled at the luxurious Caprice Hotel. Sam had completed the trip exceptionally well, and in keeping with her usual positive outlook, she was delighted with the ambience of the hotel and the remarkable scenery of the view from the deck outside our room.

I chose not to ski the next day, still feeling a bit sluggish from the trip, so the two of us relaxed and enjoyed the gorgeous day and a lovely lunch on the restaurant deck. All was right with the world that day and I probably could easily have been talked into spending each day that same way. But I chose to ski the next day—after all, it was one of the principal reasons we were in Wengen rather than simply driving to the Colorado mountains—but that decision was to prove to be a critical one.

The two Toms (Anderson, who is known as T. I., and House, who goes by Tom) and I set off at a decent, gentlemanly hour and ended our morning at a restaurant high up on the mountains at the base of the Eiger Glacier. Once again the weather was perfect. We were exhilarated by the morning and looked forward to wending our way back on the other side of the mountain to the village way below. Upon reaching a fork in the trails, so to speak, we elected to ski down the Lauberhorn World Cup downhill run, where the annual race had taken place just ten days previously (though we would ski much more slowly than the racers).

Without going into any of the hows and whys of the incident, I was run into by a young Swiss man who was out of control and skiing far too fast for the conditions. He hit me full force with the top of his helmet in the left rib cage, leaving both him and me writhing in pain on the side of the slope. As soon as they could, my friends evacuated me from the immediate area to avoid a further collision and a likely calamity, due to the blind nature of the curve we were on.

Unlike U.S. ski areas, one rarely finds a ski patroller on the vast, open European slopes, so I elected to ski the rest of the way back to the village—a run of four or five kilometers with Tom leading and T. I. bringing up the rear. It was seriously painful but we managed to handle the return without much difficulty. Soon after, I was taken to the local clinic by the hotel owner, Christian Aubert, our most solicitous and accommodating innkeeper. The clinic doctor, using very low-resolution x-ray equipment, thought she saw a fractured rib, so she gave me some pain medication and sent me back to the hotel. I had broken ribs before and knew there was little but time that would heal them, so I ended my ski vacation and looked forward to Sam's and my quiet time together for the remainder of the week. But that was not to be.

A few nights later, I was wakened in the wee hours with excruciating pain in my chest and thus began a three-hour odyssey of a visit to the clinic (the head doctor claimed I needed immediate hospitalization), a cog train ride to Lauterbrunnen, and an ambulance ride to the hospital in Interlaken. There they quickly discovered that I was in critical condition with a huge buildup of fluid in my pleural cavity, apparent damage to the left lung and thirteen fractures in eight of my ribs on the left side. After immediate emergency surgery, I was placed in the intensive care unit where I was to remain for the next thirteen days.

My first and only thoughts were for Sam: How was she going to cope without me as her caregiver? Certainly she could not stay in Interlaken by herself. All of our friends persuaded her that she had no option but to go home to Colorado, and she finally agreed when T.I. promised to take her by the hospital to see me on their way to Zurich the next morning. She told me later that leaving me there in Interlaken was the most difficult decision she could ever recall. But I don't remember much about her coming as I was heavily sedated at the time.

The wonderful combination of friends and family members did all they could for her, especially our daughter, Christine, who left her job and family once again to come from Florida to stay with her mother until I arrived home nearly a month later. But despite her excellent care and Sam's and my ability to talk to one another by telephone every day, she worried constantly, which dealt an enduring blow to her indomitable spirit.

When I arrived in Colorado Springs on a stretcher via a military medical evacuation flight from Germany, she was as happy as I'd seen her in ages and greatly relieved to have me home. By contrast, I became deeply concerned by her appearance. The worry had taken a severe toll on her; she appeared washed out and looked as if she had aged a great deal in that short period of time. She was normally accustomed to exercise at least once a day, a practice that was essential to her coronary and vascular functions, but she hadn't had any exercise for the entire time wewere separated. She had spent virtually all the time worrying and it showed.

Over the next three months, our lives gradually returned pretty much to normal. I took on an accelerated physical and respiratory therapy regime while I gently nagged Sam into rebuilding her own physical well-being, trying to set the example without explicitly saying so. She worked very hard, was consistent in her routine, and it was not long before I was not just satisfied but delighted that she had worked her way back so well. Except for one thing. In what seemed like daily digression, she experienced more and more pain in her right leg. As was her way, she never complained, but I could tell that she was hurting when she began to use a cane of her own volition. And then a tell-tale ulcer erupted on her leg that would not heal. Finally, she plaintively told me that she could no longer bear any weight on her leg and asked me if I would once again get out the transport chair[50] for her.

Less than a week went by when, on Sunday evening, the first of June, she turned to me with an apologetic look in her eyes and said, "I didn't think you'd ever hear me say this, but I need to go to the hospital. My blood sugar has gone off the scale [over five hundred, which is five times her normal, comfortable reading], I feel rotten, and the pain in my leg is near unbearable."

So shortly after 2100, we arrived at the emergency clinic in Memorial Hospital, which to my anxious eye seemed to me to be filled with malingerers, most laughing, joking, and constantly using the vending machines for food and drink. The staff did the best they could to triage those who had come in, but it was not until 0430 the next morning that she was moved to a hospital room. And she hadn't closed her eyes for even a moment.

It appeared that she was in good hands so I left and went home for an hour's rest and a shower, returning at 0700. When I went into her room, she was fitfully asleep, but apparently quite a bit more comfortable than she had been when I had left her. She had two IVs inserted, one in each arm, each with three ports in the tubing. She had four different fluid containers hanging from the "tree" beside the bed and, thankfully, had been given a morphine pump to control her pain. Meanwhile, I called her three principal physicians, Paul Sherry, her cardiologist, Rick Meinig, her orthopedic surgeon, and Pat Miller, her internist, to let them know her status. Each was to come by the room within a short space of time that morning

Later that day, two more doctors became part of the team: Peter Brookmeyer, an infectious disease specialist, and Eric Anderson,

---

50   A transport chair is for all intents and purposes a wheelchair, except that it doesn't have large rear wheels so that the occupant could propel him- or herself. Someone else needs to push it.

her wound care physician. In the series of tests that had already taken place, she was diagnosed as having septicemia from a positive staph aureus infection, a greatly elevated fluid retention problem, and x-rays had revealed her tibia had once again fractured. The titanium rod that had been inserted less than two years previously had penetrated the top of the tibia and was jamming into her knee joint with every step she tried to take. No wonder she had been in horrific pain! And yet, she still never complained—just asked me apologetically to bring her to the hospital when she could bear it no longer.

Even as she lay in the bed, seriously ill, her concerns were exclusively for me: the fact that I was spending all my time with her; the chair in the room was very uncomfortable; I wasn't eating enough; I wasn't getting enough rest at night; and so on. Nothing could have exemplified her unselfish character more than those initial days of hospitalization.

Over the next two days, the team of doctors conferred regularly and tried to reach the proper decisions that would benefit Joan the most. Sam had never been shy about making her preferences known during these crises—whether or not they agreed with the doctors' views—and she told me she was tired of the problems that the leg had caused for the past twenty-one years. She dreaded the thought of another prolonged rehabilitation process and finally turned to me and stated, "Please tell the doctors just to amputate the damn thing and get it over with. It didn't heal even with a titanium rod in it, it continues to harbor staph bacteria that the most extreme antibiotic therapy hasn't been able to eliminate, and I just don't think I have the strength to battle my way back for another year or more."

I held her hand and we both shed a few tears together, but I felt obligated to tell her that the amputation certainly wasn't the panacea she envisioned. She would have to have an above-the-knee amputation, which involved a much more difficult adjustment to a new prosthesis than one below the knee. She would still have to develop her upper body strength to a higher degree than she had ever achieved before just to attain minimal mobility, and she would, therefore, be considerably less able to do the things we loved to do. It would be an equally difficult, long, and tedious rehabilitation regardless of what option was chosen.

She simply avoided eye contact with me, looked at the ceiling briefly, and finally closed her eyes and went to sleep. She was clearly exhausted and hadn't been able muster the emotional strength needed to fight back yet again.

When Rick Meinig came in later that day, I told him of her wish to get rid of the leg once and for all. He took her hand, smiled at her, and said, "Hey, c'mon, Joan, we're nowhere near that point yet. If we can't heal the bone, there are a number of alternatives left. Before I would even think of amputating, I'd want to get together with some top-notch prosthetists in Denver and design a brace for you that would take up your weight with your knee joint and thigh. You could still have about the same level of mobility you have had up to this point, even if that darned tibia remained broken."

She seemed to brighten slightly when he told her that, but didn't really believe the solution could be that easy. There was still a lot of experimentation and pain left before it would ever come to that. And she was unquestionably correct.

Despite the reluctance of both Paul Sherry and Pat Miller, her surgery was scheduled for the following Thursday at 0700. It was apparent that the titanium rod had to be removed and she couldn't stay in the state shewas in. Something clearly had to be done.

During the proposed operation, Rick would remove the nail, as he called it, from her tibia and Eric Anderson would deeply debride the abscess just below her knee to assure that all the infected tissue was removed. Then she would be placed in yet another straight leg cast with a window in it so that a wound vacuum could be applied, necessitating a dressing change every forty-eight hours. She would be deeply sedated but still semi-conscious during surgery and the leg would be anesthetized locally, perhaps with a spinal block. This was all in an effort to avoid the hemolytic reactions she had experienced previously. Possibly, it was generally believed, the antibody reaction was caused by the general anesthetic.

Sam just shook her head "no," imperceptibly, saying without any words being necessary, "Here we go again!" And then she resigned herself to the fact that, for the umpteenth time, she was going to have to have more surgery on that damned leg. My admiration for her courage and determination reached a new peak as I watched her.

I arrived at her hospital room at 0530 on Thursday morning so that I could spend time with her before her expected move to the operating room an hour before the scheduled surgery. When I asked her how she had slept, she told me that she had awakened at 0300 with chest pains and had to have Nitrostat[51] in order for them to subside. Nearly coincidental with my picking up the phone to inform Paul Sherry, the nurse came into the room to tell us that her surgery had been delayed, because of an emergency, until 1400 that afternoon.

Not long after that welcome news, she began another episode of congestive heart failure. But this one wasn't relieved by two more sublingual doses of Nitrostat. The rapid sequence of these two occurrences of angina was somewhat of a shock to both of us since, as best we could recall, she hadn't had any such happening in at least three years. But then we recalled that one of the diagnoses on her recent admission was excess fluid retention. Dr. Sherry came by moments later and prescribed a dose of IV Lasix.[52] And since Joan already had a Foley catheter inserted, the rapid outpouring of excess bodily fluid was clearly evident.

Would she be ready for afternoon surgery? I asked Paul and he was reluctant to make that commitment. "Let's just wait until the time approaches and we'll see then, but in the meantime, I'll contact the others who are involved and see if there's a better alternative."

The operating room was pretty well booked up for the following day, Friday, but all of the physicians agreed that it was in Joan's best interest to delay a day—and they were most willing to settle on 1700 the next day as the most opportune time.

Because Sam was being poked and prodded at all hours of the day and night to monitor her blood and other bodily fluids, I asked if it were possible for her to have a PICC line installed. That was done that same afternoon thus saving her useless discomfort.

---

[51] Nitrostat is a trade-name medication used to relieve episodes of chest pain (angina). It is a nitrate based on nitroglycerin. It works by relaxing blood vessels and allowing more blood flow to the heart. Increasing blood flow to the heart can relieve chest pain due to angina (MediLexicon.com).

[52] Lasix is one of a family of prescription diuretics, fluid reduction medications.

Friday morning proved to be a significant turning point in Joan's condition. Her blood sugar was back under fairly good control. The most recent blood tests showed that her septicemia had been temporarily overcome and only the tissue near the wound still showed signs of staph aureus. Her fluid levels were right where they should be, so borrowing a phrase from the space program, everything was "in the green."

We spent most of the day talking more than we had in the previous four days, primarily because she had slept most of that time trying to make up for the lost rest she experienced during the horrific admission process—for which, of course, she had apologized to me repeatedly as if it had been her fault. We held hands throughout the time, and I spent most of my words trying to encourage her for the long rehabilitation process ahead. I even suggested, jokingly, that I wouldn't be such a nag but instead would let her set her own pace during post-op therapy.

As the time approached to move toward the operating room, she squeezed my hand just a little tighter. "I don't think I'm going to make it through this," she confided. "I know I told you that once before, and you know that I barely did. But I was a lot stronger, younger, and braver then."

When I started to protest, she held up her other hand to silence me and went on. "Whatever happens, I need you to know that I've always felt like the luckiest woman who ever lived from the day I found you. I know you've always loved me. You've protected me; you've encouraged me; you've nurtured me; and no one ever could have cared for me with the same love and devotion that you have given me. I love you with every ounce of emotion that is in me and I always, always will. Please remember that when I'm gone."

With tears in both of our eyes, we embraced and I vowed to honor her wishes. And moments later, I escorted her to the preparation area of the operating room.

I spent the next two hours in the surgical waiting area dividing my time between reading and worrying, drinking black coffee all the while. Finally—although not as long as I expected—Rick Meinig came out, still in his scrubs, and handed me a long, slightly bowed piece of anodized metal, twenty-eight centimeters (11.2 inches) long and a centimeter (0.4 inches) in diameter.

"This is it," he told me. "Here's the nail that has been causing her so much pain. We cleaned it all up for her and thought she might like to keep it on the mantel as a reminder some day that things have been worse. She came through like a champ. She's wide awake and Paul Sherry wants her to go to the CCU [cardiac care unit] instead of recovery. She's probably already there by now."

We talked for a few more minutes about the procedure, how things looked inside her leg, and then I headed off toward CCU. And since I was all too familiar with the unit, I didn't need any directions on how to get there. When I arrived, the medics were just getting her transferred from the gurney to a special bed with an air-filled mattress as a precaution against any bed sores on her back and feet.

When Sam saw me, she smiled weakly and motioned for me to come over to kiss her. She seemed to be reasonably comfortable and she told me that she was without any pain. Neither of us said much of anything and didn't mention her fear that she wasn't going to make it through the ordeal. I remained by her bedside, holding her hand, until late that evening when she opened her eyes, scolded me gently for still being there, and then sweetly told me to go home and get some rest.

When I arrived the next morning at about 0700, the shift was just changing and I thanked the nurse who had watched over her through the night. As was my normal habit, I checked all of the IV medications currently being administered. I noticed that one of them was an insulin drip—a normal procedure when she was prepping for and being operated on, but never used after the procedure was over. That bothered me considerably.

When the nurse who was coming on duty came into the room after completing the shift change-over, I asked why she still had the insulin drip and told her that Joan should be on her normal[53] insulin routine, not on a drip of short-acting insulin.

Ann, by name, responded that those were the doctor's orders. I countered by asking which doctor had prescribed this in the orders.

---

[53] Her normal routine was to take a basal dose of fifteen units of Lantus insulin (a long-acting dose that was time released over each twenty-four-hour period). This was supplemented by a dose of regular, Humalog insulin (a short-term, more immediate-acting dose) before each meal based entirely on the number of carbohydrates that she intended to consume during that meal. Since Joan had been returned to her normal diet, she should also be on her normal insulin regime.

When she told me that it was Dr. Anderson, I went through the roof.

"That's bullshit!" I countered, probably too loudly. "Dr. Anderson is a general surgeon. What in hell is he doing giving orders for her internal medical care? There are standing orders in her records stating very clearly that she has complete control over her diabetic care and when necessary, I have that authority."

"I'm sorry, sir, but all standing orders are cancelled after a patient undergoes surgery, so Dr. Anderson's direction to 'return to the patient's routine prior to surgery' is the current order. And prior to surgery, your wife was on an insulin drip and we checked her blood sugar every thirty minutes to determine the proper rate of delivery. I intend to continue following those orders."

I was not going to debate the semantics over the term, "patient's routine," so I simply said that it was seriously wrong and she could either call Dr. Miller to correct those orders or I would do so myself. She turned on her heels and left the room, quite graciously I thought, after I had been blunt to the point of being rude to her.

Less that fifteen minutes later she came back into the room and told me that Dr. Miller had ordered either Joan or me to oversee her insulin therapy, and then very mater-of-factly concluded, "Just tell me what you want me to do, and I'll be glad to respond."

Breakfast was ordered, Joan was disconnected from the drip, Ann did the first finger-stick blood test of the day, and then brought in her two morning insulin shots according to the dosage that we had specified. And all the while, Ann was as professional and polite as she could be.

Roughly halfway through the morning Sam said to me, "You know, Ann is a very sweet woman and she deserves an apology. Not because she was right. We both know that you were. But you were pretty mean to her in the process of asserting yourself."

I told Sam that I had intended to apologize when the right time came, and then looked out at the nurses' station. Ann was alone there, and the thought occurred to me that the time couldn't be better than it was at that moment.

Standing beside Ann I said, "You've probably read a lot in the newspaper recently about black bear sows, the mamas, having just come out of their hibernation dens and how dangerous they can be when they have new young cubs to protect."

She looked up from her work station at me as if I had suddenly lost my marbles, but nodded that she understood. "Well, I'm the papa bear and Joan's my primary responsibility when she needs protection."

With a marked change in expression on her face, yet not a word said, she stood up and embraced me. Then finally, "Thank you, but no apology is needed at all. I've watched you all morning and I could easily see how deeply you love one another. You're under a great deal of stress. I've just been reading through your wife's medical history and she's been through more difficulties than I can ever imagine for one person. I suspect that if I were in your shoes, I would have been tougher on me than you were. Please don't give it another thought."

Sam's recovery proceeded at a remarkably rapid pace. Her vital signs couldn't have been better. All of the tests that were administered on a daily basis took on a positive trend. Ann "specialed" Joan for the next two days, and at Sam's and Ann's urging, I cut back my daily hospital stays from fifteen or sixteen hours to just over ten. And I made one overdue trip to the fitness center in the process. But each day when I left, Ann came and hugged me and told me not to worry. Joan would soon be coming home and I needed my strength and energy to care for her.

On Monday morning, when I arrived at CCU, Sam was smiling and looked better than I had seen her in the past two weeks. And she told me that she felt better. After we exchanged kisses she expressed the hopes that all five of the attending physicians, rather than the weekend surrogates, would be in that morning so we could convince each of them that it was time for her to go home.

"They all know that you're fully able to give me the care I need. You can change the dressing on the wound vacuum because you've been doing so for the past month. You changed the dressings on the last PICC line that I had for nearly eight months, so that's no problem. And you know that I always do better when I'm home."

She didn't have to convince me. I wanted her at home as badly as she wanted to be there. So as each physician came during the course of the day, all but Pat Miller thought she was well enough to go home. And he just wanted her to spend one more night in

CCU to be sure there would be no reversal necessitating another emergency return to the hospital.

By 1000 on Tuesday morning, all five were in agreement that she could leave and so we began the seemingly interminable process of cashing in her "get out of jail" ticket—a process made even more complex because the physical and occupational therapists had to be satisfied that I didn't need help caring for her. In addition, arrangements had to be made for home oxygen service as she would still need it there, along with similar last-minute actions. I also called my nephew, USAF Master Sergeant Chris Vossmer, who was currently stationed at Peterson AFB in Colorado Springs, to get his assistance in getting his Aunt Joan safely into our home.

It was nearly 1700 that afternoon before we finally left, only ninety-six hours after she had major surgery. Sam just smiled broadly at me when I apologized for the delay, she said, "I don't care. We're going home and that's where I need to be."

And then she ordered her first meal at home in nine days: something she called American chop suey, a combination of macaroni, tomato sauce, ground beef, and cheddar cheese, and a little chocolate ice cream for dessert. It wasn't a recommended diet for a diabetic by any means, but she could cover it with her evening dose of regular insulin. And it was her definition of comfort food, so she deserved a treat.

It was not easy getting her into the house, despite the stair lift that had been installed four years before when she also had come home in a long, straight-leg cast. The oxygen technician came and went in the next hour, delivering the needed equipment and then I set about preparing her requested meal. I offered her a cocktail, but she didn't think it appealed at the moment. She had the same reaction to my offer of a small glass of red wine with her pasta. When we finished, she told me she thought that one of the Celtics-Lakers final playoff games was on television. Neither of us particularly cared for basketball, but she was enthused the Celtics had made it back to prominence again and so I turned it on.

The next thing I knew, she was tapping me on the hand and woke me from a sound sleep. "You're exhausted," she said. "You've had a tough ten days and you need to catch up on your rest. I'll be just fine, but I want to leave the game on until it's over."

We had already decided that she'd be more comfortable on the sofa, which had a reclining seat on either end. Sam would sleep there until she thought she could handle the flat bed again, so I set about preparing her for her night's rest. All she needed to do was to turn off the TV. The lights were on timers and would go off later. The last thing I did was put a small Korean temple gong right beside her, the same one that she had used to signal me so many times in the years before, after coming home from the hospital. It was loud enough to be heard easily in our bedroom, and I could rest better knowing that I could respond in seconds, if need be. The last thing we did was to kiss good-night and reaffirm our love for one another.

At about 2230, I awakened suddenly in the bedroom to the sound of the TV still broadcasting. But it was not unusual for her to go to sleep while it was on and I thought nothing of it. I quietly went back into the family room, turned the set off, and saw that she seemed to be resting comfortably. As I had done so many times in the past, I woke up shortly after midnight and then again at about 0300, and peeked around the corner from the hall between our bedroom and family room and found her sleeping peacefully.

By 0530 I was awake for the day, as I had been these past many days, and looked in at her. She still was not stirring, so I continued my morning routine of shower, shave, dress, and make the bed. At 0630, I went out to get the newspaper, started the coffee, and busied myself deciding what I would get Sam for her breakfast.

I then went over to where she slept and gently touched her hand. It was cold. I couldn't believe anything was wrong so I searched for a pulse in her carotid artery. Her neck was cold also, so I tried to move her arm and it was stiff. Rigor mortis had already set in.

All those times I had checked on her through the night and she may have been gone already. The most courageous person I have ever known had finally exhausted all the grit and determination that she had in her, and it became clear to me that Sam had simply come home to die, just where she wanted to be.

"Oh, God," I cried out to no one who could hear me, "My Sam is gone and I'll never see her again." And in abject despair, I laid my head in her lap and sobbed uncontrollably.

* * *

Epilogue

From the time of her first heart attack, Sam and I had always prayed that when her time came to go, it would happen quietly, in her sleep—no prolonged suffering, no slow deterioration, no heavy medication to ease her pain—and now, when it had happened in just that exact manner, I was stunned and devastated. How many times had I awakened in the stillness of the night or the early dawn hours and either listened carefully to see if she was breathing calmly and quietly or if I could detect any subtle rise and fall of her chest? Perhaps it had been a bad dream, or perhaps it was just a premonition that roused me. But each time that had happened, she was sleeping soundly and was her bright and cheery self when she awakened.

On the rare times that I would tell her what had happened during the night, she would smile sweetly at me and tell me that she'd be with me for a while yet. "You can't get rid of me that easily," she would joke. But both of us knew that that would be the best way for her to go. We just wanted to forestall the inevitable for as long as possible.

When I recovered my wits sufficiently, I called 911 to report what I had found, harboring the very faintest of hopes that somehow I had been wrong and they could bring my Sam back to me again. Both the police and the fire and rescue squad were at the house in a matter of minutes, shattering the early morning calm as they came. And a matter of seconds after they were in the house, they confirmed my judgment and dismissed all possibility that I could have been wrong.

My first thought was to call Patti Friesen, knowing full well that neither she nor Paul Sherry could help Sam in any way; but perhaps it was I who needed that help and instinctively reached out to people who had been immeasurably supportive in the past.

My next call was to Elaine and Roger Williamson. They were nearby, our best friends in the area, and as Elaine and Sam would frequently say, she and Joan seemed more like the sisters each had never had, than just good friends. And though both Elaine and Patti had been expecting this day to come, they were as stunned and devastated as I was. All three were on their way to my side within minutes of my call.

Meanwhile, I tried to build up adequate emotional strength to call our children and tell them the terrible news that their mother was gone. Still moving by instinct more than logic, I found a soft cloth, wet it, and began to wipe the small trail of vomit that had spilled out of Sam's mouth as her soul departed its tabernacle. Paul Sherry was later to tell me that this was a certain sign of a massive heart attack that she never felt.

As gently and kindly as he possibly could, Rich Payne, one of the police officers, came over to me, put his arm around my shoulder and said, "I'm sorry, sir. I know how much it bothers you to see your wife that way, but you can't do anything like that until after the coroner arrives and assesses the situation."

I then called our daughter, Christine, and as rationally as I could, I told her what had happened. Christine also happens to be a very courageous woman, a quality she later told me she learned exclusively from following her mom's example, but she broke down in deep wrenching sobs. And no matter how we both tried, neither of us could regain control for what seemed like a very long time. Finally, through bitter, anguished tears, she told me that she would be with me as soon as humanly possible. And, of course, she was.

My next call was to Janet Edwards, the mortuary affairs officer at the Air Force Academy. For years, I had told the younger people who worked for me that whenever a death occurred in the family, this official should be very high on the list of people to notify. The U.S. Air Force family always takes care of its own, I would tell them, and now it was my time to test that aphorism. I was not to be disappointed in the least. Janet asked me if I had previously decided on the mortuary that we wanted and the proper disposition of the remains. Sam and I had had many opportunities in the recent past to make those decisions, and I told her what they were.

When she had the minimal information needed, she assured me, "Please don't worry about anything right now. I know what you want and we will follow your wishes in the most precise and compassionate way possible."

When the coroner completed his inquiry, expressing obviously sincere and heartfelt compassion as he questioned me, Patti and Elaine asked me to go into the living room so they could clean my beloved and change her stained top. The same police officer who comforted me earlier heard them and escorted me into the next room. There he very artfully kept my mind occupied with my telling him about our life together so that I wouldn't dwell on what those two dear ladies were doing in the next room.

Soon the mortuary team arrived and began their preparations to take Sam from the house. Elaine and Patti had completed their ablutions and fixed her hair more neatly, and this time I knew I had to be present. The men were as respectful and dignified as anyone could possibly wish for in what they did. When her body was secured on the gurney, they took out a very nice plush blanket that happened to be in Joan's favorite shade of blue. As they began to place the blanket over her face, I stopped them, reached over and kissed her lightly on her lips. And then I covered her myself.

I followed them out of the house to the driveway where they gently placed her in the back of the hearse. When the rear door was closed and they began to drive off, I felt a major portion of my own heart and soul go with her.

My dear, sweet, courageous, and loving Sam was gone—forever.

Afterword

Joan Althea (Nobis) Toner's remains were cremated under the auspices of the Swan-Law Funeral Home in Colorado Springs, Colorado. On June 18, 2008, she was honored at a ceremony in the newly constructed Memorial Pavilion of the United States Air Force Academy cemetery, which faces toward the Front Range of the Rocky Mountains that she so dearly loved. Her ashes were inurned at the adjacent columbarium immediately following the service. My Sam was only the ninth person and the first woman whose remains are inurned there.

I would have been totally bereft without the unstinting and generous support of our children, Scott, Christine and Michael, and Anne and Dan, along with the family members and friends who rallied to prop me up during this critical juncture of my life. I owe a special debt of gratitude to Master Sergeant Chris Vossmer, my sister Nan's youngest son, and his wife, Kim. They took the huge burden of minutia off my back and my mind and made my task much more endurable. I loved them all—family and close friends—from times long past, but the love I feel for them at this point in my life is very special and deeply meaningful to me. Somehow I'm sure Sam agrees with me.

As I was going through all of Sam's things a few days after her memorial service, I found a wrinkled up, tiny piece of newsprint crumpled up in one of the pockets of her wallet. I started to throw it away but wisely decided to see if there was anything important on it. I'm glad I did because I'm sure that I was intended to find it so that she could say good-bye in her own way. It was an untitled little poem that had been loosely attributed to Clarence Day:

Farewell my friends, farewell and hail;
I'm off to seek the Holy Grail.
I cannot tell you why.
Remember please when I am gone,
'Twas aspiration led me on.
Twiddley-widdily-toodle-oo,
All I want is to stay with you.
But here I go—Goodbye!

The great irony of this little ditty is that one of the causes of death listed on her death certificate is "aspiration pneumonia." Sam was my reason for existing and I will always miss her terribly.

I'll always love you, Sam—Requiescat in Pacem.

*   *   *

www.ingramcontent.com/pod-product-compliance
Lightning Source LLC
Chambersburg PA
CBHW061356280526
45784CB00001B/271